DAVID PEPPERCORN'S
GUIDE TO
THE WINES OF
BORDEAUX

D0493913

DAVID PEPPERCORN'S
GUIDE TO
THE WINES OF
BORDEAUX

Mitchell Beazley

Edited and designed by
Mitchell Beazley Publishers
part of Reed International Books Ltd
Michelin House
81 Fulham Road
London SW3 6RB

First published 1986 as *David Peppercorn's Pocket Guide to The Wines of Bordeaux*.
This edition, revised, updated and expanded, published 1992.

A CIP catalogue record for this book
is available from the British Library.

ISBN 1 85732 914 7

Editor: Susan Keevil
Art Editor: Paul Tilby
Index: Ann Barrett
Production: Sarah Schuman

Executive Editor: Anne Ryland
Art Director: Tim Foster

Illustrations: Madeleine David
Maps: Eugene Fleury

Typeset in Bembo by
Servis Filmsetting Ltd
Manchester, England
Produced by Mandarin Offset, Hong Kong
Printed and bound in Malaysia
Colour Reproduction by Scantrans Pte Ltd, Singapore

Contents

Introduction

Access to the personal files of a top professional is surely the most that any serious amateur of wine could ask. The new generation of wine books represented by David Peppercorn's guide to the wines of Bordeaux and Serena Sutcliffe's companion guide for Burgundy amounts almost to such a privileged snoop.

The situation reports and critical opinions that form the basis of buying decisions are normally classified information. But wine literature has moved with quite startling speed from the phase of enthusiastic generalization to that of precise wine-by-wine commentary. In these two books it drops at least its sixth, if not its seventh, veil. Now we are allowed to know as much as the most experienced professionals.

David Peppercorn is one of the most perceptive and respected of that ancient aristocracy of Anglo-Saxon merchants whose speciality is the wine of Bordeaux. He inherited both skill and passion from his father, one of the great 'claret men' of the previous generation. Indirectly, one might say, he inherited them from a long line of predecessors stretching right back to the *negotiator brittanicus* who was identified on the waterfront of Burdigala, Roman Bordeaux, 18 centuries ago.

Accumulated experience is a serious merchant's vital stock in trade. It allows him to watch the passing show with a sense of historical perspective, to interpret as well as to observe. But to keep up with such a complex scene as Bordeaux demands above all perpetual tastings and almost daily communication with the market-place. Thousands of properties vary from one vintage to another in their relative success or failure, while their older wines develop – not always in predictable ways.

David Peppercorn combines these two essential elements – a background of experience and a fund of knowledge constantly kept up to date – as well as any merchant-turned-author has ever done. It is a remarkable privilege to be able, as it were, to look over his shoulder at the enthralling pageant of Bordeaux.

Hugh Johnson

How to Use this Book

This book has three main sections: first, an introductory one giving a general picture of the Bordeaux wine region and how it works; second, a general A–Z of châteaux; third, a series of château profiles arranged by *appellation*, with a short briefing on each *appellation*. Out of the 4,000 or so châteaux in the region, a careful selection has been made of some 1,100 properties, ranging from the most illustrious growths to many lesser-known *crus* that are worth seeking out. These include not only châteaux but also some domaines and cooperatives.

To look up a name, turn first to the alphabetical listings. If the name appears only in the A–Z it will be followed by brief factual details such as *appellation*, ownership, vineyard area and production figures. If the château merits a profile, the A–Z entry will merely tell you its *appellation* and refer you to the page on which the profile appears. If the name is that of a secondary label the parent château is listed. A star beside one of the A–Z entries indicates that, although not profiled, the wine is above average in its class.

To save space, a number of abbreviations have been used. Vineyard areas are expressed in hectares (shortened to ha), and yields are given in hectolitres per hectare (hl/ha).

Where a company owns a property, the company name may be preceded by the following abbreviations. These indicate types of company as follows:

Ets	Etablissements	**SARL**	Société à Responsibilité Limité
GAEC	Groupement Agricole d'Exploitation en Commun	**SC**	Société Civile
		SCA	Société Civile Agricole
GFA	Groupement Foncier Agricole	**SCI**	Société Civile Immobilière
SA	Société Anonyme		

The following abbreviations are used for grape varieties:

CF	Cabernet Franc		**Musc**	Muscadelle
Col	Colombard		**PV**	Petit Verdot
CS	Cabernet Sauvignon		**Sauv**	Sauvignon Blanc
Mal	Malbec		**Sém**	Sémillon
Mer	Merlot			

The Region and its Wines

Bordeaux occupies a pre-eminent place among the world's wine regions. Its special geographical situation enables it to produce more fine wines with more regularity than any other part of France, or any other country.

Nowhere else are the greatest wines made in such quantity (only Ausone and Pétrus are in really short supply). And if world-wide acclaim has driven the prices of the First Growths beyond the reach of most of us, there are a number of excellent wines at far more reasonable prices which can often rival the First Growths, especially when young. For if Bordeaux can claim nine Premiers Crus (eight red and one white), how many other remarkable and exceptional wines does it not make? Tot up the best of the classified Médocs (and some of the unclassified ones) and the best of the Graves and St-Emilion classified growths, to say nothing of the best Pomerols, and you arrive at a figure of around 100 growths that can or do produce great bottles of wine. An impressive roll call. This, of course, covers only red wines, but there are also great sweet white wines and good dry whites.

Of course, this small elite is only the tip of the iceberg. The Bordeaux bible, *Bordeaux et Ses Vins*, by Cocks & Féret, lists over 4,000 property names in its 1982 edition, while just over 17,800 growers made wine in the department of Gironde in 1989 (this includes *vin de table*) and over 100,000 hectares of vineyards were dedicated to the growing of vines with the right to an *appellation contrôlée*. Bordeaux wines are indeed within the reach of all today and its most modest wines have never been better made.

The Bordeaux Region and its Wine Areas

ATLANTIC OCEAN

1

0   10km
0   5mls

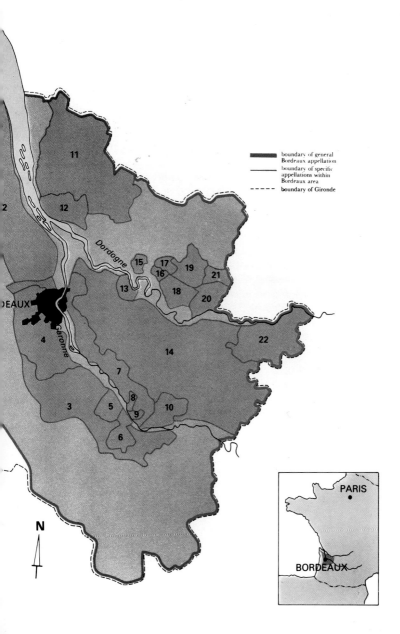

	boundary of general Bordeaux appellation
	boundary of specific appellations within Bordeaux area
---	boundary of Gironde

Geography

Physically Bordeaux lies in the southwest of France, on the 45°
latitude, with the often stormy waters of the Atlantic Ocean in the
Bay of Biscay only a few miles to the west. Its vineyards spread out
along the rivers Gironde, Garonne and Dordogne. Here the
warming influence of the Gulf Stream is crucial – bear in mind that
on the other side of the Atlantic the same latitude goes through
Nova Scotia and Maine. The Gulf Stream and the Atlantic provide
Bordeaux with hot summers, long mild autumns, often extending
to the very end of October, relatively mild but wet winters, and
mild springs. The consistency of the weather is emphasized by the
way in which years of bitter cold (1709, 1740, 1820, 1956, 1985) or
years of excessive rain (1930–32, 1965 and 1968) stand out.

The geology of the region is also important – not so much, it is
now thought, for what the soils contain as for the drainage they
provide. Going south from the Pointe de Grave and the ocean, the
riverside land to the west of the Gironde and Garonne is basically
gravel, that to the east predominantly sand, limestone and clay, in
constantly changing patterns and proportions. There are exceptions, however, such as the important outcrops of gravel found in
parts of Pomerol and the part of St-Emilion that adjoins it, and the
limestone and clay under the gravel which gives Sauternes its
special character.

The flat, gravelly ridges of the Médoc and Graves are protected
from the Atlantic gales by the thick pine forests bordering the ocean
which also buffer the rainfall. The hills in the Premières Côtes and
Entre-Deux-Mers, together with the rivers, also provide important
differences in microclimate between those vineyards to the west of
the Gironde and Garonne (Médoc and Graves) and those to the east
of the Dordogne (the Libournais). The sheer distances involved are
also significant. From the Pointe de Grave in the north to Langon in
the south is 148 kilometres (92 miles), from the city of Bordeaux
eastwards to Ste-Foy-la-Grande is 70 kilometres (44 miles), so
important climatic variations are hardly surprising.

Historical Background

Three centuries of allegiance to the English crown (1152–1453) gave Bordeaux a sense of unity as a region set apart from the rest of France and helped to orientate it firmly towards the Atlantic and its associated seafaring trade routes.

During these centuries the relative strengths and weaknesses of the sides ebbed and flowed. In the long term the development of sea trade was to have the most far-reaching consequences of all. The evolution of the city of Bordeaux, both as the commercial centre of the region and as its principal port, was natural enough in view of its position. But the development of Libourne as the main port on the Dordogne resulted from a deliberate act of policy by the English to expand trade by creating in 1270 an entirely new town and port.

After the inevitable trading setback caused by the severance of the political ties between Bordeaux and England, it took some time for the region to recover, but, as it did, the value of the sea routes and the trading links built up through them became clear. Not only was trade with England, and soon Scotland and Ireland, restored on a lesser scale, but trade with other maritime powers, such as Holland and the Hanseatic ports, was developed. Sea links were also important in establishing trade with Brittany, Normandy and Dunkirk. It was also quite logical that the lucrative West Indies business should have been built up and carried on through the port of Bordeaux. This brought considerable wealth to the city in the 18th century.

The 18th century also saw significant developments in the pattern of land ownership. The movement to build up important estates in the Médoc had begun in the previous century, but now it really began to take shape. This consolidation of land holdings in the hands of the so-called *noblesse de robe* (the legal and political aristocracy of Bordeaux) has had a vital influence in creating the château system which gives the Bordeaux vineyards their unique character. At the same time, a new and prosperous merchant class began to assert itself, first as *courtiers* (brokers) and *négociants*, and later as château proprietors.

This gave Bordeaux as a region a structure which was durable and resilient enough to withstand the vast social and political upheavals of the French revolutionary period (1789–96). Of course there were many important changes in ownership. A British general even acquired a château and gave it his name, Palmer, after the final defeat of Napoleon in 1815. But many châteaux changed ownership in name only, having been bought by relatives of exiles whose absence abroad led to their lands being forfeited, and the eventual return of these exiles, in many cases, saw a restoration of the status quo.

In the post-Napoleonic era the importance of the new merchant class, often enriched by commerce with the West Indies, greatly increased. Families such as Barton, Guestier, and Johnston became château proprietors as well as *négociants*. The growing success of the Médoc was crowned by the Paris Exhibition of 1855 for which the famous Classification was prepared, covering the red wines of the Médoc, with the exception of Haut-Brion, and the great sweet wines of Sauternes and Barsac.

In 1853 the Paris-Bordeaux railway was opened. This was to have a vital impact on the opening of much of the French market to Bordeaux wines at a period of increasing prosperity. It was especially important for the development of St-Emilion, which had lagged behind Médoc until this time. Napoleon III had ushered in the Second Empire in 1851, and a period of new buoyancy enabled France increasingly to share in the fruits of the industrial revolution, which had been launched in Britain.

Parisian bankers like the Rothschilds (Lafite and Mouton) and the Péreires (Palmer) invested in properties in the Médoc. Even more important in the long run, the Libournais (St-Emilion, Pomerol and Fronsac) began to emerge from their long obscurity and make their mark. But just as the whole region seemed set on the greatest period of expansion and prosperity in its history, disaster struck. The period often called the Grande Belle Epoque was effectively ended in 1878 by the devastations of phylloxera. Not until 1893 was there a large vintage of fine quality again.

It said much for the resources built up during the previous years, as well as the energy and determination of the large landowners who led the way in combating the disease, that Bordeaux recovered in the way it did. Once it was discovered that grafting the original French vines on to disease-resistant American rootstock was the only sure remedy, the reconstitution of the vineyards began. But an undertaking of this magnitude could not be accomplished overnight, nor without a great deal of cost and much experimentation.

The picture of what actually happened during these years is a complex one. The need to produce large quantities of serviceable wines quickly was met by planting on marginal lands not previously used for vines and on the Palus (riverside plain) where treatment by flooding and the sandy soil inhibited the spread of the disease. At the same time, the owners of quality vineyards fought, with a good deal of success, to preserve their ungrafted vines, realizing that fine wines needed mature vines. That is why many of the great vineyards of the Médoc, as well as some in St-Emilion and Pomerol such as Cheval Blanc, Figeac and La Conseillante, were able to continue making great wines during the years of transition.

But a new Belle Epoque was not yet in sight. After two great years in 1899 and 1900, there was to be no outstanding vintage again until 1920. Economically the years leading up to the First World War were depressed in Europe as a whole, and the Bordeaux trade did not experience the same degree of prosperity it had known in the 1850s, 1860s and 1870s. Although the 1920s produced some splendid vintages, economic conditions became steadily worse. The price of the 1926 vintage collapsed, and the world slump soon followed. Poor vintages and a disastrous economic climate spelt ruin for many growers and merchants during the 1930s.

Bordeaux Since 1945

It was against this background that Bordeaux celebrated peace in 1945 with a series of wonderful vintages, but it took some time for the region to repair the years of neglect and begin to rebuild its prosperity. It was not until the late 1950s that one could say with confidence that a new age was dawning. Prices, and with them investment in vineyards and buildings, began to rise. The real prosperity of the 1960s culminated in the speculation and spiralling prices of 1971–73, which ended in disaster precipitated by the oil crisis of 1974 and exacerbated by a thoroughly unhealthy market situation in Bordeaux itself. But after only two years of disorder the Bordeaux market recovered, and since then progress, prosperity and good vintages have been the region's hallmarks.

Technical Progress and Innovation

The 1960s and 1970s were years of enormous technical progress. In the vineyards, the success of sprays in preventing rot have meant that not since 1968 has a Bordeaux vintage been harvested in an unhealthy condition. The vinification of these healthy grapes has also seen important improvements. The temperature at which wine is fermented is now much more carefully controlled than it used to be. This means that even in very hot years, such as 1982, 1983, 1985, 1989 and 1990, very few wines become acetic, whereas in 1947 this misfortune was commonplace. The quality of dry white wines has improved almost beyond recognition now that fermentation is carried out at around 18°C (64°F) and the wine is aged in steel rather than wooden barrels.

Great improvements have been made among top growths, especially in the Médoc where the properties are large, by taking much more care over the selection of grapes before the final *assemblage* for the *grand vin*. This has been one of Professor Emile Peynaud's many contributions to the improvements in quality which have been so widely achieved over the past 25 years.

Bordeaux tends to be rather more schizophrenic about a modernization that not everyone would hail as an improvement: the introduction of mechanical harvesters. Nowhere in France has their use spread more rapidly, and today more machines are employed in the Gironde than in any other *vignoble* of France – 1,050 were in use by 1983 and 1,500 by 1986, harvesting more than half the area under vine. The large estates in Médoc and Entre-Deux-Mers are especially well adapted to their use as the land is rather flat and the *cuviers* where the wine is vinified are usually adjacent to the vineyards. The major advantage of mechanical harvesting is its speed, enabling a much more precise decision to be made as to when the picking should take place, permitting all the grapes to be harvested when perfectly ripe without running the risk of part of the harvest being overripe or the weather breaking.

Many of the Crus Classés are still resisting the introduction of machines on the grounds that it would be detrimental to quality. One suspects that they are also concerned about the image created by the machine in the context of an expensive, high-quality product. The present indications are that, with the progress that has been made in adapting these machines to French vineyards, excellent results can be obtained. For white wines, the cylindrical presses now in use in the winery – the horizontal screw press and, especially in recent years, the pneumatic press – can press the destalked white grapes although the presence of stalks certainly helps to drain the *marc* (pulp left after pressing) better. Machines also leave unripe grapes unpicked, and in this respect make a better selection 'on the vine' than would most pickers.

The Appellations

The concept of *appellations*, developed in France immediately after the First World War, and the final legislation giving effect to the system we now know, was enacted in 1935. It meant that any wine of more than purely local fame was given the designation *Appellation d'Origine Contrôlée* (AOC), usually shortened to *Appellation Contrôlée* (AC). The original purpose was to protect the famous wine names of France from cheap imitations at a time of surplus production and low prices. It also spearheaded an important campaign to remove hybrid vines from French *appellation* vineyards. These are crosses between European vines and phylloxera-resistant American vines, as distinct from grafted vines or crosses between different European vines (eg Müller-Thurgau). These hybrids, which often carry over something of the odd 'foxy' flavour to be found in American vines, were planted in many vineyards after the phylloxera as an alternative to grafting.

The principal functions of an *appellation* regulation are:

1   To define the area entitled to a name (eg Médoc).

2   To list what grape varieties may be planted.

3   To lay down the density per hectare of vines to be planted, and how they shall be pruned.

4   To set maximum yields per hectare.

5   To set minimum degrees of alcohol (and sometimes for
     white wines, maximum degrees) and regulate chaptalization
     (addition of sugar to must to increase alcoholic degree in
     years of deficient ripeness).

6   Since 1974 to insist on analyses and tastings before finished
     wines may receive their *appellation* documents.

7   To require growers to make a declaration of their
     production after each vintage, and a declaration of the
     stocks they hold as at August 31 each year.

To administer this system and liaise with the syndicates of growers
in each *appellation*, the Institut National des Appellations d'Origine
(INAO) was formed, and remains today the key body for watching
over and reforming the system.

    In the Bordeaux region the definition of a particular area entitled
to an *appellation* of its own caused fewer problems than in some
other parts of France. But in the Libournais there was much local
controversy as to the use of the name St-Emilion. In the 19th
century its use was very widespread, as old copies of Cocks & Féret
bear witness. St-Emilion at this time included not only Pomerol
and the communes to the north but also the area to the east now
known as the Côtes de Castillon. In 1921, the situation was finally
resolved when the Tribunal of Libourne judged that the name of
St-Emilion should refer only to those parishes contained within the
ancient jurisdiction of the Jurade de St-Emilion. But in 1936 the
communes that had been refused the right to sell their wines as St-
Emilion were permitted to add the name to their own, thus
Montagne-St-Emilion, etc – now known as the St-Emilion
satellites.

    In the Médoc, the area north of St-Estèphe known as the Bas-
Médoc received the simple AC Médoc, while the best part
southwards as far as Blanquefort was made Haut-Médoc. However, within the Haut-Médoc, the growers of the most renowned
villages sought, and eventually received, their own *appellations*. A
similar situation has recently arisen in Graves where the growers in
the best parts of the northern Graves sought to use the names of
Pessac and Léognan instead of Graves. A compromise was agreed in

1984, each château concerned adding one of the two names to that of Graves. In 1987 however, after a long campaign, the new *appellation* Pessac-Léognan was granted. One rather odd anomaly exists in Sauternes, where the commune of Barsac, one of the five within the *appellation*, also has its own AC, and growers here may choose to call their wines either Barsac or Sauternes.

The control of what grape varieties may be planted ensures that the traditional character of each wine is preserved and prevents the use of inferior, and possibly higher-yielding, varieties. At the same time, of course, it prevents experimentation, not that this is something much sought after in Bordeaux.

The significance of the density with which vines are planted may not at first be obvious. However, it has been shown that if vines are planted more widely apart than is traditional in Bordeaux they produce higher yields, and the character and quality of the wine changes. A decree in 1974 fixed 2,000 vines per hectare for the Bordeaux AC, and this compares with 5,000 to 10,000 for the Médoc ACs. Traditionally, 8,000 to 9,000 vines are planted per hectare in the Médoc, against 6,000 per hectare in St-Emilion.

The relationship between quantity and quality has long been a vexed one. While it is clear that very high yields normally lead to lower quality, at what stage this occurs is not always easy to determine. Several points need to be made. The more effective control of disease, more extensive use of fertilizers and the cloning of the most successful vines have all produced higher yields. The vintage of 1953 produced an average yield of 40·8 hectolitres per hectare, and 1955 yielded 41·1, compared to 24 in 1949 and 25·7 in 1961. But 1970 produced 52·6, and 1973 achieved 55·3, which seemed remarkable by all historic standards. However, 1979 saw a figure of 62·9 hectolitres per hectare reached, and the great 1982 vintage yielded 60. 1984, with its disastrous flowering of the Merlot, achieved only 36·9, but that should be compared with the figure of 17 in 1956 after the infamous frost.

It is clear then that the red grape varieties planted in Bordeaux are capable of producing fine wines from relatively high yields, certainly much higher than would have been thought possible a few years ago. In Burgundy, by contrast, the Pinot Noir's quality falls very significantly when yields rise over 50 hectolitres per hectare in hillside vineyards. There were many examples of this in 1982. But in the same vintage in Bordeaux both the Merlot and the Cabernet Sauvignon produced magnificent wines of real concentration at this level of yield and higher. White wines are less susceptible to loss of quality from high yields, and in Bordeaux the best growths for dry wines tend to use the high-yielding Sémillon and the low-yielding Sauvignon.

The minimum degrees of alcohol are supposed to provide some guarantee of quality and, unless they are achieved, chaptalization (the addition of sugar) is illegal. But it is interesting to note that the great clarets of the past were very low in alcohol, often between 9 percent and 10 percent by volume, and many have lasted superbly. Even as recently as the 1940s some great wines scarcely reached 11 percent. Certainly, there is no call for a Médoc to be more than 12 percent alcohol if it has to be chaptalized, or for a St-Emilion to be more than 12·5 percent. In exceptional vintages it is, of course, possible to produce wines of over 13 percent quite naturally in St-Emilion.

Bordeaux was the first major wine region in France to institute tastings before the granting of an *appellation*. St-Emilion had made this part of its new classification system, in itself the first classification to be tied to AC regulations, in 1955. In the Médoc tasting was introduced on a voluntary basis. After the major overhaul of the whole AC system in 1974, tastings became compulsory throughout the whole of France in the awarding of *appellations*. There is a certain cynicism about the tastings because it is said wines are rarely turned down. The panels consist of growers, *courtiers* (brokers) and *négociants* (merchants). The cask or vat samples have to represent an assemblage of all wines at a given property (including *vin de presse* and second-label wines) for which the *appellation* is required. So the quality of a sample is usually inferior to the quality which will go out under the château label, especially at the larger properties. Proprietors are often requested to resubmit samples because, at the early stage at which they are tasted, wines often show minor faults which subsequently disappear. My own experience of these tastings is that they are serious.

The declaration of stocks, which is another stipulation of the AC system, is more or less self-explanatory. It enables the authorities and the trade to know precisely how the last year's sales have gone and thus what there is to sell in the coming year. By adding together the stocks at August 31 with the declarations for the new vintage, the amount available for the coming sales campaign becomes clear. A comparison of the level of stocks from year to year also provides a valuable barometer of the health of the market and has an influence on price levels.

The overhaul of the AC system in 1974 was a far-reaching one which did much to remove the inflexibility of the old system and its insensitivity towards vintage variations. The essence of the new system revolves around three new concepts:

1   *Rendement de Base* (basic permitted yield). This corresponds to the old maximum yields which were established in 1935 and had remained little changed since. For Bordeaux they were revised in 1984 (backdated to apply to the 1983 vintage), and most *appellations* were given higher allowances, sometimes by as much as 5 hectolitres per hectare. But, as we shall see, under the new system, this *rendement de base* simply represents a norm and has less significance than previously.

2   *Rendement Annuel* (annual yield). Now, each year, the growers in each *appellation*, through their syndicate, make a proposal to the INAO, bearing in mind the actual conditions of the year, as to what normal production levels should be. This figure may be above or below the *rendement de base*.

3   *Plafond Limite de Classement* (PLC). This is a fixed proportion (usually 20 percent), given in the decrees governing each *appellation* which, when applied to the *rendement annuel*, gives the maximum permitted yield for that particular year. If the *rendement annuel* allows a flexibility for the conditions of a particular year, the PLC allows for flexibility between different vineyards and growers. To apply for this extra allowance, all the wines on the property must be offered for tasting, and anything over and above this limit has to go for distillation.

Grape Varieties

Today five grape varieties, three red and two white, dominate the vineyards of Bordeaux, but it was not always so. At the end of the 18th century, nine red and four white varieties were recorded in the Médoc, but this was nothing compared with the 34 red and 29 white varieties in the Libournais. The process of selection made rapid progress in the 19th century and its completion was finally precipitated by the phylloxera crisis which, over a period of years, led to the replanting of all vineyards. Today the most important varieties are the following:

Red

Cabernet Sauvignon
> This is the most important variety in Médoc and Graves, especially for the Grands Crus. It produces wine with a deep, brilliant colour, a marked bouquet, often reminiscent of blackcurrants, and a flavour which is markedly tannic when young but which develops great finesse and complexity. This is a very hardy variety and it is notably resistant to *coulure* at the flowering and to grey rot before the harvest. It has a thick skin and is a late ripener. It does best on gravelly soils and has a relatively low yield.

Cabernet Franc
> This is an important secondary variety in both St-Emilion and Médoc. In St-Emilion it is known generally as the Bouchet. It produces very perfumed wines with less colour and tannin than the Cabernet Sauvignon, but in other respects it is very similar.

Merlot
> The most important variety in St-Emilion and Pomerol, but also important in Médoc and Graves since it harmonizes so well with Cabernet Sauvignon. It produces wines which are deep in colour, less tannic and higher in alcohol than the Cabernet Sauvignon, supple and full-flavoured. It does well

in the presence of clay, precisely where the Cabernet Sauvignon does less well. It is an early ripener and generous yielder, but it is very susceptible to *coulure* during the flowering and to rot in wet weather. However, new sprays have helped overcome this last deficiency.

Malbec

Also known as Pressac in the Libournais and as Côt in Cahors. This variety used to be particularly important in Fronsac, Pomerol and the Côtes de Bourg, as well as having a minor role in most Médoc vineyards. Today, because of its flowering problems, its importance has seriously declined, and only in Bourg and Blaye does it remain a significant element, although many châteaux in the Médoc, St-Emilion and Pomerol still have a few old Malbec vines left. This is a high-yielding, early-ripening variety, producing soft, delicate wines with good colour. It is especially useful for blending with more tannic varieties such as Cabernet Sauvignon.

Petit Verdot

This is used in small quantities in the Médoc, especially on the lighter soils of Margaux, but is of declining importance. It is late in ripening and produces highly coloured wines, high in alcohol and tannin, and adds complexity to wines for long ageing.

White

Sémillon

This is the most distinctively Bordelais of the white varieties. Although it has suffered a decline as a result of the popularity of the Sauvignon it is now making something of a comeback. It is the most important component of all the great sweet wines, and provides complexity and ageing potential in dry Graves. Its distinctive and complex bouquet requires bottle-age to develop in dry wines, and becomes richer and more honeyed with age. The wine is taut and firm at first, before becoming increasingly full-flavoured and complex with ageing. It blends very well with Sauvignon. Its susceptibility to *pourriture noble* (noble rot) is responsible for its success in making great dessert wines.

Sauvignon Blanc

This has been traditionally planted as a minor partner to the Sémillon in the sweet wine areas and as an equal component of the dry wines. In recent years it has been increasingly used on its own, especially in the Entre-Deux-Mers, to produce wines sold as Bordeaux Blanc Sauvignon. This variety, also widely planted in other parts of France, tends, when unblended, to have a character which is so strong that it obliterates regional characteristics, especially when complete ripeness is not obtained. However, in Bordeaux it can produce wines high in natural sugar and therefore in alcohol, with more finesse and style, especially when aged in oak. The Pavillon Blanc of Château Margaux is an outstanding example of this. Sauvignon tends to be a lower and more erratic yielder than the Sémillon, so that where a vineyard is planted half and half with Sémillon, there will always be more Sémillon in the resulting blend.

Muscadelle

An extremely perfumed and aromatic variety that can be useful in small doses. It is particularly favoured in the Premières Côtes for producing sweet wines for early drinking, and as an adjunct to the Sémillon and Sauvignon.

The essence of winemaking in Bordeaux is to mix the different varieties in the right proportions for the soil in each particular vineyard and the style of wine the proprietor is trying to make. It is the small but important variations from château to château, coupled with soil and microclimatic differences, that give Bordeaux wines their remarkable variations and individuality. Thus, in the Médoc, where the Cabernet Sauvignon dominates, some proprietors will use Merlot as their second variety, with very little Cabernet Franc; others will use less Merlot and more Cabernet Franc. In St-Emilion and Pomerol, where Merlot is dominant, some proprietors have 80 percent Merlot, while others plant it half and half with Cabernet Franc or mix it with Cabernet Franc and Cabernet Sauvignon in a ratio of one third each – in fact you will find every conceivable variation in the proportions.

Châteaux

The château system has been a crucial factor in building the prestige of the great Bordeaux wines. In the Médoc, the putting together of many small farms in the 18th century enabled large estates to be formed, capable of producing sufficient quantities of wine to create a wide reputation on many markets. The First Growths led the way in England in the early years of the 18th century; the others followed, creating a unique image of excellence for Bordeaux.

In the Médoc, the château names have in effect become marques, whose proprietors can increase the size of their vineyards at will, provided they remain in the same *appellation*. Nobody controls the extent of an individual vineyard now. Only the reputation of the wine and its consistent quality counts. But in St-Emilion, where the 1954 classification system is under the control of the INAO, vineyards of classified wines cannot be expanded at will, and when Beau-Séjour-Bécot took over two other properties and incorporated their production into its Premier Grand Cru Classé wine, it lost its status in the 1985 revision of the classification.

The very success of the château system, however, has produced its own problems. It is difficult for the consumer to remember the names of more than a handful of châteaux, let alone the thousands that exist in the whole region. But because the consumer knows that good Bordeaux wines come from châteaux it is hard to create successful brands which cannot of their nature have a château name. It is not without significance that the most successful brand of claret by far is Mouton-Cadet, precisely because most people believe, erroneously, that it is directly connected with the famous Château Mouton-Rothschild. Even the Caves-Coopératives now sell many of their wines under château names.

Cooperatives

Cooperatives are of increasing importance in Bordeaux, and their role is changing. Initially much of the wine they sold went to *négociants* for their generic blends and brands. Increasingly however, they are vinifying the wines of their best members separately and marketing them under their château labels, on which they have the right to put '*mis à la propriété*'. In addition they are creating their own brands and selling these and some of their château wines directly to wholesalers in France and to importers in foreign markets, rather than through the traditional Bordeaux trade, although the latter remains a significant part of their business. The most important cooperative in Médoc is at Bégadan, with 170 members producing some 27,000 hectolitres of Médoc AC. In St-Emilion the Union des Producteurs has 330 members producing some 50,000 hectolitres, including over 11,000 hectolitres of St-Emilion Grand Cru, the best of it aged in casks. In the Haut-Médoc, the most important cooperative is at St-Estèphe. It has 200 members and produces some 18,000 hectolitres of this important AC, nearly one third of the total production of the *appellation*.

Négociants

Traditionally, the Bordeaux trade has been carried out by the *négociants*. In Bordeaux itself this has centred on the Quai des Chartrons, conveniently placed for the docks. *Négociants* not only distributed Bordeaux wines in France and on export markets, they also effectively acted as bankers for the château proprietors, buying their wines when they were a few months old, then either taking them into their own cellars, where they would be looked after until ready for bottling, or keeping them at the château for château-bottling. They also kept substantial bottle stocks and could always supply mature wines ready for drinking or old vintages for special occasions.

Inflation and high interest rates, however, have provided a challenge to which the *négociants* have not found an answer. None has been able to achieve the size and financial muscle to meet the new problems while retaining their traditional role, which has inevitably contracted. Far more wines are now château-bottled, and far more stock is now held and financed at the property than ever before. Many firms now work on minimum stocks or act purely as brokers, not buying wines until they have sold them, which puts them at the mercy of the notoriously volatile Bordeaux market. The *courtiers* themselves still have an important role as the link between the growers and the *négociants*; largely because there are so many growers, the bigger merchants in particular simply could not select from the huge range of wines.

The following are the leading *négociant* houses today:

B d'Arfeuille A small, well-respected family firm in Libourne that is also proprietor of Châteaux La Pointe, Pomerol, and La Serre, Grand Cru Classé, St-Emilion. The firm naturally specializes in Libournais wines, but also covers the full range of other Bordeaux districts.

Baron Philippe de Rothschild SA (formerly La Bergerie and then La Baronnie) After the legendary Baron's death in 1987 it was decided to perpetuate his name in this, the commercial arm of his enterprise. Apart from selling its property wines, d'Armailhac and Clerc-Milon, the principal business is Mouton Cadet and its associated brands. (Mouton-Rothschild is sold via the Bordeaux market, and not exclusively through Baron Philippe de Rothschild SA.) The firm is very strong on export markets.

Barton & Guestier This famous old concern is now part of Seagrams and is only a pale reflection of the firm it used to be, largely concentrating on brands sold on the US market.

Borie-Manoux A dynamic family firm with some important properties as a basis for its quality business (Châteaux Batailley, Trottevieille, Beau-Site etc). Its wines are well distributed on export markets as well as in France.

Calvet Once one of the great names of Bordeaux, now only a shadow of its former self, it was sold to British brewers Whitbread in the early 1980s, and was then taken over by European Cellars (France) – a subsidiary of the Allied group. Now mostly selling generic brands.

Castel Frères A large firm specializing in cheap wines,

especially its *vin de table* marque, Castelvin. It has purchased and restored the extensive buildings of the cooperative in Arcins where it vinifies the production of a number of small properties from the *appellations* Margaux, Haut-Médoc, Médoc and Bordeaux Supérieur. Most of the firm's business is concentrated in France. A recent acquisition was Nicolas – the famous Parisian chain of wine shops.

Cordier One of the leading firms in Bordeaux, which also owns Châteaux Gruaud-Larose, Talbot, Meyney, Lafaurie-Peyraguey and Clos-des-Jacobins – as well as managing Cantemerle. The Cordier family sold control of the company in 1984 to an important financial group whose other interests include the Domaines des Salins du Midi. The Cordier properties are sold on an exclusive basis and not through the market, so it specializes in selling a very limited range of its own exclusivities and generic brands. Over half its business is export.

Edmond Coste This family firm operating from Langon in the Graves has become well known, under the directorship of Pierre Coste, for its advocacy of wines vinified to be drunk young. Coste works very closely with a number of growers in his region, and his white wines were among the first to set the trend for low-temperature fermented wines. His reds are soft and fruity, but sometimes lack regional characteristics as a result of this vinification.

Cruse Another household name which no longer holds its former position. The family sold out during the 1974 crisis to Société des Vins de France. Brands are important, but some château wines are still offered.

CVBG (Consortium Vinicole de Bordeaux et de Gironde) This group includes Dourthe and Kressmann, and the wines are marketed under these old company names. In 1983 the families sold out to a Dutch company. These companies have a good reputation and sell a wide range of wines, many on an exclusive basis. Château Maucaillou belongs to the Dourthe family while they manage Château Belgrave, 5e Cru Classé. The Kressmanns own the classified Graves Château La Tour-Martillac.

Dulong Frères & Fils A family business situated at Floirac just across the bridge from Bordeaux. It enjoys a good reputation for its Petits Châteaux and Cru Bourgeois exported to the UK and the USA.

Louis Eschenauer This was one of the first of the old Chartronnais firms to be sold, originally to John Holt of Liverpool (now part of Lonrho) in 1959, who also owned Châteaux Rausan-Ségla and Smith-Haut-Lafitte. It is now owned and run by private shareholders.

Gilbey de Loudenne This is part of IDV, the wine and spirit division of Grand Metropolitan, the international hotel and leisure group. It markets Château de Pez worldwide, as well as a small portfolio of brands headed by La Cour Pavillon. An export-orientated company.

Nathaniel Johnston Formed in 1734 and still run by the same family. If it no longer owns great châteaux like Ducru-Beaucaillou, it still specializes in selling a wide range of Bordeaux's leading growths, especially for export.

J Lebègue & Cie The emphasis here is on bulk wines, both AC and *vin de table*, much of it for export.

Alexis Lichine & Cie There is now no connection at all between the Lichine family and the company that bears their name, and that belonged to the British brewers Bass Charrington before being sold to Pernod-Ricard. This is an important company selling a wide range of wines and operating widely in export markets. Château Lascombes, also belonging to Bass, is its flagship, and is marketed on an exclusive basis.

A de Luze & Fils This old family firm was sold to a British paper group during the oil crisis, but now belongs to Rémy Martin of Cognac. The business is still run along fairly traditional lines with the emphasis on quality wine, but is now run jointly by Rémy's other Bordeaux house, De Rivoyre and Diprovin.

Mähler-Besse A family firm still firmly rooted in its Dutch origins. Part-owner of Château Palmer.

Yvon Mau & Fils A firm specializing in generic wines and Petits Châteaux, situated near La Réole in Entre-Deux-Mers.

Mestrezat SA A house specializing in a wide range of wines, mostly château-bottled. It part owns, or participates in the management of, Grand-Puy-Ducasse and Rayne-Vigneau, as well as several lesser *crus*.

A Moueix Armand Moueix's business, run from Château Taillefer in Pomerol, may not have the glamour of his cousin's firm in Libourne, but this is a serious quality house nevertheless. It is also firmly based on properties, of which the two Grands Crus Classés of St-Emilion, Châteaux La-Tour-du-Pin-Figeac and Fonplégade, are the best. Very much a Libournais specialist, its association with Schröder & Schÿler has enabled it to present a more comprehensive range for export.

J-P Moueix Jean-Pierre Moueix is a legend in his own lifetime. No one has done more to carry the fame of Libournais wines into the US and UK markets and raise their prestige worldwide. Now Christian, his son, and Jean-Jacques, his nephew, are there to carry on the tradition, and the old Bordeaux house of Duclot has been transformed into Moueix-Export, with a classic range of Médocs, Graves and Sauternes to complement the St-Emilions and Pomerols. This firm has the ownership or exclusive distribution of many châteaux, headed by Pétrus, Trotanoy, La Fleur-Pétrus and Magdelaine.

Les Fils de Marcel Quancard A family firm, based at La Grave-d'Ambarès in Entre-Deux-Mers, which has grown considerably in the past 25 years. It owns several properties, including Château Terrefort, and offers a wide range of Petits Châteaux and brands.

De Rivoyre & Diprovin Not an easy name to trip off the Anglo-Saxon tongue, so, for export, the names Louis Dubroca and Rineau are used. Specializing in a large selection of Petits Châteaux and Cru Bourgeois, as well as the big names *en primeur*, this firm has substantial business in France as well as exporting to the UK and USA. Now part of Rémy Martin and run jointly with its other Bordeaux house, de Luze.

Schröder & Schÿler A famous old business founded in 1739 and still with Schÿlers working in the company. The main markets are still its traditional ones of Scandinavia and

Holland. Proprietor of Château Kirwan.

SDVF (Société de Distribution des Vins Fins) Founded in 1973 by M Hernandez at a time when many firms were in trouble. He bought large stocks of Crus Classés at low prices when no one else wanted them – and has never looked back.

Maison Sichel This well-respected family firm has a share of Château Palmer, and its head, Peter A Sichel, owns and lives at Château d'Angludet. Since it separated from H Sichel of Mainz and London, all Sichel brands in Germany, the UK, Eire and the USA (where Shieffelin own the rights) have passed out of its hands. On these markets it sells as Gallaire, although in the UK Peter A Sichel trades under his own name. H Sichel has its own company in Bordeaux which furnishes the wines for the Sichel brands in Germany, the UK, Eire and the USA.

Understanding a Bordeaux Label

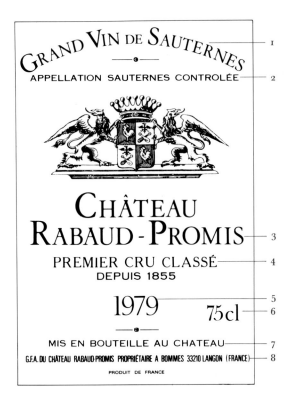

I   Almost every Bordeaux wine describes itself as a 'Grand Vin', whether it is a Cru Classé or a simple Bordeaux rouge.

2   It is a legal requirement that the *appellation* be indicated. The name has to appear between the words 'Appellation' and 'Contrôlée'.

3   The majority of Bordeaux wines are sold under a château name. In addition, many wines that are sent to be vinified at *caves coopératives*, but kept separate, are allowed to use their property names.

4   Classification. The wines of Sauternes and Barsac were classified in 1855 at the same time as those of the Médoc. More recently there have been classifications for St-Emilion and Graves.

5   Year of vintage.

6   This is the standard bottle size in the EC.

7   'Bottled at the château'. Until a few years ago the majority of Bordeaux wines were bottled either in the Bordeaux cellars of *négociants* or abroad in such places as London and Brussels. Château-bottling became obligatory for all Crus Classés in the early 1970s. The words *'mis en bouteille à la propriété'* indicate that the wine has been bottled by the *cave coopérative* where it was made.

8   Name and address of producer.

Classifications

1855 Classification of the Médoc

The Médoc First Growths had emerged as such in the 18th century and, by the early 19th century, classifications were being made covering a range of Médocs and some Graves. They were essentially based on market prices and were produced by *courtiers* and *négociants* as guides for their customers.

When the newly fledged Second Empire was preparing its answer to London's Great Exhibition of 1851, it was decided to show a range of Bordeaux wines, and the question arose as to which châteaux should represent the region. A commission of *courtiers* was given the task, and the result was the Classification of 1855 encompassing the red wines of Médoc plus Château Haut-Brion, and the great sweet wines of Sauternes. It was rather an accident of history that this particular list should have become enshrined as an immutable and permanent order of merit, something its authors certainly never intended. When, in 1867, a group of St-Emilions was shown at a subsequent Paris Exhibition, no such permanent value was accorded to the list.

There have been various attempts to update the 1855 classification, but the vested interests opposed to it seem more powerful than those who would like to see change. I will indicate under the individual entries which growths I consider to be superior or otherwise to their classification. The only official change was the elevation of Mouton-Rothschild to the status of First Growth in 1973, recognizing a position it had in reality long held. It is important to remember that there is no control over the vineyards of any of the listed châteaux. Some have remained virtually unchanged since 1855, while others have expanded or contracted.

This is essentially the original 1855 list. Apart from the promotion of Mouton-Rothschild to Premier Cru in 1973 there have been no fundamental changes, except that certain *crus* have disappeared, while others have been divided or have changed their names. The list encompasses the great red wines of the Médoc, the sole exception being the inclusion of Haut-Brion in the Graves.

Premiers Crus

Lafite-Rothschild	Pauillac
Margaux	Margaux
Latour	Pauillac
Haut-Brion	Pessac (Graves)
Mouton-Rothschild	Pauillac

Deuxièmes Crus

Rausan-Ségla	Margaux
Rauzan-Gassies	Margaux
Léoville-Las-Cases	St-Julien
Léoville-Poyferré	St-Julien
Léoville-Barton	St-Julien
Durfort-Vivens	Margaux
Gruaud-Larose	St-Julien
Lascombes	Margaux
Brane-Cantenac	Cantenac
Pichon-Longueville Baron	Pauillac
Pichon-Longueville Comtesse	Pauillac
Ducru-Beaucaillou	St-Julien
Cos d'Estournel	St-Estèphe
Montrose	St-Estèphe

Troisièmes Crus

Kirwan	Cantenac
d'Issan	Cantenac
Lagrange	St-Julien

Langoa-Barton	St-Julien	Prieuré-Lichine	Cantenac
Giscours	Labarde	Marquis-de-Terme	Margaux
Malescot-St-Exupéry	Margaux		
Boyd-Cantenac	Cantenac	**Cinquièmes Crus**	
Cantenac-Brown	Cantenac	Pontet-Canet	Pauillac
Palmer	Cantenac	Batailley	Pauillac
La Lagune	Ludon	Haut-Batailley	Pauillac
Desmirail	Margaux	Grand-Puy-Lacoste	Pauillac
Calon-Ségur	St-Estèphe	Grand-Puy-Ducasse	Pauillac
Ferrière	Margaux	Lynch-Bages	Pauillac
Marquis-d'Alesme-		Lynch-Moussas	Pauillac
Becker	Margaux	Dauzac	Labarde
		d'Armailhac	Pauillac
Quatrièmes Crus		du Tertre	Arsac
St-Pierre	St-Julien	Haut-Bages-Libéral	Pauillac
Talbot	St-Julien	Pédesclaux	Pauillac
Branaire-Ducru	St-Julien	Belgrave	St-Laurent
Duhart-Milon	Pauillac	Camensac	St-Laurent
Pouget	Cantenac	Cos-Labory	St-Estèphe
La Tour-Carnet	St-Laurent	Clerc-Milon	Pauillac
Lafon-Rochet	St Estèphe	Croizet-Bages	Pauillac
Beychevelle	St-Julien	Cantemerle	Macau

1855 Classification of the Sauternes

Again, the original list, apart from divisions and changes of name.

Grand Premier Cru		**Deuxièmes Crus**	
Yquem	Sauternes	de Myrat	Barsac
		Doisy-Daëne	Barsac
Premiers Crus		Doisy-Dubroca	Barsac
La Tour-Blanche	Bommes	Doisy-Védrines	Barsac
Lafaurie-Peyraguey	Bommes	d'Arche	Sauternes
Clos Haut-Peyraguey	Bommes	Filhot	Sauternes
Rayne-Vigneau	Bommes	Broustet	Barsac
Suduiraut	Preignac	Nairac	Barsac
Coutet	Barsac	Caillou	Barsac
Climens	Barsac	Suau	Barsac
Guiraud	Sauternes	de Malle	Preignac
Rieussec	Fargues	Romer	Fargues
Rabaud-Promis	Bommes	Lamothe	Sauternes
Sigalas-Rabaud	Bommes		

Classed Growths of the Graves

After the Second World War, interest in classification revived, and both Graves and St-Emilion began to negotiate with the INAO for their own. The Graves classification, which was a great deal simpler to agree, came out first in 1953, encompassing only red wines, and this was revised in 1959 to include white wines as well. With such a small number of wines actually classified, there is, not surprisingly, no attempt to place the wines in different categories, with the result that the wines vary in quality considerably, from Haut-Brion with its Premier Cru status, to wines that sell at prices of Médoc Fifth Growths or top Crus Bourgeois. Again, I shall assess the standing of each wine under its individual entry.

Red Wines

Bouscaut	Cadaujac
Haut-Bailly	Léognan
Carbonnieux	Léognan
Domaine de Chevalier	Léognan
Fieuzal	Léognan
Olivier	Léognan
Malartic-Lagravière	Léognan
La Tour-Martillac	Martillac
Smith-Haut-Lafitte	Martillac
Haut-Brion	Pessac
La Mission-Haut-Brion	Talence
Pape-Clément	Pessac
Latour-Haut-Brion	Talence

White Wines

Bouscaut	Cadaujac
Carbonnieux	Léognan
Domaine de Chevalier	Léognan
Olivier	Léognan
Malartic-Lagravière	Léognan
La Tour-Martillac	Martillac
Laville-Haut-Brion	Talence
Couhins	Villenave d'Ornon

The 1985 St-Emilion Classification

St-Emilion had long been in a chaotic state, posing special problems for the consumer. A large number of *crus* described themselves as Premiers Crus, and the properties, mostly small, and many with similar names, also have a way of changing more often than elsewhere. Although there are over 5,000 hectares now under vine in the St-Emilion *appellation*, only 14 domaines are of more than 25 hectares in size, and there are only 34 properties with between 12 and 25 hectares, the total area of these covering 589 hectares. The classification divides the châteaux of the region into two categories – Premiers Grands Crus Classés and Grands Crus Classés, with the

Premiers Ausone and Cheval Blanc singled out as category A, the rest as B. The first list was published in 1955, comprising 12 Premiers Grands Crus and 63 Grands Crus. In 1969, at the first revision, the Grands Crus were increased to 71, while in 1985 a second revision reduced the Premiers Crus to 11, and the Grand Crus to 63.

Premiers Grands Crus Classés
(A) Ausone
     Cheval-Blanc
(B) Beauséjour (Duffau-Lagarosse)
     Belair
     Canon
     Clos Fourtet
     Figeac
     La Gaffelière
     Magdelaine
     Pavie
     Trottevieille
Grands Crus Classés
L'Angelus
L'Arrosée
Balestard la Tonnelle
Beau Séjour Bécot
Bellevue
Bergat
Berliquet
Cadet-Piola
Canon-la-Gaffelière
Cap de Mourlin
Chauvin
Clos des Jacobins
Clos la Madeleine
Clos de l'Oratoire
Clos Saint Martin
La Clotte
La Clusière
Corbin
Corbin-Michotte
Couvent des Jacobins
Croque-Michotte
Curé-Bon-La-Madeleine
Dassault
La Dominique
Faurie-de-Souchard

Fonplégade
Fonroque
Franc-Mayne
Grand-Barrail-Lamarzelle-Figeac
Grand-Corbin-Despagne
Grand-Corbin
Grand-Mayne
Grand-Pontet
Guadet-Saint-Julien
Haut-Corbin
Haut-Sarpe
Laniote
Larcis-Ducasse
Lamarzelle
Larmande
Laroze
Matras
Mauvezin
Moulin-du-Cadet
Pavie-Decesse
Pavie-Macquin
Pavillon-Cadet
Petit-Faurie de Soutard
Le Prieuré
Ripeau
Sansonnet
Saint-Georges-Côte-Pavie
La Serre
Soutard
Tertre-Daugay
La Tour-du-Pin-Figeac
    (Giraud-Bélivier)
La Tour-du-Pin-Figeac (Moueix)
La Tour-Figeac
Trimoulet
Troplong-Mondot
Villemaurine
Yon-Figeac

1978 Classification of the Crus Bourgeois of the Médoc and Haut-Médoc

The Crus Bourgeois of the Médoc were originally classified in 1920, but by 1962 there were only 94 members compared with the 444 properties that existed in 1932. Today there are over 200 *crus* claiming to be Crus Bourgeois, and of these 150 belong to the Syndicat. The first *classement* was issued in 1966, and a revision in 1978 divided the members into Grands Bourgeois Exceptionnels, Grands Bourgeois, and Bourgeois. But unfortunately EC regulations permit only the words 'Cru Bourgeois' to appear on a label. The distinctions made in 1978 are useful, however, because of the criteria used.

Cru Bourgeois must have a minimum of seven hectares, the wine must be made on the property (not at a cooperative), and the Syndicat must be satisfied that the wine is of good quality. There are 68 properties in this category.

In the case of **Cru Grand Bourgeois**, in addition to these stipulations, the wine must be wood-matured in cask. There are 41 such *crus*.

Cru Grand Bourgeois Exceptionnel is the tightest category. In addition to the requirements for the above categories, these *crus* must be in the communes of the Haut-Médoc, the area covered by the Crus Classés, and the wine must be château-bottled. There are 18 of these (indicated by the letter *E*).

The château name is followed by that of the commune.

Grand Bourgeois

Agassac	Ludon *E*	Cissac	Cissac *E*
Andron-Blanquet	St-Estèphe *E*	Citran	Avensan *E*
Beaumont	Cussac	Colombier-	
Beau-Site	St-Estèphe *E*	Monpelou	Pauillac
Bel-Orme	St-Seurin-de-	Coufran	St-Seurin-de-
	Cadourne		Cadourne
		Coutelin-Merville	St-Estèphe
Brillette	Moulis	Le Crock	St-Estèphe *E*
Capbern	St-Estèphe *E*	Duplessis	
La Cardonne	Blaignan	(Hauchecorne)	Moulis
Caronne-Ste-		Dutruch Grand	
Gemme	St-Laurent *E*	Poujeaux	Moulis *E*
Chasse-Spleen	Moulis *E*	La Fleur-Milon	Pauillac

Fontesteau	St-Sauveur	Balac	St-Laurent-de-Médoc
Fourcas-Dupré	Listrac *E*		
Fourcas-Hosten	Listrac *E*	La Bécade	Listrac
du Glana	St-Julien *E*	Bellerive	Valeyrac
Greysac	Bégadan	Belle Rose	Pauillac
Hanteillan	Cissac	Bonneau-Livran	St-Seurin-de-Cadourne
Haut-Marbuzet	St-Estèphe *E*		
Lafon	Listrac	Le Boscq	St-Christoly
de Lamarque	Lamarque	du Breuil	Cissac
Lamothe	Cissac	La Bridane	St-Julien
Larose-Trintaudon	St-Laurent	de By	Bégadan
		Castéra	St-Germain-d'Esteuil
Laujac	Bégadan		
Liversan	St-Sauveur	Cap-Léon-Veyrin	Listrac
Loudenne	St-Yzans	Carcanieux	Queyrac
MacCarthy	St-Estèphe	Chambert-Marbuzet	St-Estèphe
Malleret	Le-Pian		
Marbuzet	St-Estèphe *E*	La Clare	Bégadan
Martinens	Margaux	La Closerie	Moulis
Meyney	St-Estèphe *E*	Duplessis-Fabre	Moulis
Le Meynieu	Vertheuil	Fonréaud	Listrac
Morin	St-Estèphe	Fonpiqueyre	St-Sauveur
Moulin-à-Vent	Moulis	Fort Vauban	Cussac
Les Ormes-de-Pez	St-Estèphe	La France	Blaignan
Les Ormes-Sorbet	Couquèques	Gallais Bellevue	Potensac
Patache d'Aux	Bégadan	Grand-Duroc-Milon	Pauillac
Paveil-de-Luze	Soussans		
Peyrabon	St-Saveur	Grand-Moulin	St-Seurin-de-Cadourne
Phélan-Ségur	St-Estèphe *E*		
Pontoise-Cabarrus	St-Seurin-de-Cadourne	Haut-Bages-Monpelou	Pauillac
		Haut-Canteloup	Couquèques
Potensac	Potensac	Haut-Garin	Bégadan
Poujeaux	Moulis *E*	Haut-Padarnac	Pauillac
Reysson	Vertheuil	Houbanon	Prignac
Sigognac	St-Yzans	Hourtin-Ducasse	St-Sauveur
Sociando-Mallet	St-Seurin-de-Cadourne	de Labat	St-Laurent
		Lamothe-Bergeron	Cussac
du Taillan	Le Taillan	Le Landat	Cissac
La Tour-de-By	Bégadan	Landon	Bégadan
Tour-du-Haut-Moulin	Cussac	Lartigue-de-Brochon	St-Seurin-de-Cadourne
Tronquoy-Lalande	St-Estèphe	Cru Lassalle	Potensac
Verdignan	St-Seurin-de-Cadourne	Lestage	Listrac
		MacCarthy-Moula	St-Estèphe
Bourgeois		Monthil	Bégadan
Aney	Cussac		

Moulin Rouge	Cussac	La Tour-Haut-	
Panigon	Civrac	Caussan	Blaignan
Pibran	Pauillac	Tour-du-Mirail	Cissac
Plantey-de-la-Croix	St-Seurin-de-	La Tour-St-Bonnet	St-Christoly
	Cadourne	La Tour-St-Joseph	Cissac
Pontet	Blaignan	des Tourelles	Blaignan
Ramage-la-Bâtisse	St-Sauveur	Vieux Robin	Bégadan
La Roque-de-By	Bégadan		
La Rose-		**Vineyards at present being**	
Maréchale	St-Seurin-de-	**reconstituted**	
	Cadourne	Les Bertins	Valeyrac
St-Bonnet	St-Christoly	Clarke	Listrac
Saransot	Listrac	Larivière	Blaignan
Soudars	Avensan	Lavalière	St-Christoly
Tayac	Soussans	Romefort	Cussac
La Tour Blanche	St-Christoly	Vernous	Lesparre

The following properties have joined the Syndicate of Bourgeois Growths of the Médòc since 1978 but are at present not classified because of EC regulations.

Anthonic	Moulis	Lacombe-de-	
Beau-Site	St-Estèphe	Noaillac	Jau
Bellevue	Valeyrac	Lagorce	Blaignan
Les Bertins	Valeyrac	Lagrave	St-Sauveur
Blaignan	Blaignan	Lestage Simon	St-Seurin
Bonneau	Avensan	Lieujan	St-Sauveur
Bourdieu	Vertheuil	Liouner	Listrac
Bournac	Civrac St-Julien	Magnol Dehez	Blanquefort
Cailloux-de-By	Bégadan	Malescasse	Lamarque
Canuet	Margaux	Malmaison	Listrac
Charmail	St-Seurin	Marsac-Seguineau	Soussans
La Commanderie	St-Estèphe	Martinens	Cantenac
de Conques	Couquèques	Maucaillou	Moulis
Domaine de la		Maucamps	Macau
Croix	Ordonnac	Monbrison	Arsac
L'Estruelle	St-Yzans	Moulin-de-	
Goudy-la-		Castillon	St-Christoly
Cardonne	Ordonnac	Moulin-de-Laborde	Listrac
Grivière	Blaignan	Moulin-de-la-	
Hauterive	St-Germain-	Roque	Bégadan
	d'Esteuil	Moulin Riche	St-Julien
Haut Logat	Cissac	Moulin-de-St-	
Lalande	Listrac	Vincent	Moulis

Moulis	Moulis	St-Paul	St-Seurin
Pey-Martin	Ordonnac	St-Roch	St-Estèphe
Peyredon-		Sestignan	Jau Dignac-
Lagravette	Medrac-Listrac		Loirac
Le Plantey	St-Yzans	Terrey-Gros-	
Pomys	St-Estèphe	Cailloux	St-Julien
Preuilhac	Lesparre	La Tour-de-Mons	Margaux
Puy-Castéra	Cissac	Tour-du-Roc	Arcins
Domaine de la		Tourteran	St-Sauveur
Ronceray	St-Estèphe	Troupian	St Seurin-de-
St-Ahon	Caychac		Cadourne
Saint Aubin	Jau	Les Tuileries	St-Yzans
St-Estèphe	St-Estèphe	Vieux-Robin	Bégadan

What Happens in the Vineyard

Good wine begins with good grapes, and good grapes in turn depend on good viticulture and the weather. A leading proprietor said to me recently that, after the enormous progress made in the past 20 years' winemaking, there was not much more to be done in this respect, but there were still improvements possible in viticulture.

If we start with a new vine, the first important decision made is what American rootstock to use and which clone of the European vine to select. Different varieties perform better in different soils. For instance, much work has been done in recent years by the Station de Recherches Viticoles du Sud-Ouest to discover rootstocks that are resistant to chlorosis in limestone soils. Furthermore, some varieties do better than others in poorly-drained, humid soils as against dry, well-drained ones. Less work has been done on the cloning of vines here than in Burgundy, to say nothing of Germany. The yearly pattern of work in the vineyards roughly proceeds as follows:

January The work of the *taille* (pruning), begun in December, continues. New stakes are put in place and secured, and the pruned canes are attached to the vines.

February The pruning continues, together with the clearing of the vineyard, gathering of the bundled canes, and so on. The first treatment of the vines against excoriose (a fungus which attacks the wood), esca (another fungus, also called black measles), and red and yellow spider (which would later attack the young leaves).

March The first buds normally break in late March, between the 20th and 30th of the month. The first ploughing removes the earth from around the foot of the vine in order to aerate it after the winter.

April Spring begins. Any dead vines are replaced and the first hoeing takes place. The vines may be dusted with sulphur against oidium and sprayed with a copper sulphate solution against mildew.

May The work begun in the previous month continues according to weather conditions, as do the treatments against disease. The first pinching back of the young shoots is carried out to limit the growth of the vine and direct it towards the production of grapes. Stray shoots from the base of the vine are cut back.

June This is classically the month of the flowering. In the years 1975–84 the earliest flowering began on May 26 (1982), and the latest on June 15 (1977). Most typically it happens between the 2nd and 10th of the month. This gives the approximate timing for the vintage, which normally occurs 100 to 110 days after the flowering. Ploughing continues, the new shoots are tied up, and the length of the new growth permits it to be trained between the second and third row of wires, though not attached to them.

July The soil is now ploughed away from the vines again so there is a mound of soil running between each row of vines, and weeds are hoed. Treatment continues according to the conditions. The *véraison* (the changing of the colour of the grapes, the most important indication of ripening between the flowering and the vintage) can begin in late July. (This happened in 1975, 1976, 1981, 1982 and 1989.)

August A quiet period when many *vignerons* go on holiday, this can nevertheless be a crucial time for treating the vines if the weather is damp and humid, especially against premature rot. If the *véraison* has not occurred in July it usually happens in the first week of August (but in 1980 it did not occur until the 18th).

September The preferred month for beginning the harvest. Over the period 1975–84 half the vintages began in this month. In the weeks before the harvest the last preventative treatments are carried out, but at this time the *vigneron* hopes to be able to concentrate his efforts on preparing for the vintage in the *cuvier*.

October The month of the harvest (vintage or *récolte*) and hence the key month in the viticultural calendar. Even if the vintage began in September, most of it will take place and be completed in October. Sometimes the vintage in Sauternes will go on until the end of the month.

November The harvest is over and the plough returns to the vineyard to earth up the vines for the winter. The manuring also takes place.

December The pruning begins. First the foliage is cut back to make the work of pruning easier. The cuttings are bundled up and burnt. Any vines that have been damaged or have died during the year are noted for replacement next year. The work goes on.

Making Wine

Red Wine

Thirty years ago it was almost true to say that in most years the great red Bordeaux made themselves. They are still not complicated wines to make, but the art has been refined, at least at most properties.

The process is as follows:

1   The grapes arrive in the *cuvier* and are moved via an Archimedian screw mechanism to the *fouloir-égrappoir*, which crushes and destalks the grapes. The word 'crush' is perhaps an exaggeration of what actually happens; this machine breaks the skins rather than crushing the grapes, as can be clearly seen when the pulp is then pumped into the fermenting vat. Mechanically-harvested grapes do not usually need to be de-stemmed. There has been much refinement of the basic *fouloir-égrappoir* in recent years to make the process gentler and to ensure that no tannins from the stalks are released into the pulp.

2   The traditional fermentation *cuve* (vat) in Bordeaux is wooden, and the top is often reached by a wooden gallery. Many of these old *cuves* are still in use, but are steadily being replaced by vats of stainless steel, metal lined with enamel, or concrete lined with enamel. The advantages of the new *cuves* are that: (a) they are easier to clean; (b) they

make it easier to control the temperature of the fermentation; (c) they are often of smaller size to assist selection and temperature control. The fermentation usually lasts from five to ten days, and the object is to ferment at 28–30°C (82–86°F), instead of allowing the temperature to rise to 34°C (93°F) as formerly.

3 After the fermentation has been in progress a few hours, the solid matter, mostly skins, rises to the top of the vat to form what is known as the cap. At regular intervals the fermenting must is pumped over the top of the cap to keep it moist, keep its temperature down, and extract colour. A variation on this classic system is that in which the cap is submerged. This is a method whereby the cap is prevented by a mesh from rising to the top of the *cuve*.

4 In Bordeaux natural yeasts are usually allowed to bring about and sustain the fermentation. Normally there is an abundance of them, and the results they give usually prove satisfactory. Only when the grapes are unhealthy (affected by rot) can problems arise with this approach, and this is now rare.

5 The temperature is controlled by a variety of means. The most traditional in Bordeaux is a contraption that looks like a milk cooler. The must passes through a coil while cold water runs over the outside. With stainless steel vats, either the cold water can run down their exterior sides, or interior cooling coils can be used, as they can be for other types of vat. All this is a long way from throwing blocks of ice into vats, a system still in use in 1961 in many cellars.

6 Chaptalization (the addition of sugar to fermenting must in order to increase its potential alcohol) is now much more frequent in Bordeaux where, prior to 1962, it was almost unknown and illegal. Most Médocs are now chaptalized to 12 percent and St-Emilions and Pomerols to 12·5 percent, except in the best years when the natural degrees are quite sufficient. The sugar is normally added at the beginning of

fermentation after the composition of the must has been carefully checked.

7   The progress of the fermentation, the fall in density and the temperature, is normally shown in chart-form on each vat and checked every few hours. When no sugar remains to ferment, the wine (as it has now become) is either drawn off or left to macerate for some days in the presence of the skins. In the past this often continued for several weeks, but now the view is that most of the colour extraction takes place during fermentation, owing to the high temperatures, and that afterwards any improvement in the colour is minimal but tannins are still extracted, and these may not always be desirable. Bacterial infections may also be caused by prolonged skin contact and many winemakers like to draw the wine off immediately it has finished to avoid this.

8   After the new wine has been drawn off, the remaining solid matter (mostly what was contained in the cap) is removed from the vat and pressed. The result is what is known as *vin de presse*. The first *vin de presse* is usually of superior quality and will later be added back to the finished wine at the *assemblage*. The result of the second pressing is not normally of sufficient quality to be included. These two *vins de presse* between them account for about 15 percent of the wine produced. While *vin de presse* is not usually a desirable element in ordinary wines made for early consumption, it is richer in all its elements than the free-run wine, except in alcoholic degree, and so adds an important element in fine wines intended for long maturation and keeping.

9   The next stage is known as malolactic fermentation. Ideally, this should follow immediately after the alcoholic fermentation. It is the process by which the astringent malic acid is converted into the more supple lactic acid, and in the process the total acidity is also diminished. Some winemakers like this to take place in *cuve*, others put the wine straight in cask. This secondary fermentation occurs most easily at 20–25°C (68–77°F), so much emphasis is

placed on completing it before the weather turns too cold as the large *cuviers* of Bordeaux are hard to heat, particularly in comparison with the small cellars of Burgundy. If vats are equipped with an internal cooling system this can also be used, if necessary, for warming, thus facilitating the onset of malolactic fermentation. Until this process is finished the wine is not truly stable and it is also vulnerable to bacterial infections. In the past it was often observed that the wine would begin 'working' in the spring, at the time when the vine began to push out its first buds; this was, in reality, carbon dioxide released when the malolactic fermentation began again, the warm weather permitting the bacteria to become active once more. It is preferable though, to finish the process in the autumn rather than leaving the wine unstable through the winter.

10 Most, but not all, properties leave the new wine in *cuve* until the final selection or *assemblage* (blending) has been completed. This usually happens in January, sometimes later, depending on the year. All the *cuves* are tasted and decisions taken as to what will go into the *grand vin* (the main château label) and what should be eliminated in order to maintain the quality and reputation of the château. Sometimes there is a second label (such as Pavillon Rouge of Château Margaux, Réserve de la Comtesse of Pichon-Lalande, Clos du Marquis of Léoville-Las-Cases), but most of the rejected wine is usually sold under a simple generic label. This applies only to large properties and, therefore, mostly to the Médoc.

One of the less publicized but important decisions taken at this time is the addition of *vin de presse*. This gives the wine more tannin and extracts, and provides an important element in wines of quality, intended for ageing.

11 All the best Bordeaux châteaux mature their wines in oak casks of 225 litres, the finest using 100 percent new casks each year. But the wine has to have the power and composition to withstand such handling and, apart from the First Growths, most Crus Classés use around one third new wood each year. While wooden barrels are an important factor in giving complexity and 'finish' to a wine, they must be in good condition and not, in any case, more than about five years old. In the past many lesser *crus*, not being able to afford to buy new casks regularly, spoilt their wines by keeping them in old casks; these can easily taint the wine, making it seem mouldy or just not clean. It is better to keep the wine in vat rather than do this, and this is the policy of many lesser *crus* today, with resulting benefit to the wine. Bottling dates vary according to style and quality. The old system for the First Growths was to bottle only after the third winter in cask, that is in the spring of the third year. Now, most are bottled either after the vintage in the second year (at latest) or several months earlier in the late spring or summer of the second year (most commonly).

Dry White Wines

Over the past few years in Bordeaux the preparation of these has changed much more radically than in the case of the reds. The use of stainless steel horizontal presses, pneumatic presses and of low-temperature fermentation, has really revolutionized the style and quality of dry wines. In the past, Bordeaux made a few superb white Graves, but much of its white wine production was over-sulphured, heavy and dull. Now the wines are fruity and perfumed, fresh and clean.

The basic process is as follows:

1   The grapes are fed into a horizontal press as they come from the vineyard, stalks and all. The pressing must be very gentle, and the *marc* (solid cake or pomace of skins and other solid matter left after pressing) is continuously broken up by chains inside the press, which rotates at the same time as the grapes are squeezed.

2   The juice runs from the press and is collected in a stainless steel *cuve*. This will often nowadays be chilled and held as

grape juice over a period of 12 to 24 hours, in order to precipitate its solids. This process is known as *débourbage*. Some of the best Graves *vignerons* run the must straight into new barrels, which are often kept in an air-conditioned *chai*. The must is lightly sulphured to guard against oxidation.

3   Fermentation then takes place after the must has been racked off its solids after the *débourbage*, either into another *cuve* or into barrel. Fermentation is now usually controlled at 15–20°C (59–68°F).

4   Again, as with reds, white wines in Bordeaux normally undergo a malolactic fermentation.

5   As soon as the second fermentation is finished, it is clarified to prevent it from picking up any undesirable odours. This is usually done by filtration, or in large cellars by centrifuge.

6   Since the object nowadays is to prevent oxidation, wines spend much less time in pre-bottle maturation. Only the finest Graves spend more than a few months in cask; most wines are kept in *cuve* and bottled in the spring, some six months after the vintage, to conserve their freshness and fruit.

Sweet White Wines

Because of the state of grapes affected by *pourriture noble* (noble rot or *Botrytis cinerea*, to give the scientific name), both the harvesting and vinifying of grapes for sweet wines pose special problems. The grapes cannot be picked as for dry wines, because the infection by *Botrytis cinerea* does not occur uniformly, either in the vineyard or even in single bunches. This means that the workers must go through a vineyard several times (four to six times at the best properties) selecting the best grapes from each bunch, a method requiring a certain amount of skill. Such grapes obviously cannot be mechanically harvested.

Botrytis cinerea itself is a fungus which, when it attacks overripe grapes, dehydrates them thus concentrating their sugar content. Mild humid conditions, typical of a Bordeaux autumn, are required for this infection to thrive. If conditions are too dry, the fungus will not attack even very ripe grapes. This happened in 1978. On the other hand, if it rains at the wrong moment the vintage can be ruined, or only a small part of it will be any good. For these reasons there are far fewer successful vintages in Sauternes than in the neighbouring Graves.

The process of vinification is as follows:

1   Because of the condition of the grapes they are not crushed in a separate operation but go straight into the press. The pressing is difficult because the grapes are so rich in sugar (20–25° baumé – 360–450 grams per litre) and the juice so viscous. Three pressings are usual for Sauternes.

2   A *débourbage* is not usual because of the danger of sulphur dioxide binding the yeast cells and thus inhibiting their activity, and because a must so rich in sugar and bacteria is very susceptible to oxidation at this stage. The best method of clarification is to centrifuge and then chill the must before beginning the fermentation, which can still be in barrel, but is now more usually and safely in *cuve*.

3   The fermentation is slow and often continues for many weeks. It must be controlled very carefully in order to obtain a balanced wine. Thus, a wine with 12·5 percent alcohol is well balanced with 30–35 grams of sugar per litre but not with 50. This sort of result would be typical of wines made in the Premières Côtes. But a wine with 14 percent alcohol needs 60–70 grams to be balanced. Although the yeast becomes tired and 'blocked' when the level of alcohol rises to around 14 percent, the wine will still not be permanently stable, and must therefore be stabilized by the addition of sulphur dioxide. Stabilization is often assisted by filtration and chilling. Wines with less sugar must, in any case, be stopped from further fermentation in this way in order to ensure a balance.

4   The *élevage* (literally raising the wine, as one would
     children or cattle) then proceeds in much the same way as
     for dry wines, except that the best sweet wines seem to
     benefit from maturing in cask, and the process is more
     lengthy, often two to two and a half years before bottling.
     Selection, between *cuves* and even casks, is also very
     important when seeking to obtain really fine Sauternes, or
     indeed Loupiac or Ste-Croix-du-Mont.

Vintages

In temperate climates vintages are always important. Although
there are fewer poor vintages than there used to be in Bordeaux, it is
still important to know how the vintages vary, because this can tell
you broadly which wines should be laid down and which can be
drunk early. But each year has its distinctive character. Indeed the
finer the year, the stronger the vintage character, and the more
pronounced the character of each *cru*.

1990

Weather and General Assessment The pattern of 1989 was
     followed to a degree which is rare. The flowering was in
     May and but for a combination of heat and drought in July,
     which simply stopped the vines in their tracks, the vintage
     would have been even earlier than in 1989. As it was the
     vintage for the Merlots began around September 10, while
     the Cabernet Sauvignons in the Médoc needed to wait until
     the beginning of October. The wines have outstanding fruit
     and good structure, in the mould of 1982 and 1989.
Médoc and Graves The more northerly regions of the Médoc,
     with their heavier soils, did especially well. There are many
     outstanding successes among the Crus Bourgeois, and many
     exceptional wines in St-Estèphe, Pauillac and St-Julien, but
     Margaux is more varied. Graves are often opulent but also
     have elegance and great individuality.
St-Emilion and Pomerol The St-Emilions are characterized by their
     combination of rich, luscious fruit and good structure,

while Pomerol is notable for the concentration of its wines.

Dry Whites The aromatic quality of the fruit is outstanding, producers often achieving better balance and acidity than experienced with the 1989 vintage.

Sweet Whites The *annus mirabilis* for Sauternes, with the richest wines seen since 1929, even surpassing the wonderful 1989s. They are wines which are remarkably exotic in character.

1989

Weather and General Assessment The warmest, sunniest and driest summer, on average, in 30 years, with a flowering that began on May 20, and the earliest vintage since 1893, beginning on August 28. The wines are high in alcohol, with luscious fruit and soft ripe tannins reminiscent of 1982. The yields for red AC wines set a new record, surpassing 1986 by over 350,000 hectolitres.

Médoc and Graves The St-Juliens are a stunning group, but there are lovely wines in all the main communes. Selection of the best fruit, due to high yields, has meant that the leading growths have done correspondingly better than the lesser *crus*. There are some gloriously rich fruity wines. The Graves are lighter and more elegant in structure.

St-Emilion and Pomerol Amazingly dense-textured and forceful wines, with exceptional structure to add to the opulence of a great Merlot vintage.

Dry Whites Very big fat fruity wines, but many suffer from shortage of acidity and could, with advantage, have been harvested even earlier. For early drinking.

Sweet Whites After the classic 1988s, this is an exceptional year, comparable with 1947 and with more of everything. 1989 and 1990 must be the greatest pair of Sauternes perhaps since 1928 and 1929, coming at the end of a decade of fine vintages.

1988

Weather and General Assessment A wet winter and spring were followed by a drier than average summer and a very warm October. Significant variations in maturity between the grape varieties, and between the same variety at different

sites, caused noticeable variations in quality. In style, the
wines began as forbiddingly tannic, in the mould of 1986,
but have become classically elegant and fine.

Médoc and Graves Classically structured wines that seem finer,
but have less power, than the 1986s. They should be long-
lived and very harmonious.

St-Emilion and Pomerol The St-Emilions are exceptionally rich
and concentrated, usually superior to the 1986s, while the
Pomerols are really opulent with great depth of flavour.

Dry Whites The wines have pronounced fruit, with the best
Graves having complexity and elegance.

Sweet Whites Another classic botrytis year to set beside 1983 and
1986. The wines have character and great breed, they are
well balanced and the top wines are very consistent.

1987

Weather and General Assessment After above average temperatures
in July, August and September, it rained more intensely
during the second half of the vintage than in any year since
1964. In general the wines are soft, fruity and easy to drink
young.

Médoc and Graves The Cabernets were caught by the rain, so the
Merlots are of more than usual importance for this vintage.
The wines have plenty of fruit and charm, if light in body
and rather short. Pleasing, early-drinking wines.

St-Emilion and Pomerol With their high proportion of Merlot,
these regions did better than Médoc and Graves. The wines
are supple and fruity and are developing quickly.

Dry Whites The whites were picked in good condition and are
well balanced with pleasing fruit character.

Sweet Whites A small quantity of ripe botrytised grapes were
harvested before the rain. Where strict selections were
made, good wines have resulted.

1986

Weather and General Assessment There was a very successful
flowering and a good summer, but heavy rain, especially
around Bordeaux, in late September. The situation was
saved by exceptional conditions during the harvest, when

not a drop of rain fell. The red wine crop beat the record established the previous year. The quality of the best wines is excellent, with some classic wines for long keeping. The most tannic year since 1975, and a complete contrast to 1985.

Médoc and Graves Very much a Cabernet year, with many vats of Merlot remaining unused. The wines have great power, depth and promise but will need patience.

St-Emilion and Pomerol Here there was less rain and the Merlot did much better. The Pomerols are very powerful and tannic, the St-Emilions have more charm but are generally less powerful.

Dry Whites Very perfumed and attractive, sometimes better balanced than the 1985s.

Sweet Whites Another great Sauternes vintage. The onset of botrytis was more general and rapid than in 1985, and the quality more consistent than in 1983.

1985

Weather and General Assessment In spite of rain during eight out of ten of the 17 days' flowering, there was an excellent setting of the fruit. The character of the vintage was formed by the driest September on record combined with sustained heat, and a warm and dry October. This was the largest crop of AC reds, beating 1982. The overall quality is very high, and the wines have more charm and breed, classic in the style of 1983, but they are more outstanding across the board.

Médoc and Graves Outstanding in Margaux and Graves, more rigorous selection was necessary in Pauillac, St-Julien and Médoc: yields were very high. Properties that delayed picking their Cabernets until the second week of October did best. The wines are rich in fruit and tannin and very harmonious.

St-Emilion and Pomerol The sugar levels in the Merlot here were higher than in 1982, and the general level amongst the leading growths is more uniform than usual. There were lower yields than in 1982 but still excellent considering the exceptionally cold January.

Dry Whites Extremely perfumed fruity wines, but acidity low.
Sweet Whites The dryness of the year inhibited the growth of
    botrytis, but the few properties which prolonged picking
    have made excellent wines with great elegance, if less
    length than 1983.

1984

Weather and General Assessment A cold wet May seems to have
    been responsible for the worst *coulure* (failure of flowers to
    set) in the Merlot in living memory. Then rain and storms
    in late September gave way to perfect October weather for
    harvesting. There are a few successes, but in general rather
    mean wines.
Médoc and Graves Average yields produced wines that have not
    lived up to early expectations. There are a few pleasant
    surprises.
St-Emilion and Pomerol A very small crop of rather average wine
    which lacks character and can appear mean.
Dry Whites Excellent quality, normal yield. The wines have
    more delicacy and are lighter than the 1983s, with
    pronounced character.
Sweet Whites The potential for quality was reduced by the wet
    weather at the end of September, but some fine wines were
    made.

1983

Weather and General Assessment After a wet spring the weather
    for the flowering in June was perfect, and the result
    promised a large vintage to begin around September 25.
    The first part of September caused anxiety, with too much
    rain, but from September 18 until October 16 the weather
    was ideal for the vintage. A very fine year, not quite as
    consistent as 1982, but producing classic wines with depth
    and character.
Médoc and Graves Another large vintage, quality not so regular
    as in 1982 but very fine at Crus Classés level with some
    very stylish wines. Many wines now pleasant to drink.
St-Emilion and Pomerol A high yield with some outstanding
    wines but again more variation than in 1982. Wines

developing attractively.

Dry Whites Wines have more acidity and style than the 1982s. Very good.

Sweet Wines A great year, probably the best since 1976. Very luscious wines, but well-balanced.

1982

Weather and General Assessment A classic hot year, with a large yield; but sustained warm weather led to perfect ripeness. Certainly the most outstanding vintage since 1961. The wines have a very special vintage character.

Médoc and Graves Wines of exceptional concentration and power, with plenty of fruit to cover the high tannin levels. An exceptional year, the most individual since 1961.

St-Emilion and Pomerol Wines of exceptional opulence and power, reminiscent of 1947. As in 1947, some of the top wines have proved remarkable for early drinking, but are still improving.

Dry Whites These wines have charm but are short of acidity. Mostly for early drinking.

Sweet Whites The dry hot weather delayed the noble rot, and then the rain in October started too early, resulting in medium-weight wines that are no more than good.

1981

Weather and General Assessment Good weather right through the growing period, but some rain during the vintage. Wines have more breed but less body than in 1979.

Médoc and Graves Classic wines, with length and finish. Not as powerful as the 1979s nor as firm as the 1978s but with all the breed of a really fine year.

St-Emilion and Pomerol The wines have elegance and style; at the same time the best are full and luscious in flavour, although many are rather light, developing fairly quickly.

Dry Whites Elegant wines of medium weight. Now mostly drunk.

Sweet Whites The best are luscious, better than the 1982s.

1980

Weather and General Assessment The coldest June since 1946 caused prolonged flowering and widespread *coulure*. A very cold July was followed by a warm August and September. For many châteaux this was the latest harvest since 1922, with the smallest crop since 1969, mainly due to a very small harvest of white wines. A very useful vintage of early-developing stylish wines.

Médoc and Graves Very attractive wines for early drinking, now at their best or beginning to show their age. The selection carried out by the leading châteaux produced dividends. A good follow-up to 1976.

St-Emilion and Pomerol More variable than Médoc but, since the Merlot ripened better than the Cabernet Sauvignon, these areas produced many supple, fruity wines for early drinking.

Dry Whites Light, pleasant wines that should have been drunk by now.

Sweet Whites The wines are rather light, but the best have a pleasant fruitiness and charm without real lusciousness.

1979

Weather and General Assessment A late flowering in warm, sunny conditions led to an excellent setting and the prospect of a large vintage. There was a setback in August with cold, wet weather, but better conditions in September enabled a large crop to be gathered. The wines have great depth of fruit and vigour, lots of charm, but are slightly lacking in backbone and breed.

Médoc and Graves The wines have a marked vintage character and are rich and dense in texture. They have developed more slowly than expected, with the best wines still improving but lacking the finesse of 1978.

St-Emilion and Pomerol The exceptional ripeness of the Merlot produced much more luscious, dense and opulent wines than in 1978. This is the sort of year that brings out the best in these districts.

Dry Whites Very stylish wines, with fruit and breed.

Sweet Whites Vies with 1981 as the best vintage between 1976 and 1983. Luscious, fruity wines, developing well.

1978

Weather and General Assessment A year of contrasts. The wettest
March since 1870, then exceptionally dry weather in July,
August and September. The vintage – of average size – was
late, but, thanks to a dry October, harvested in ideal
conditions. These are classic wines, which many will prefer
to 1975 because of their harmonious balance. They have
developed more quickly than expected and are ideal for
drinking now.

Médoc and Graves Although not a year of perfect ripeness, the
wines have great character and finesse. Their considerable
tannin, well blended with fruit and richness, has given them
a long development. They are now mostly at their best.

St-Emilion and Pomerol At first these wines seem to lack the
power and richness of the Médocs, but they have developed
very attractively. Some wines are rather lean, but most are
decidedly stylish. Not such typical wines as the 1979s.

Dry Whites A fine year, with the best Graves needing longer to
develop than the 1979s.

Sweet Whites A freak year, with perfect ripeness but almost no
noble rot, leaving the wines lacking in classic character.

1977

Weather and General Assessment Frost at the end of March caused
serious damage, especially in Pomerol and St-Emilion. A
cold summer threatened disaster on a scale far exceeding
1972. Then came the driest September, with the most hours
of sunshine (not the highest temperatures) for 100 years.
Some useful commercial wines, but they tend to lack
appellation character.

Médoc and Graves Many light, pleasing wines, but mostly lacking
a real character of *appellation* or *cru*. With few exceptions,
these are wines which should have been drunk.

St-Emilion and Pomerol Small wines, not without charm, but
lacking individuality. Should have been drunk.

Dry Whites A few Graves are stylish and pleasing.

Sweet Whites A year to forget.

1976

Weather and General Assessment An unusual year, with very dry, hot weather from April to the end of August. By then, conditions resembled 1921, 1947 and 1949. The vintage began early (September 13), but there was considerable rain during the month, which diluted the musts. The thick skins and very small, concentrated berries would have produced something even more tannic and rich than 1975 had it not been for the rain. As it was, this mixture of tannin and concentrated fruit, diluted with rainwater, produced wines which vary considerably. Some are deeply coloured, rich and fruity. In others tannin and fruit seem to have separated. It has also affected the whole development cycle of the wines, which has been relatively rapid.

Médoc and Graves The best wines are supple, powerful and attractive, but there are also disappointments. The wines have developed well and are by now mostly at their best. To drink rather than to keep.

St-Emilion and Pomerol Overripeness and diluted colours are a feature here. Many wines suffer from low acidity and have aged rapidly. A few have more structure and are delicious now.

Dry Whites Wines low in acidity that needed drinking early. Some top Graves are rich and fine.

Sweet Whites A great vintage, with luscious wines which are more elegant and stylish than the 1975s.

1975

Weather and General Assessment Excellent flowering was followed by a very dry, hot summer. Some rain in September was just what was needed. A year of moderate yields, good alcoholic degrees and thick skins resulted in very tannic, slow-developing wines. They lack the balance and charm of the 1961s which some optimists believed them to resemble at an early stage.

Médoc and Graves At some châteaux this is now looking the best vintage of the decade, with the tannins peeling away to reveal rich concentrated classic wines with power and fruit. Elsewhere the tannins can seem too dry.

St-Emilion and Pomerol As often happens in a very tannic year,
the best wines seem better balanced than in the Médoc.
Here the emphasis is on ripeness and opulence and there are
many successful wines.

Dry Whites The best Graves are concentrated and powerful but
lack the elegance of the 1976s.

Sweet Whites Many wines have too much botrytis and are too
alcoholic, resulting in clumsy, tarry wines which are ageing
rapidly (Yquem, Climens, Coutet and Doisy-Daëne are
notable exceptions).

1974

Weather and General Assessment A good flowering ensured a large
vintage. A fine summer promised good quality, but a cold,
wet September changed all that. These are austere,
charmless wines for the most part, which lack any real
appellation or *cru* character. Some white Graves could
provide nice surprises, but a year to forget in Sauternes.

1973

Weather and General Assessment Good flowering conditions
ensured a large crop, but the summer alternated between
hot and sunny (August) and very wet (July and the second
half of September). A good October enabled the vintage to
be gathered in good conditions. A big commercial vintage,
with a wide spectrum of qualities. The best wines have lots
of unaffected charm.

Médoc and Graves Very attractive early-developing wines. The
majority should have been drunk by now, but some are
holding up surprisingly well.

St-Emilion and Pomerol Rather overblown wines which had great
charm but were short-lived, with a few notable exceptions.

Dry Whites Some stylish Graves have lasted well, but most
should have been drunk some time ago.

Sweet Whites Pleasant but moderate wines, on the light side.

1972

Weather and General Assessment A cold spring led to a late and
protracted flowering; then a poor summer, with more than

its share of rain in August, resulted in a very late harvest and unripe grapes. The year is more remembered for its high prices than for its mean, dull wines which are best forgotten.

1971

Weather and General Assessment A cold, wet spring caused a poor flowering and a correspondingly small crop. Then the summer turned warm and sunny with just the right amount of rain. A complete contrast to the previous vintage, the sprinter against the long-distance runner.

Médoc and Graves Very flattering, charming wines that developed quickly and have been at their peak since the late 1970s. With their low acidities, they now need drinking, and many have already turned the corner.

St-Emilion and Pomerol Some great successes here, with rich, luscious but rather overblown wines. They should be drunk up, except for a few Pomerols.

Dry Whites Very perfumed, elegant Graves at the top level and lasting well.

Sweet Whites A great classic Sauternes year, combining richness with elegance, usually better than 1970.

1970

Weather and General Assessment Ideal growing conditions produced the rare combination of quantity and perfect ripeness. For the first time the new plantings of the 1960s yielded quality wines, and 1970 marked the beginning of the great switch from white to red wines and heralded the large yields of the 1970s and 1980s. This was the largest quality year since 1934. This fine vintage has been slow to develop but generally worth waiting for.

Médoc and Graves These wines have taken much longer to develop than expected, due perhaps to a lack of maturity in parts of the vineyards at this period. Nevertheless, these are classic long-distance wines, well structured, with breed and fruit to match the tannin. They are now becoming enjoyable to drink, especially the Margaux, St-Juliens and Graves, but there are some disappointments.

St-Emilion and Pomerol Also slow to evolve, but they have more
charm now than many Médocs and can mostly be drunk
with pleasure. The power and the structure of these wines
also promise a long life.

Dry Whites The best Graves are rich and solid and holding well.

Sweet Whites Big luscious wines, with less style for the most part
than 1971. Long-lasting wines.

1969

Weather and General Assessment A poor spring and flowering
ensured a small crop. There was rain in early September,
but then conditions turned fine for the vintage. The
growers persuaded themselves and others that the wines
would be 'useful', but they deteriorated during the second
winter. Then, even with some assistance from 1970, the
wines were never better than dull and meagre. Now to be
avoided, except for some pleasant honourable Sauternes.

1968

Weather and General Assessment The last great year of rot in
Bordeaux. A bad summer (August the coldest and wettest
for 20 years), ensured that even fine weather in October
could not save matters. A few wines were pleasant when
young, if light and short, but they are dead and buried now
– or should be!

1967

Weather and General Assessment A good flowering, July and
August hot and dry, then three weeks of wet and cold
conditions in September, with the final week hot. Mixed
conditions during the vintage, good weather punctuated by
heavy rain. This was the largest harvest of red AC wines of
the decade, but the quality was uneven, and many wines
have a characteristic bitter finish.

Médoc and Graves A few pleasant surprises still, but most wines
are now going dry and were better a few years ago. Drink
up!

St-Emilion and Pomerol In general, superior to Médoc and Graves.
The wines have more charm, with Pomerol leading the

way and the St-Emilion Côtes generally superior to the
Graves. But these wines are mostly fading now and should
be drunk.

Sweet Whites A great year for Sauternes, much better than 1966.
The wines have great fruit and style and are still fresh. A
long-lived classic vintage.

1966

Weather and General Assessment After a good flowering the
summer was cool and dry, and it was not until September
that there was any real heat, emphasizing once again that
the quality of the vintage is made in September. Harvesting
conditions were ideal, and there was no rot. After 1961, this
was the decade's best vintage, also a very consistent one.

Médoc and Graves Very classic wines, with structure, length and
great style. After a long period of gestation, these wines
have really come into their own and should continue to
give enjoyment for many years to come.

St-Emilion and Pomerol There was a tendency to say that the
1967s were better here, but I have found the 1966s have
remained fresher, even when they seemed lighter. Wine of
great charm and style, with some outstanding bottles. At
their best.

Sweet Whites These wines have less sugar and style than the
1967s.

1965

Weather and General Assessment An appalling summer of heavy
rains, with a wet, humid September, leading to grapes that
were both unripe and rotten. The worst of the three bad
years of the 1960s. The wines were thin and nondescript.

1964

Weather and General Assessment Very good flowering conditions
were followed by a hot, dry summer so that, when the
vintage began (September 21), expectations were high.
Unfortunately torrential rains fell from October 8 to 17,
and a number of leading Médoc châteaux were seriously
affected. So this was a vintage of very varied fortunes. Both

1962 and 1966 provided more consistent wines.

Médoc and Graves Graves, St-Julien, Margaux and those Pauillacs which were picked early fared best. Such wines are generous and supple, if a little lacking in backbone. The wines affected by rain are thin and washed out and should be avoided.

St-Emilion and Pomerol Wines of real concentration, powerful, full of fruit and richness, the best of which are keeping well. In spite of their extra weight, many lack the staying power of 1961 or 1966.

Sweet Whites The October rain ruined the Sauternes harvest, and few decent wines were made.

1963

Weather and General Assessment A cold, wet summer led to widespread rot and a lack of ripeness, although conditions during the harvest were good. A year best forgotten.

1962

Weather and General Assessment Late flowering in good conditions, a moderate summer interspersed with rain, then a hot Indian summer in September and good harvest conditions in October saved the vintage. A year overshadowed by 1961, but with a large crop of consistent, sound, attractive wines.

Médoc and Graves These wines have developed real depth and complexity in their maturity. Classic wines for enjoying now, although there is some mileage left in the top wines.

St-Emilion and Pomerol Lovely, mature wines, some now showing their age. Should be enjoyed now.

Sweet Whites An excellent vintage for Sauternes, the wines are well balanced and elegant, at their peak now.

1961

Weather and General Assessment Cold, wet weather during the flowering ensured that this would be a small crop, then drought conditions further reduced yields. The result: a small crop of wines, high in extract and alcohol, which have developed into the most outstanding year since the

Second World War, with no rival until the 1982s.

Médoc and Graves These wines continue to gain in complexity
with age. They have plenty of tannin matched by fruit and
richness and are marvellously harmonious. They still seem
to have a long life ahead.

St-Emilion and Pomerol At some châteaux the vines were still
suffering from the effect of the 1956 frost. The best wines
are opulent and almost opaque. More advanced than
Médocs, now at their best.

Sweet Whites Some wines are over botrytized and seem top-
heavy. Others are superbly balanced like the 1962s.

Older Vintages Still Drinking Well

1959 – Wines have a very roasted character. Some are not far
behind 1961 but most lack their harmony.

1955 – Some still remarkably fresh, solid and more interesting
than a few years ago.

What Makes Great Bordeaux

The following is a list, with brief notes, of the main factors that
determine the quality of a great Bordeaux wine.

Red

Vineyard
Well-drained, relatively poor soil, high in gravel (Médoc and
Graves), limestone (St-Emilion Côtes), gravel and sand (St-
Emilion Graves) or gravel and clay (Pomerol).
Grape varieties
Cabernet Sauvignon, Cabernet Franc and Merlot.
Mature healthy grapes
The right balance of sugar and acidity, no rot.
Careful vinification
No extraction of acids from the stalks. Fermentation at 28–30°C
(82–86°F).

Careful selection
Rejection of any sub-standard *cuves* (young vines, grapes from
an inferior part of the vineyard, *cuves* affected by rain or rot).
Addition of vin de presse (*see* page 46)
This adds colour and extracts and so provides additional
elements to assist ageing.
Use of new barrels
The percentage of new barrels should be correct for the weight
of the wine; it ranges from 30–100 percent.
Bottling at the right time
After 18–24 months, depending on the wine's tannin and power.

Sweet White

Vineyard
Well-drained, poor soil, characterized by the presence of clay
with gravel and limestone.
Grape varieties
Sémillon and Sauvignon.
Overripe grapes affected by noble rot
This must be carefully controlled by selection. Too little botrytis
and the wine lacks character; too much, and the wine becomes
clumsy.
Selection in the vineyard
The pickers must go through the vineyard from three to six
times to select overripe and botrytized grapes.
Slow and long fermentation in cask
The ideal temperature is normally about 20°C (68°F). Because of
this and the high concentration of sugar, the fermentation
usually lasts two to five weeks.
Cask ageing
The best *crus* still keep their wines two to three years in cask. A
proportion of the casks are new.
Selection for bottling
Selection is made between pressings (the third is usually the best)
and between casks.

A–Z of Châteaux

This alphabetical listing is both an index to the profile section and a directory of some 400 châteaux that are not profiled. In the case of the latter, certain basic information is contained in the A–Z entries. Where possible, the following details are given, and in the corresponding order: château name, *appellation*, classification (if any), owner (see page 7 for types of company), size of vineyard in hectares, colour of wine (R or W for red or white), and the average number of cases produced annually. If a star appears after the name it means that the wine concerned is one that, although not profiled, is above average and worth investigating. The initials SL indicate that the wine is a second label, AL indicating an alternative label. The *appellations* are abbreviated as follows:

Name	Abbreviation
Barsac	Bars
Blaye	Bl
Bourg	Bg
Bordeaux	Bord
Bordeaux Supérieur	Bord Sup
Canon-Fronsac	C-Fron
Côtes de Castillon	Cast
Entre-Deux-Mers	E-D-M
Fronsac	Fron
Graves	Gr
Haut-Médoc	H-Méd
Lalande-de-Pomerol	L-de-Pom
Listrac	List
Loupiac	Loup
Lussac-St-Emilion	L-St-Em
Margaux	Marg
Médoc	Méd
Montagne-St-Emilion	M-St-Em
Moulis	Moul
Pauillac	Pau
Pomerol	Pom
Premières Côtes de Bordeaux	Prem Côtes
Puisseguin-St-Emilion	P-St-Em
Ste-Croix-du-Mont	Ste-Cr

St-Emilion   St-Em
St-Estèphe   St-Est
Sauternes   Saut

This is not a comprehensive list of Bordeaux châteaux, but aims to give as broad and useful a selection as possible within the limits of the space available.

d'Agassac p154
de l'Amiral, SL of Labégorce-Zédé
Andron-Blanquet p141
Aney, H-Méd, CB, Raimond Père & Fils, 20ha, R10,000
L'Angélus p235
d'Angludet p90
des Annereaux p297
Anthonic p106
d'Archambeau p205
d'Arche p217
d'Arche-Lafaurie, SL of d'Arche, not used since 1981
d'Arcins p155
Ardennes p205
d'Armailhac p127
Arnaud-Jouan, Prem Côtes, M Darriet, R3,000, W18,000
Arnauld p155
d'Arricaud p205
L'Arrosée p235
d'Arsac p155
Artiges-Arnaud, SL of Grand-Puy-Ducasse
Ausone p236
Balac, H-Méd, CB, L Touchais, 15ha, R10,000
Balardin, Domaine du, SL of Malescot-St-Exupéry
Balestard-la-Tonnelle p236
de Barbe p299
Barbé★, Bl, C Carreau, 25ha, R10,000, W2,500

La Barde, Bg, A Darricarrère, 16ha, R6,600
Barde-Haut, St-Em, J-C Gasparoux, R7,500
Baret p189
Barrabaque p307
du Barrail, Cér, G Uteau, W8,000
Barreyres p156
Bastor-Lamontagne p217
Batailley p127
Les Baziliques p237
Beau Mayne★, Bord, Brand of Dourthe, R & W
Beau Mazerat, SL of Grand-Mayne
Beaumont p156
de Beaumont, Bl, L Schweitzer, 9ha, R4,000
Beauregard p280
Beau-Rivage, Bord, Brand of Borie-Manoux, R & W
Beau-Rivage, Prem Côtes, Languens, 34·5ha. R & W
Beauséjour, St-Est, CB 1932, Jacques Brossard, 17ha, R7,000
Beau-Séjour Bécot, p237
Beauséjour (Duffau-Lagarrosse) p237
Beau-Site, Prem Côtes, Desmerie, 20ha, R18,000, W6,000
Beau-Site p141
Beau-Site-Haut-Vignoble p141

La Bécade p112
La Bécasse, Pau, Georges
Fonteneau, 5ha, R2,000
Belair, Bl, P Mourlot, 15ha,
R4,000, W4,000
Belair p238
de Bel-Air, L-de-Pom, p298
Bel-Air, H-Méd, p156
Bel-Air, Pom, F F Sudrat, 13ha,
R6,000
Bel-Air, Ste-Cr, M Méric, W
Bel-Air, St-Em, p274
Bel-Air-Lagrave p106
Bel-Air-Marquis-d'Aligre p91
Bel-Air-Marquis-de-Pomereu,
SL of Bel-Air-Marquis-
d'Aligre
Belair-Montaiguillon p274
de Belcier, Cast, SC, 34ha,
R20,000
Belgrave p157
Bellefont-Belcier p238
Bellegarde, SL of Siran
Bellerive, Méd, CB 1932, Guy
Perrin, 12ha, R5,000
Belle-Rose, Pau, CB 1932,
Bernard Jugla, R35,000
Bellevue, Bl, M de la Garcie,
18ha, R8,000
Bellevue★, Méd, CB, Yves
Lassalle et Fils, 13ha, R6,000
Bellevue, Pom, R Brieux, 5ha,
R1,300
Bellevue, Cave Coop p175
Bellevue, St-Em, p239
Bellonne-St-Georges, SL of
Maquin St-Georges
Belon p206
**Bel-Orme-Tronquoy-de-
Lalande** p157
Bergat p239

Berliquet p239
des Bertins, Méd, CB 1932,
Domaines de Codem SA, 22ha,
R10,000
Beychevelle p116
du Biac, Prem Côtes, Mme N-H
Ducatez, 10ha, R & W
Bigaroux★, St-Em, GC, D
Dizier, 14ha, R7,000
Birot p314
Biston-Brillette p106
Blaignan★, Méd, CB 1932, SC,
55ha, R25,000
La Blancherie p206
Blanquet, SL of
Andron-Blanquet
Blason de Maucaillou, Bord,
Brand of Dourthe Frères, W
Bonalgue p280
Bon-Dieu-des-Vignes, SL of de
Chantegrive
Bonneau, H-Méd, CB, Lucien
Eyquem, 5ha, R2,500
Bonnet, St-Em, GC, R Bonnet,
18·5ha, R11,000
Bonnet p311
Le Bon Pasteur p280
Le Boscq★, Méd, CB 1932,
Claude Lapalu, 21ha, R8,300
Le Bosq, St-Est, CB 1932,
Philippe Durand, 15ha, R8,500
du Bouilh, Bord Sup, Comte P
de Feuilhade de Chauvin, 50ha,
R22,500, W4,000
Bourdieu, Bl, p301
Le Bourdieu, H-Méd, p157
Bourgneuf-Vayron p281
de Bourgueneuf★, Pom, E & J-
M Meyer, 5ha, R1,800
Bournac★, Méd, P Secret, 12ha,
R4,500
Bouscaut p190

du Bousquet, Bg, Castel, 60ha,
    R44,000
Bouteilley, Dom de, Prem
    Côtes, J Guillot, 20ha, R10,000
Boyd-Cantenac p91
Braidoire, SL of Launay
Brame-les-Tours, St-Est,
    Vicomte Aimery de Foulhiac
    de Padirac, 8ha, R4,000
Branaire-Ducru p117
Branas-Grand-Poujeaux p107
Brane-Cantenac p92
Brethous p314
du Breuil p158
La Bridane p118
Brillette p107
Brondelle p206
des Brousteras, Méd, GFA du
    château, 18ha, R7,000
Broustet p217
Brown p190
Brûle-Sécaille, Bg, J Rodet,
    15ha, R7,000
de By p176
Cabanes, SL of Toumilon
La Cabanne p281
Cabannieux p206
Cadet-Bon p240
Cadet-Piola p240
Cadet-Pontet, St-Em, GC, M
    Merias, 7ha, R3,350
de Caillavet★, Prem Côtes, SC,
    R16,000, W3,000
Caillou p218
Le Caillou, Pom, L Giraud, 7ha,
    R1,700
Caillou-Blanc, SL of Talbot
Calon p274
Calon-Ségur p142
de Calvimont★, Gr, J Perromat,
    12ha, R2,000, W4,000
de Camarsac★, E-D-M, L

Lurton, 150ha, R20,000,
    W2,000
Cambon-la-Pelouse p158
Camélon, Dom de *see* Léon
de Camensac p158
Canet★, E-D-M, J & B Large,
    42ha, R12,000, W15,000
Canon, C-Fron, p307
Canon, C-Fron, p307
Canon, St-Em, p241
Canon-de-Brem p307
Canon-la-Gaffelière p241
Canon-Moueix p308
Cantebeau, SL of La Louvière
Cantegril, SL of Doisy-Daëne
Cantemerle p159
Cantenac-Brown p92
Canterayne p159
Capbern-Gasqueton p142
Cap-de-Mourlin p242
Cap-Léon-Veyrin p113
Carbonnieux p191
Carcanieux★, Méd, CB 1978,
    SC, 21ha, R8,000
du Cardaillan★, SL of de Malle
Cardeneau p303
Cardinal-Villemaurine p242
La Cardonne p176
de Carles p303
Les Carmes Haut-Brion p191
Caronne-Ste-Gemme p160
Les Carrelles, Bl, C Carreau,
    30ha, R10,000, W3,500
Carteau-Côtes-Daugay, St-Em,
    GC, J Bertrand, 12ha, R6,000
du Cartillon★, H-Méd, CB
    1932, G & H Maltête, 25ha, R
Cassagne-Haut-Canon p308
Cassevert, SL of Grand-Mayne
Castegens p318
Le Castelot p243
Castéra p177

Cayla p314
Cazebonne p207
de Cérons★, Cér, J Perromat,
  12ha, R2,000, W4,000
Certan-de-May p281
Certan-Giraud p282
Chambert-Marbuzet p143
Chantalouette, SL of de Sales
Chantegrive p207
de Chantegrive p207
La Chapelle-Lescours, St-Em,
  GC, P Quentin, 7ha, R4,500
Charmail p160
Charron p301
La Chartreuse★, SL of
  St-Amand
Chasse-Spleen p107
Chastelet p314
Le Châtelet, St-Em, H & P
  Berjal, 6ha, R3,000
Châtelleine p161
Les Chaumes, Bl, R Parmentier,
  20ha, R10,000
Chauvin p243
Cheret-Pitres p208
Cheval-Blanc p243
Chevalier, Dom de p191
Chevalier Lascombes★, Méd, A
  Lichine & Co Lichine Brand
Chevalier de Malle, SL of de
  Malle
Chevalier-de-Malle, SL of
  Cardaillan, W
Chevalier de Védrines, Bord,
  Brand of Roger Joanne,
  R & W
Chevaliers du Roi Soleil p171
Chicane p208
Cissac p161
Citran p161
de Civrac★, Bg, J-P Jaubert,
  14ha, R5,500

La Clare p177
de Clairefort, SL of
  Prieuré-Lichine
Clarke p113
Clément-Pichon p162
Clerc-Milon p128
Climens p218
Clinet p282
Cloquet★, Pom, M Vigier, 6·5ha,
  R1,300
Clos du Clocher p283
Closerie-Grand-Poujeaux p108
de Clotte, Cast, Mme J Guerret-
  Denies, 15ha, R8,000
La Clotte p244
La Clusière p245
Colombier-Monpelou p128
La Commanderie, St-Est, p143
La Commanderie, Pom, F &
  Mlle M H Dé, 5·8ha, R2,500
de la Commanderie★, L-de-
  Pom, Dr H-R Lafon, 19ha,
  R8,000
**Commanderie du Bontemps,
  Cuvée de la** p177
Connétable Talbot, SL of
  Talbot
La Conseillante p283
Copet-Bégaud p308
Corbin p245
Corbin-Michotte p246
Cordat, Clos, SL of Monbrison
Cormeil-Figeac p246
Cos-d'Estournel p143
Cos-Labory p144
de la Coste, SL of Paveil de Luze
Côte-Baleau p246
Coucheroy, SL of La Louvière
Coudert p247
Coudert-Pelletan p247
Coufran p162

Couhins p192
Couhins-Lurton p193
Coulac, Ste-Cr, G Despujols,
7ha, W3,000
La Cour Pavillon, Bord, Brand
of Gilbey de Loudenne,
R & W
de Courbon p208
La Couronne p129
de Courteillac, E-D-M, Baron
du Foussat, 30ha, R6,000,
W8,000
La Couspaude p247
Coustolle p308
Coutelin-Merville p145
Coutet, Gr, p208
Coutet, St-Em, p247
Coutet, Saut, p219
Le Couvent p247
Couvent-des-Jacobins p247
Crabitey★, Gr, SC, 18ha, R3,000,
W400
Le Crock p145
La Croix, Pom, p283
La Croix, SL of
Ducru-Beaucaillou
La Croix-Blanche, SL of des
Tours
La Croix du Casse p284
La Croix-de-Gay p283
La Croix-Landon, Méd, J P B
Laforgue, 9ha, R4,000
Le Croix de Mazerat, SL of
Beauséjour (Duffau-Lagarosse)
La Croix de Millorit, Bg, A
Jambert, 17ha, R7,500
La Croix de Pez★, St-Est, Guy
Guyonnard, 7ha, R2,750
La-Croix-St-André, L-de-Pom,
M Carayon, 15ha, R6,000
La Croix-St-Georges p284
La Croix-Toulifaut p284

Croizet-Bages p129
Croque-Michotte p248
du Cros★, Loup, M Boyer, 38ha,
W3,500
Cru St-Marc, SL of La
Tour-Blanche
du Cruzeau p193
de Cugat, E-D-M, B Meyer,
25ha, R11,500, W4,500
Curé-Bon-La-Madeleine p248
Curebourse, Domaine de, SL
of Durfort-Viviens
Dalem p303
La Dame Blanche, White wine
of du Taillan
Dassault p248
Le Dauphin-Château-Guiraud,
SL of Guiraud
Le Dauphin-de-Lalague, SL of
Guiraud
de la Dauphine p303
Dauphiné-Rondillon, Loup, J
Darriet, W10,000
Dauzac p92
Desmirail p93
Despagnet★, St-Em, P Faure,
8ha, R4,400
Deyrem-Valentin p93
Dillon p163
Doisy-Daëne p219
Doisy-Dubroca p220
Doisy-Védrines p220
Domaine des Douves, SL of
Beauregard
La Dominique p249
Doms★, Gr, M Duvigneau & L
Parage, 22ha, R3,000, W3,500
Dubory, SL of Launay
Ducluzeau p113
Ducru-Beaucaillou p118
Duhart-Milon-Rothschild p129
Dupeyron, SL of Cannet

Duplessis-Fabre p108
Duplessis (Hauchecorne) p108
Durfort-Vivens p93
Dutellier, SL of
 Ramage-la-Bâtisse
Dutruch-Grand-Poujeaux p109
de l'Eglise p284
Clos L'Eglise p285
L'Eglise-Clinet p285
L'Enclos p285
L'Escadre p302
de l'Espinglet, Prem Côtes, R
 Raynaud, 30ha, R & W
L'Estang, Cast, Robert Filliol,
 23ha, R10,000
L'Estruelle, Méd, GFA Ladra,
 R5,000
L'Etoile p209
L'Evangile p286
La Fagnouse, St-E, Mme
 Coutant, R3,500
Falfas, Bg, Mme M Jaubert,
 17ha, R8,750
de Fargues p221
Faubernet★, Bord Sup, Adrien &
 Guy Dufis, 80ha, R33,000,
 W7,000
Faurie-de-Souchard p249
Fayau p314
de Ferbos★, Cér, J Perromat,
 W3,000
Ferran p194
Ferrand★, Pom, SC, 15ha, W
de Ferrand p250
Ferrande p209
Ferrière p94
Feytit-Clinet p287
Les Fiefs-de-Lagrange, SL of
 Lagrange
de Fieuzal p194
Figeac p250
Filhot p221

La Fleur p251
La Fleur-Cailleau p309
La Fleur-Canon p309
Fleur-Cardinale p251
La Fleur-de-Gay p287
La Fleur-Milon p130
La Fleur-Pétrus p287
La Fleur-Pourret p251
**Fleuron Blanc de Château
 Loubens**, SL of Loubens
de Florimond, Bl, L Marinier,
 44·5ha, R7,000, W8,000
Fombrauge p251
Fonbadet p130
Fonchereau, E-D-M, Mme
 Georges Vinot-Postry, 27ha,
 R5,000
Fondarzac p312
Fongrave p312
Fonplégade p252
Fonrazade, St-Em, GC, G
 Balotte, 9ha, R4,500
Fonréaud p114
Fonroque p252
Fonsèche, SL of Lamothe-Cissac
La Fontanelle, SL of
 Cantenac-Brown
Fontenay p318
Fontenil p304
Fontesteau p163
Fort-de-Vauban, H-Méd, A
 Noleau, 7ha, R2,500
Les Forts-de-Latour, SL of
 Latour
Fourcas-Dupré p114
Fourcas-Hosten p114
Fourney, St-Em, GC, Vignobles
 Rollet, 18ha, R7,000
Fourtet p252
de France p195
La France, E-D-M, SC, 60ha,
 R8,000, W26,000

La France, Méd, CB 1932, A
Feuvrier, 7ha, R3,000
Franc-Grâce-Dieu p253
Franc-Maillet★, Pom, G Arpin,
5ha, R1,500
Franc-Mayne p253
Franquet-Grand-Poujeaux★,
Moul, CB, P Lambert, 6ha,
R2,500
de Fronsac, Fron, Seurin, 7ha,
R2,200
La-Fuie-St-Bonnet, SL of La
Tour-St-Bonnet
'G' Château Guiraud, SL of
Guiraud
du Gaby p309
La Gaffelière p253
Gagnard p304
Gaillard, St-Em, GC, J-J
Nouvel, 20ha, R10,000
de Gaillat p209
Gallais-Bellevue, SL of Potensac
Galius, Cuvée p272
La Garde p195
Le Gardera p314
Gardour, SL of Moncets
Le Gay p288
Le Gay, E-D-M, R Maison,
40ha, R12,000, W4,000
Gazin, Gr, P Michotte, 10ha,
R4,000
Gazin, Pom, p288
du Gazin p309
Gibeau, P-St-E, Bourlon-
Masseron family, 70ha, R7,500
Gilette p222
Giscours p94
du Glana p119
Gloria p119
de Goélane, E-D-M, A Castel,
50ha, R20,000, W5,000

Gombaude-Guillot★, Pom,
GFA, 7ha, R2,400
Gontier, Bl, M F Levrand, 30ha,
R12,500
Goumin, SL of Bonnet
La Grâce-Dieu★, St-Em, GC, M
Pauty, 11ha, R7,000
La Grâce-Dieu-Les-Menuts
p254
du Grand-Abord p210
Grand-Barrail-Lamarzelle-
Figeac p254
Grand-Corbin p254
Grand-Corbin-Despagne p255
Grand-Duroc-Milon, Pau, CB
1932, Bernard Jugla, 6ha,
R22,500
Le Grand-Enclos, Cér, Lataste,
30ha, W13,000
Grand-Jour, Bg, Mme
Gaignerot, 25·5ha, R12,500,
W1,500
Grand-Listrac p115
Grand-Mayne p255
Grand-Monteil, Bord Sup, Soc
du Grand Monteil des Pontons
et de Lafite, 70ha, R38,000,
W1,200
du Grand-Moueys, Prem Côtes,
N Lacour & A Icard, 42ha,
R9,200, W3,800
Grand-Moulin, H-Méd, CB,
SC, 35ha, R7,000
Grand-Moulinet, Pom, J-M
Garde, 16ha, R6,900
Grand-Pontet p256
de Grand-Puch, E-D-M, Société
Viticole, 175ha, R40,000,
W5,500
Grand-Puy-Ducasse p131
Grand-Puy-Lacoste p131

Grand-Renouil p309
Le Grand-Village-Capbern, SL
of Capbern-Gasqueton
Grandes Murailles p255
Grandis p163
Grangeneuve, Dom de, Pom,
Veuve Gos & Fils, 6ha, R3,000
Grate-Cap, Pom, A Janoueix,
10ha, R2,900
du Grava★, Prem Côtes, J-L
Duale, 100ha, R40,000
La Grave, Domaine p210
de la Grave★, Bg, R & P Y
Bassereau, 40ha, R20,000
La Grave-Martillac, SL of La
Tour-Martillac
La Grave-Trigant-de-Boisset
p288
Gravelines, Prem Côtes,
Dubourg, 30ha, R6,000,
W8,000
Gravet, St-Em, GC, J Faure, 8ha,
R5,000
La Gravière, L-de-Pom, Mme
Cascarret, R3,000
Gravières-de-Marsac, SL of
Marsac-Séguineau
Graville-Lacoste★, Gr, Mme S
Doubourdieu-Bouchet & Fils,
6ha, W4,000
Gressier-Grand-Poujeaux p109
Greysac p178
Grimond, Prem Côtes, P
Young, 80ha, R33,000
Grivière, Méd, CB, F de
Rozières, 20ha, R7,000
Grolet, Bl, J B Mallambic,
34·5ha, R & W 20,000
Gros-Moulin, Bg, P-M Eymas,
27ha, R10,000
Gruaud-Larose p120

Guadet-Franc-Grâce-Dieu now
called Franc-Grâce-Dieu
Guadet-St-Julien p256
Guerry p299
Gueyrot, St-Em, SC, R4,000
Guibeau p275
Guibon, E-D-M, A Lurton,
25ha, R5,000, W5,000
Guionne p300
Guiraud p222
Guiraud, SL of Guiraud
Guiteronde p223
La Gurgue p95
Hanteillan p164
Haut-Badette p256
Haut-Bages-Averous, SL of
Lynch-Bages
Haut-Bages-Libéral p132
Haut-Bages-Monpelou p133
Haut-Bailly p105
Haut-Batailley p133
Haut-Bergey p196
Haut-Beychevelle-Gloria, SL
of Gloria
Haut-Bommes, Saut, CB, J
Pauly, W2,000 (adjoining and
with same owner as
Haut-Peyraguey)
Haut-Breton-Larigaudière,
Marg, CB 1932, G de Mour,
7ha, R3,500
Haut-Brignon, Prem Côtes, R
Fourès, 60ha, R25,000
Haut-Brion p196
Haut-Canteloup, Méd, CB
1932, J Sarrazy, 17ha, R7,500
Haut-Castenet, SL of Launay
Haut-Chaigneau p298
Haut-Corbin p256
Haut-Courgeaux, SL of Launay
Hauterive, Méd, CB, Vignobles

Rocher-Cap de Rive SA, 57ha, R30,000

Haut-Gueyrot p257

Haut-Lavallade★, St-Em, J-P Chagneau, R5,500

Haut-Lignan★, Méd, Jean Castet, R4,000

Haut-Logat★, H-Méd, CB, C & M Quancard, 19ha, R6,000

Haut-Macau, Bg, B & J Mallet, 22ha, R13,000

Haut-Madrac p164

Haut-Maillat, Pom, P Delteil, 5ha, R1,120

Haut-Marbuzet p145

Haut-Mazeris p310

Haut-Peyraguey p223

Haut-Pontet p257

Haut-Quercus p272

Haut-Sarpe p257

Haut Ségottes, St-Em, GC, D André, 7ha, R2,650

Haut-Tayac★, Marg, CB 1932, C & V Saux, 10ha, R4,000

Haut-Tuquet p318

Les Hauts-Conseillants p298

Les Hauts-de-Pontet, SL of Pontet-Canet

Les Hauts-Tuilleries p298

de Haux p315

La Haye, St-Est, CBS 1932, André Vincent, 6ha, R2,000

Les Heaumes, Bg, M Robin, 15ha, R8,500

Hortevie p120

Houbanon, Méd, CB 1978, SC, 9·5ha, R4,000

Houissant p146

Hourtin-Ducasse★, H-Méd, CB, M Marengo, 16ha, R6,000

d'Issan p95

Clos-des-Jacobins p244

Jacques-Blanc, St-Em, GFA, 21ha, R12,500

des Jaubertes★, Gr, Marquis de Pontac, 14ha, R3,000, W3,500

Jauga, SL of Rabaud-Promis

Jeandeman p304

Jean-Faure p257

Jean-Gervais, Gr, Counilh & Fils, 30ha, W10,000

Jean-Voisin, St-Em, GC, S C Chassagnoux, 12ha, R3,700

La Joncarde★, Bg, Mme M Jaubert, 16ha, R8,000

Jourdan, Prem Côtes, A Guillot de Suduiraut, 45ha, R4,000, W8,000

du Juge★, Bord Sup (Cadillac), P Dupleich, 30ha, R6,000, W9,000

du Juge, Bord Sup (Haux), J Mèdeville, 24ha, R9,000, W5,500

Junayme p310

Le Jurat, St-Em, GC, E Guinaudie, 8ha, R3,500

Justa★, Prem Côtes, Y Mas, 20ha, R8,000, W5,000

Les Justices p223

Kirwan p95–6

de Labat★, H-Méd, Nony-Borie, R2,500

Labégorce p96

Labégorce-Zédé p96

Clos Labère, SL of Rieussec

Laborde, L-de-Pom, J-M Trocard, 15ha, R4,000

Labottière, Bord, Brand of Cordier, R & W

Lachesnaye★, H-Méd, CBS, H Bouteiller, 20ha, R5,000

Lacoste-Borie, SL of Grand-Puy-Lacoste

Lafaurie, Prem Côtes, A
  Croizet-Sauvestre, 25ha,
  R5,000, W5,000
Lafaurie-Peyraguey p224
Lafayette, Bord, Brand of
  Nathaniel Johnston, R
Laffitte-Carcasset p146
Laffitte-Laujac, SL of Laujac
Lafite, Prem Côtes, SCE,
  R11,500
Lafite-Canteloup, H-Méd, CB
  1932, GFA, 10ha, R5,000
Lafite-Rothschild p133
Lafleur p289
Lafleur-Gazin p289
Lafleur-du-Roy, Pom, Y
  Dubost, 3ha, R1,750
Lafon p115
Lafon-Rochet p147
Lagarosse p315
Lafüe, Ste-Cr, J Sicres, R2,000
Lagrange, Pom, p290
Lagrange, St-Jul, p121
Lagrange-de-Lescure p258
Lagrave, Ste-Cr, J-M Tinon,
  18ha, R2,000, W6,000
Lagüe★, Fron, Roux-Oulié, 10ha,
  R4,000
La Lagune p164
Lalande★, List, CB 1932, Mmes
  Dubosc & Darriet, 10ha,
  R5,000
Lalande, St Jul Société
  d'Exploitation, 30ha, R10,000
Lalande-Borie p121
Lalibarde, Bg, R Dumas, 34·5ha,
  R20,000, W2,000
Lamarque, Ste-Cr, R Bernard,
  R4,000, W5,000
de Lamarque p165
Lamartine, SL of
  Cantenac-Brown

Lamothe, Saut, p224
Lamothe, Bg, P Pessonier, 20ha,
  R7,000
Lamothe, Prem Côtes, J
  Perriquet & F Neel, 25ha,
  R3,000, W6,000
Lamothe-Bergeron p166
Lamothe-Cissac p166
Lamothe-Guignard p225
Landat, H-Méd, CB 1978, SC du
  Château Lamothe, 14ha,
  R7,000
Landiras p210
Lanessan p166
Langoa-Barton p122
Laniote p258
Lapelletrie, St-Em, GC, Jean
  family, 12ha, R6,000
Larcis-Ducasse p258
Lardit, Cast, Jacques Trepout,
  11·5ha, R
Larmande p258
Laroche-Bel-Air p315
Laroque p259
Larose-Trintaudon p167
Laroze p259
Laroze-Bayard p275
Larrivaux, H-Méd, CB 1932,
  GFA, 20ha, R6,000
Larrivaux-Hanteillan, SL of
  Hanteillan
Larrivet-Haut-Brion p197
Lartigue★, St-Est, SC, 7ha,
  R3,000
Lartigue-de-Brochon, SL of
  Sociando-Mallet
Lascombes p96
Lassalle, SL of Potensac
Lassèque, St-Em, GC, J P
  Freylon, 22·5ha, R13,000
Latour p134
Latour à Pomerol p290

Laujac p178
Launay p312
Laurensanne, Bb, J-F Levraud,
  20ha, R10,000, W2,000
Laurétan p314
des Laurets p275
Laurette, Ste-Cr, F Pons, R
  1,000, W7,000
Lavalière, Méd, CB, Cailloux
  family, 15ha, R7,500
Laville-Haut-Brion p197
Lavillotte p147
Lemoine-Nexon, SL of de
  Malleret
Léon, & Dom de Camélon,
  Prem Côtes, M F Mähler-
  Besse, R3,000, W2,000
Léoville-Barton p122
Léoville-Las-Cases p123
Léoville-Poyferré p124
Lestage p115
Lestage-Darquier p109
Lestage-Simon p167
Letourt, SL of Hauterive
Ligondras, Marg, 1er Artisan, P
  Augeau, 7ha, R3,000
Ligondras, Marg, Pierre Augeau,
  7ha, R3,500
Lilian Ladoueys p148
Liot p225
Liouner★, List, CB 1932, P Bosq,
  15ha, R7,500
Clos des Litanies p290
Liversan p168
Livran p178
Lognac, SL of Ferrande
Loubens p317
Loudenne p179
Louloumet, SL of Chicane
Loupiac-Gaudiet p318
La Louvière p198

de Loyac, SL of
  Malescot-St-Exupéry
Lucas, SL of Dillon
Ludon-Pomiés-Agassac, SL of
  Lagune
Lynch-Bages p135
Lynch-Moussas p136
du Lyonnat p276
MacCarthy p148
MacCarthy-Moula, St-Est, CB,
  see Haut-Marbuzet
Macquin-St-Georges p276
La Madeleine p259
Magdelaine p260
Magence p210
Magneau p211
Magnol p168
Maillard, Prem Côtes, F Germe,
  20ha, R4,000, W4,000
Maison-Blanche p276
Maison Blanche, Pom, G
  Despagne, 4ha, R1,500
Maison-Rose, SL of des Laurets
Maître d'Estournel, Bord,
  Brand of Le Cercle d'Estournel,
  R & W
Malagar, Prem Côtes, M
  Dubourg, 13ha, R2,000,
  W4,500
Malartic-Lagravière p198
Malescasse p168
Malescot-St-Exupéry p87
de Malle p225
de Malleret p169
Malmaison, SL of Clarke
de Marbuzet p148
de Marbuzet, SL of
  Cos-d'Estournel
Margaux p97
Marquis-d'Alesme-Becker p99
Marquis-de-Bressane, SL of
  Hauterive

Marquis, Clos du, SL of
Léoville-Las-Cases
Marquis de St-Estèphe p149
Marquis-de-Terme p99
Marsac-Séguineau p99
Martinens p100
Martinon, E-D-M, Trollier,
35ha, R5,000, W15,000
de Martouret, E-D-M, D
Lurton, 30ha, R12,000, W5,500
La Marzelle p254
Matras p260
Maucaillou p110
Maucamps★, H-Méd, CB, I
Tessandier, 15ha, R12,000
Mausse p310
Mauvesin p110
Mauvezin p260
du Mayne p226
Mayne-d'Anice, SL of de
Chantegrive
Mayne-Binet, Cér, J Perromat,
W2,000
Mayne-Lévêque, SL of de
Chantegrive
Mayne-Vieil p304
Mazarin, Loup, Courbin-
Meyssan, 25ha, W15,000
Mazeris p310
Mazeris-Bellevue p310
Mazeyres p290
Clos Mazeyres, Pom, Laymarie
& Fils, 9ha, R3,500
Méaume★, Bord Sup, (Guitres &
Coutras), A Johnson-Hill, 24ha,
R7,500
Menota p226
Le Menotat, Bl, E Cruse, 10ha,
R6,000, W1,000
Mendoce p300
de Menota p226

Close des Menuts★, St-Em, GC,
P Rivière, 20ha, R5,500
de la Meulière p316
Meyney p149
Le Meynieu p169
Mille-Sescousses★, Bord Sup, J
Darricarrère, 75ha, R & W
45,000
Millet p211
La Mission-Haut-Brion p199
Les Moines, Méd, Claude
Pourreau, 21ha, R12,000
des Moines, L-de-Pom, H
Darnazou, 12ha, R2,000
Monbousquet p261
Monbrison p100
Moncabon, Enclos de, SL of
Rauzan-Gassies
Moncets p298
Monconseil-Gazin, Bl, M
Baudet, 15ha, R5,000
Montalbert, St-Em, GC, SC,
12·5ha, R6,000
Montalivet p211
Montbrun p100
Le Monteil-d'Arsac, SL of
d'Arsac
du Monthil p179
Montlabert p261
Montrose p150 ·
Mony, Prem Côtes, Marquis de
Barbentane, 25ha, R3,000,
W10,000
Morange, Ste-Cr, F Durr,
W6,000
Morin p150
Moulin-d'Arvigny, SL of
Beaumont
Moulin du Cadet p261
Moulin-des-Carruades, SL of
Lafite-Rothschild

Moulin-Duhart, SL of Duhart-Milon-Rothschild

Moulin-Haut-Laroque p304

Moulin-Haut-Villars p305

Moulin-de-Laborde, List, Michel Hostens, 9·5ha, R4,500

Moulin-de-Launay p312

Moulin-Pey-Labrie, C-Fr, Yvette Seurt, 8ha, R3,500

Moulin-Riche★, SL of Léoville-Poyferré

Moulin-de-la-Roque, SL of La Tour-de-By

Moulin de la Rose, St Jul, CB 1932, Guy Delon, 4ha, R2,000

Moulin Rouge, Cast, J-C Bassilieaux, 23ha, R14,000

du Moulin Rouge★, H-Méd, CB, Veyries-Pelon family, 15ha, R6,000

Moulin-St-Georges p261

Moulin-de-St-Vincent, SL of Moulin-à-Vent

Moulin de Taffard★, Méd, Pierre Peyruse, 6ha, R3,000

Moulin-à-Vent★, L-de-Pom, SC, 6ha, R2,250

Moulin-à-Vent, Moul, p110

Moulinet p291

Moulinet-Lasserre, AL of René

Moulis p111

Mourlet, SL of d'Archambeau

Mouton-Baronne–Philippe, (*see* d'Armailhac)

Mouton-Cadet, Bord Brand of La Baronnie, R & W

Mouton-Rothschild p137

Myrat p226

Nairac p226

Nenin p291

Nenin, Prem Côtes p316

Notton, SL of Brane-Cantenac

Olivier p200

L'Oratoire p261

Les Ormes-de-Pez p151

Les Ormes-Sorbet p179

Palais-Cardinal-La-Fuie p262

Palmer p101

Panigon★, Méd, CB, G Lamolière, 25ha, R12,500, W300

Le Pape p200

Pape-Clément p201

du Parc, H-Méd, René Gonzalvez, 10ha, R6,000

Pardaillan, Bl, C Carreau, 15ha, R4,000, W2,000

La Parde de Haut-Bailly, SL of Haut-Bailly

La Paroisse p169

La Patache, Pom, Mme Forton, 5ha, R2,250

Patache-d'Aux p179

Patris p262

Paveil-de-Luze p101

Pavie p262

Pavie-Decesse p263

Pavie-Macquin p263

du Pavillon, Ste-Cr, d'Arfeuille, 11ha, W5,000

Pavillon Blanc and Pavillon Rouge, SLs of Margaux

Le Pavillon-de-Boyrein p211

Pavillon-Cadet p263

du Pavillon & Grand-Renouil, C-Fron, Jean Ponty & Fils, 10ha, R4,000

Pêcheur, Blanc du, Bord, Brand of Borie-Manoux, W

Péconnet★, Prem Côtes, Amiel family, 20ha, R9,000

Pédesclaux p137

Perenne, Bl, M & P Oudinot, 48ha, R20,000

Pernaud★, Saut, CB, P Pascaud, 20ha, W5,500
Perron, L-de-Pom, Massonié, 10ha, R6,000
Pessan-St-Hilaire p212
Petit-Faurie-de-Soutard p264
Petit-Village p291
Pétrus p292
Peychaud p300
Peymartin, SL of Gloria
Pey-Martin, Méd, CB, Jean Signoret, 10ha, R6,500
Peyrabon p169
Peyrat, Prem Côtes (Beguey), Mme David, 40ha, R5,000, W20,000
du Peyrat★, Prem Côtes (Capian), SC, 63·5ha, R6,000, W15,000
Peyraud, SL of Bonnet
Peyreau★, St-Em, GC, M Boutet, 13ha, R6,200
Peyredon-Lagravette★, List, CB, P Hostein, 6ha, R3,000
Peyredoulle, Bl, J & B Germain, 16ha, R6,200, W1,500
de Peyrelongue, St-Em, GC, P Cassat, 12ha, R6,000
de Pez p151
Phélan-Ségur p152
Piada, Saut, CB, J Lalande, 13ha, R1,300, W2,500
Pibran p138
Pichelèbre (*see* Canon-Moueix)
Pichon, H-Méd, C Fayat, 23ha, R8,000
Pichon-Longueville Baron p138
  Pichon-Longueville Comtesse-de-Lalande p139
Picourneau, SL of Le Bourdieu
Picque-Caillou p201

Pierredon★, Bord Sup (Gornac), P Perromat, 45ha, R10,000
Le Pin p292
Pipeau p264
Piron★, Gr, P Boyreau, 20ha, R2,000, W7,500
Pitray, Cast, Vicomte L de Pitray, 26ha, R
Plagnac p180
Plain-Point p305
Plaisance, p316
Plantey, Pau, G Meffre, 30ha, R13,000
Plantey-de-la-Croix★, SL of Verdignan
Plassan p316
Plessis, SL of Moulin-de-Launay
Plince p293
La Pointe p293
Pomeys p111
Pomys p152
de Poncet, Prem Côtes, J L David, 40ha, R7,000, W15,000
Pontac-Lynch p102
Pontac-Monplaisir p201
Pontet, Méd, CB 1978, Emile Courrian, 11ha, R7,000
Pontet-Canet p139
Pontet-Chappaz, Marg, Vignobles Rocher-Cap de Rive SA, 6·5ha, R3,500
Pontet-Clauzure p264
Pontoise-Cabarrus p170
de Portets★, Gr, J-P Théron, 14·5ha, R6,000, W2,000
Potensac p180
Pouget p102
Poujeaux p111
Les Pradines p153
de Pressac p264
Preuillac p181

Prieur du Château Meyney, SL of Meyney

Le Prieuré p265

Prieurs de la Commanderie p293

Prieuré-Lichine p102

Les Productions Réunies de Puisseguin et Lussac-St-Emilion p276

La Providence, Bord Sup, Francis Cuvelier, 6ha, R3,000

La Providence, Pom, J Dupuy, 3ha, R250

Puy-Blanquet★, St-Em, GC, R Jacquet, 23ha, R10,000

Puyblanquet-Carille, St-Em, GC, J-F Carille, 17ha, R7,400

Puycarpin p318

Puy-Castéra p170

Puyguilhem p305

Puymiran, E-D-M, Degueil, 45ha, R23,000, W13,000

Quentin, St-Em, GC, SC, 30ha, R1,800

Les Queyrats★, Gr, Dulac family, 38·5ha, W10,000, (*see also* St-Pierre, p214)

de Quinsac, E-D-M, SC, R5,000

'R', SL of Rieussec

Rabaud-Promis p227

Rahoul p212

Ramage-la-Bâtisse p170

La Rame, Ste-Cr, C Armand, 36ha, R5,000, W15,000

de Ramondon, Prem Côtes, M Sangers & Mme van Pé, 80ha, R7,000, W6,000

Rausan-Ségla p103

du Raux, H-Méd, SCI du Raux, 10ha, R5,000

Rauzan-Gassies p103

Raymond, E-D-M, Baron R de Montesquieu, R20,000, W5,000

Raymond-Lafon p227

Rayne Sec, Dry wine of de Rayne-Vigneau, p228

de Rayne-Vigneau p228

Clos René p294

Réserve de la Comtesse, SL of Pichon-Longueville Comtesse

Réserve du Marquis d'Evry, SL of de Lamarque

de Respide, Gr, P Bonnet & Fils, 40ha, R & W

Respide-Médeville p212

du Retout p171

Le Reverdon, *see* Coutet, p208

Reynier★, E-D-M, D Lurton, 60ha, R25,000, W11,000

Reynon p316

Reysson p171

de Ricaud p318

Richelieu, Fron, Y Viaud, 20ha, R6,000

Rieussec p228

Ripeau p265

La Rivalerie, Bl, M Bauchet, R20,000

La Rivière p305

La Roche, Prem Côtes, J Palau, 20ha, R4,000, W4,000

de Rochemorin p202

du Rocher, St-Em, GC, Baron S de Montfort, 14ha, R6,250

Rocher-Bellevue, Cast, Vignobles Rocher-Cap de Rive SA, 15ha, R

La Rochette, SL of des Laurets

Côtes Rocheuses p272

Clos du Roi, SL of La Louvière

de Rol, St-Em, GC, J Sautereau, 7ha, R3,000

de Rolland p229

Romer-du-Hayot p229
de la Ronceray, St-Est, CB,
  Jacques Pedro, 8ha, R32,500
La Roque–de-By p
Roquegrave, Méd, CB 1932,
  Joannon & Lleu, 25ha, R13,000
de Roques p276
Roquetaillade-le-Bernet, SL of
  de Roquetaillade-la-Grange
de Roquetaillade-la-Grange
  p213
Rosechatel, Bord, Brand of
  Schröder & Schÿler, R & W
de la Rose p313
La-Rose–Côte-de-Rol, St-Em,
  GC, Y Mirande, 8·5ha, R3,500
La Rose–Maréchale, SL of
  Coufran
La Rose Pauillac p140
La Rose–Peruchon, SL of du
  Lyonnat
La Rose Pourret★, St-Em, GC,
  B Warion, 7ha, R2,500
Roudier p277
Rouet p306
Rouget p294
de Rouillac p202
Roumieu★, Bars, P Goyaud,
  14ha, W3,500
Roumieu, Saut, CB, R Bernadet,
  20ha, W2,000
Roumieu-Goyaud, Saut, CB,
  Mme C Cravcia-Goyaud,
  14ha, W
Roumieu-Lacoste★, Saut, CB
  Mme S Dubourdier-Bouchet,
  12ha, W2,500
Rousset p300
Royal St-Emilion p271
Rozier p265
Ruat, SL of Ruat-Petit-Poujeaux

Ruat-Petit-Poujeaux p112
de la Sablière-Fongrave and
  Domaine de Fongrave★, E-
  D-M, P Perromat, 45ha.
  R & W
St-Agrèves p213
St-Amand p230
St-André-Corbin p277
St-Bonnet p181
St-Christoly, Méd, CB 1932,
  Hervé Héraud, 15ha, R8,000
Ste-Colombe p318
St-Estèphe p153
St-Georges p277
St-Georges–Côte-Pavie p265
Ste-Hélène, SL of de Malle
St-Jean p181
St-Martin p266
St-Paul, H-Méd, SC, 20ha, R
St-Pierre, St-Jul, p125
de St-Pierre, Gr, p214
de St-Pierre, St-Em, GC, L & J
  P Musset, 18ha, R9,000
St-Roch, SL of Andron-Blanquet
St-Roch, Cave Coop p182
St-Saturnin p182
de St-Yzans-de-Médoc p182
de Sales p294
La Salle-de-Poujeaux, SL of
  Poujeaux
Sansonnet p266
Saransot-Dupré p116
Sarget du Gruaud-Larose, SL
  of Gruaud-Larose
Le Sartre p203
Segonnes, SL of Lascombes
Segonzac p302
Ségur, H-Méd, CGB 1932, SC,
  33ha, R15,000
Ségur-d'Arsac, SL of d'Arsac
Sémeillan Mazeau, List, CBS

1932, SC, 11ha, R5,200

Senailhac★, E-D-M, Magnat, 60ha, R15,000, W8,000

Sénéjac p172

Senilhac★, H-Méd, CB 1932, M & J-L Grassin, 12ha, R6,000

Sergant, L-de-Pom, GFA des Vignobles Jean Milhade, R6,000

La Serre p266

Sestignan p182

Siaurac p298

Sigalas-Rabaud p230

Sigognac p183

Simon, Saut, CB, J Dufour, 10ha, W2,000

Siran p103

Smith-Haut-Lafitte p203

Sociando-Mallet p172

Soleil, P-St-Em, J Soleil, 15ha, R7,000

Soudars p172

Le Souley-Ste Croix, H-Méd, CB 1932, Jean Riffaud, 19ha, R10,000

Soutard p267

Suau, Prem Côtes, M Raoux, 45ha, R20,000

Suau, Saut, p230

Suduiraut p230

Taffard★, Méd, Paul Mottes, 16·5ha, R7,500

du Tailhas, Pom, p295

du Taillan, H-Méd, p173

Taillefer p295

Talbot p125

Tanesse p314

du Tasta★, Prem Côtes, R5,000, W500

de Tastes p317

Tayac p104

Tayac, Bg, P Saturny, 23ha, R

des Templiers, SL of Larmande

Templiers, Clos des, L-de-Pom, E & J-M Meyer, 9·6ha, R3,800

Terfort, SL of Loubens

de Terrefort-Quancard, Bord Sup, Quancard family, 70ha, R38,000

Terrey-Gros-Caillou p126

du Tertre p104

Tertre-Daugay p267

Le Tertre-Caussan p183

Tertre-de-Launay, SL of Moulin-de-Launay

Tertre-Rôteboeuf p268

Teysson★, L-de-Pom, Mme Servant, 13ha, R6,000

de Thau, Bg, L Schweitzer, 45ha, 15,000

Thibauld-Bellevue p318

Thieuley p313

Timberlay★, Bord Sup, R Giraud, 75ha, R50,000, W6,000

Toinet-Fombrauge p268

La Tonnelle p268

Toumalin p311

Toumilon p214

La Tour-d'Aspic, SL of Haut-Batailley

La Tour-de-Bessan p105

La Tour-Bicheau★, Gr, Y Daubas & Fils, 20ha, R7,000, W1,300

La Tour-Blanche p231

La Tour Blanche, Méd, CB 1932, SCA, 27ha, R10,000

Tour-de-Bonnet, SL of Bonnet

La Tour-de-By p183

La Tour-Carnet p173

La Tour-Figeac p268

La Tour-Haut-Brion p203

La Tour-Haut-Caussan p184
Tour-du-Haut-Moulin p173
La Tour-Léognan★, Gr, SC,
R5,000, W3,000, run jointly
with Carbonnieux, p191
Tour de Marbuzet★, St-Est, CB
1932, Henri Duboscq, 7ha,
R3,000
La Tour-Martillac p204
Tour-du-Mirail p174
La Tour-de-Mons p105
La Tour Mont d'Or p278
Tour-Musset p278
Tour-du-Pas-St-Georges p278
La Tour-Pibran, Pau, CB 1932,
J-J Gounel, 8ha, R3,500
La Tour-du-Pin-Figeac p269
La Tour-du-Pin-Figeac
(Giraud Belivier) p269
La Tour-Prignac, Méd, CB
1932, SC, 120ha, R50,000
La Tour-Puymirand, E-D-M, E
Fazilleau, 60ha, R10,000,
W7,500
Tour-du-Roc, H-Méd, CB
1932, Philippe Robert, 12ha,
R4,500
La Tour-St-Bonnet p184
La Tour St-Joseph★, H-Méd,
CB, M & C Quancard, 13ha, R
Tour-St-Pierre, St-Em, GC, J
Goudineau, 10ha, 4,500
La Tour-Seran, Méd, CB 1932,
Patrick Peronno, 13ha, R6,000
Tour-des-Termes p153
Tour-de-Tourteau p300
La Tour-Védrines SL of
Doisy-Védrines
Tournefeuille, L-de-Pom, GFA,
Sautarel, R6,000
des Tours p278

Tourteau-Chollet p214
Tourteran, AL of
Ramage-la-Bâtisse
de Toutigeac p313
Trimoulet p269
des Troischardons, Marg, S de
Fait Chardon Père & Fils,
R800
Tronquoy-Lalande p153
Troplong-Mondot p269
Trotanoy p296
Trottevieille p270
de Tuilerie, SL of
Moulin-de-Launay
La Tuilerie★, Gr, F & B Dubrey,
20ha, R4,500, W4,500
Les Tuileries, Bl, C Alins, 25ha,
R10,000
Le Tuquet★, Gr, P Ragon, 44ha,
R12,500, W8,000
de Tustal, E-D-M, Comte
d'Armaillé, 45ha, R6,000,
W14,000
**Union des Producteurs de
St-Emilion** p270
Clos d'Uza, SL of de St-Pierre
La Vaillante, SL of Launay
La Valade p306
La Valière p184
Valrone, Bl, Bertolus & Poullet,
30ha, R12,000, W8,000
Verdignan p174
Vernous, Méd, CB 1932, SCI,
20ha, R10,000
La Vicomtesse, SL of
Laffitte-Carcasset
Videau, Prem Côtes, 30ha,
R5,000, W10,000
La Vieille France, Gr, M
Dugoua, 10ha, R1,500
Vieux Château Certan p296

Vieux Château Landon p185
Vieux Château Mazerat p272
du Vieux-Clocher p185
Vieux-Colombiers p185
La Vieille Cure p306
du Vieux-Moulin, Loup, Mme
Jean Perromat, 18ha, W5,000
Vieux-Robin, Méd, CB,
François Dufau, 13ha, R8,000
Vieux Sarpe p272
La Vigerie, SL of
Moulin-de-Launay
Villars p306
de Villegorge p174
Villemaurine p272

Vincent, Marg, CB 1932, Mme
Jean Domec, R2,000
Vin Sec de Doisy-Daëne, SL of
Doisy-Daëne
La Violette, Pom, Vignobles S
Dumas, 3·3ha, R2,000
Virou, Bl, Mme Monier,
R10,000, W10,000
Vrai-Canon-Bouché, C-Fron,
Roux-Oulié, 8ha, R3,000
Vray-Canon-Boyer p311
Vraye-Croix-de-Gay p297
'Y', SL of d'Yquem
Yon-Figeac p273
d'Yquem p232

Château Profiles by Appellation

This section focuses on properties that merit special consideration. It includes not only the great names of Bordeaux but also many less well-known producers whose wines deserve recognition. The entries are arranged by *appellation*, and each *appellation* is introduced with a description of its general character. In the case of the Médoc, which encompasses many important *appellations*, there is also a general introduction to the region.

After the name of the property, each entry begins with the following details, where obtainable and relevant: classification, owner, administrator, number of hectares planted with vines, number of cases produced annually, grape varieties and respective percentages used in production, and any secondary labels. *See* pages 7 and 8 for a key to the abbreviations.

The Médoc Appellations

Médoc has been the great ambassador for the red wines of Bordeaux the world over. From the early 18th century, when wealthy and discerning Englishmen first paid a premium to obtain better wines, until the second half of the 20th century the fame of the region has centred on the treasure trove of the Médoc.

With its proximity to the city of Bordeaux, the commercial and political centre of the Gironde, it was natural that the Médoc should be developed earlier and more thoroughly than any other piece of land in the region. In the 17th and 18th centuries, the great wine estates there were put together in much the same form as they exist today. Because of the poor, gravelly soil, mixed subsistence farming easily gave way to specialized viticulture. A glance at the map shows the Médoc to be a very narrow but lengthy strip of land running along the estuary of the Gironde from just outside the modern suburbs of northern Bordeaux, at Blanquefort and Le Taillan, to St Vivien, 70 kilometres (44 miles) to the north. In few places do the vineyards extend more than ten kilometres (6 miles) inland from the river, and most lie to the east of the main Bordeaux-Lesparre-Soulac road. This is where the ridges of gravel are at their deepest and purest. As you go north, the soils get heavier and the gravel more interspersed with clay or sand, while, to the west, the land becomes sandy and the pine forests of Les Landes begin.

Viticulturally, the Médoc is divided into two distinct areas: the Haut-Médoc in the south and the Bas-Médoc (called simply Médoc for *appellation* purposes) in the north. Within the Haut-Médoc, six communal *appellations* have been carved out. In addition, the name Haut-Médoc itself constitutes a seventh *appellation*, encompassing wines not covered by the communal *appellations*. The latter correspond to the area where the great majority of the finest vineyards lie. This is vividly illustrated by the following figures showing the proportion of the area under vine in the five *appellations* occupied by the Crus Classés (the remaining two contain no Crus Classés). Haut-Médoc 5·5 percent, Margaux 68 percent, St-Julien 75 percent, Pauillac 72·5 percent, St Estèphe 19·5 percent.

Although more and more of the Crus Bourgeois now bottle at the château at least a proportion of their wines, many smaller

The Médoc and Haut Médoc

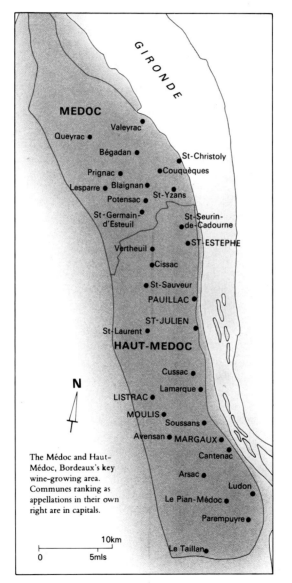

GIRONDE

MEDOC

Valeyrac

Queyrac

Bégadan

St-Christoly

Couquèques

Prignac

Lesparre Blaignan

Potensac St-Yzans

St-Germain-
d'Esteuil

St-Seurin-
de-Cadourne

Vertheuil

ST-ESTEPHE

Cissac

St-Sauveur

PAUILLAC

ST-JULIEN

St-Laurent

HAUT-MEDOC

N

Cussac

Lamarque

LISTRAC

MOULIS

Soussans

Avensan MARGAUX

Cantenac

Arsac

Ludon

Le Pian-Médoc

Parempuyre

Le Taillan

The Médoc and Haut-
Médoc, Bordeaux's key
wine-growing area.
Communes ranking as
appellations in their own
right are in capitals.

10km

0 5mls

vineyards find it makes economic sense to join cooperatives where the methods of vinification have been modernized, rather than face the large capital cost of modernizing their own *cuviers*. Members of cooperatives account for the following proportions or the areas under vine in these *appellations*: Médoc 42·5 percent, Haut-Médoc 17·5 percent, Pauillac 18 percent, St-Estèphe 26 percent, Listrac 24 percent, Moulis 6·5 percent.

Standards in cooperatives have improved considerably in the past few years and they are now undoubtedly a positive influence on quality.

The predominance of the Cabernet Sauvignon grape in all the vineyards of the Médoc ensures a certain family resemblance, a crispness of definition on nose and palate and a tendency for the tannin to be dominant in the first year or so in bottle. The development of bouquet, combined with delicacy and character of flavour, comes with bottle-ageing. Médoc wines all need to be aged, and even quite modest *crus* keep and improve very well.

Margaux

The only one of the six commune *appellations* that is not restricted to the area bearing its name. Also included under this *appellation* are most of the commune of Arsac and all of Cantenac, Labarde and Soussans. The area under vine increased by 16 percent between 1981 and 1988.

The outstanding characteristics of the *appellation*'s wines are finesse and breed, the results of deep, poor, gravelly ridges and a high proportion of Cabernet Sauvignon. But the variations of emphasis are considerable. Labarde wines tend to have more body and richness, the Cantenacs are more elegant and often shorter, as is du Tertre, the sole Cru Classé of Arsac. Many Margaux wines have more tannin and are slower to evolve.

Château d'Angludet
Cru Bourgeois Supérieur Exceptionnel 1932. Owner: **M & Mme Peter A Sichel. 33ha. 14,000 cases. CS 45%, Mer 35%, CF 15%, PV 5%.**
Angludet was unfortunate not to be classifed in 1855. At that time it

was divided up and had much declined in importance since the 18th century, when it had been ranked with the leading growths. Now, under Peter Sichel's devoted care, the wines are becoming steadily better as the vineyard matures.

This excellent vineyard, situated on the plateau of Cantenac, produces wines that are finely perfumed and combine great finesse with elegance and vigour. Since the excellent '78, the wines have been consistently impressive. I would single out the '81, '82, '85, '86, '89 and '90, all of which are fine examples of these vintages.

Château Bel-Air-Marquis-d'Aligre
Cru Bourgeois Supérieur Exceptionnel 1932. Owner: **Pierre Boyer. 17ha. 4,500 cases. Mer 35%, CS 30%, CF 20%, PV 15%.** Second label: **Château Bel-Air-Marquis-de-Pomereu.**

Confusingly, this is one of three Margaux properties sporting the name Marquis in its title, and the only one not classified. It lies at the back of Margaux, with a part of the vineyard in the adjoining commune Soissans.

Pierre Boyer is a perfectionist who makes his wines with great care from low yields. Only organic fertilizers are used in the vineyards. The wine has real finesse and a certain unctuousness combined with delicacy and freshness.

Château Boyd-Cantenac
3e Cru Classé. Owner: **Pierre Guillemet. 18ha. 7,500 cases. CS 67%, Mer 20%, CF 7%, PV 6%.**

This is a property with a chequered history. It lost many of its vineyards to Cantenac-Brown in 1860, disappeared as a name for 45 years before reappearing again in 1920, then lost its buildings to Château Margaux. Until 1982 the wine was made at Château Pouget, Pierre Guillemet's neighbouring property, but now the wines are separately made.

Although no longer as important as it was in 1855, nor of the standard expected of a Troisième Cru, it produces well-made wines, rich and supple in style and certainly worthy of a Cru Classé once more; '70, '71, '75, '78 and '79 were all very successful years here. The vintages of the 1980s have been bigger and more tannic but seem to have less finesse.

Château Brane-Cantenac
2e Cru Classé. Owner: **Lucien Lurton. 85ha. 29,000 cases. CS 70%, Mer 15%, CF 13%, PV 2%.** Second label: **Château Notton.**

Brane-Cantenac owed its name and pre-eminence in 1855 to Baron de Brane, famed as a viticulturist and responsible for the rise of Mouton. Now it belongs to another famed viticulturist, Lucien Lurton, the largest vineyard owner in the Médoc today.

With vineyards enjoying a prime position on the plateau of Cantenac, this property produces a wine noted for its delicacy, finesse and breed – quintessential Margaux qualities, and this in spite of its high proportion of Cabernet Sauvignon – a sure indication of the influence of soil on grape varieties. Like many Margaux wines it can often be drunk young with enjoyment, but lasts well, as demonstrated by its lovely '66. Among more recent vintages very good wines were made in '78, '79 and '81; the '82 is outstanding; '83 is rather light; '85 has the breed of the year; '86 is unusually tannic, and '88 and '89 combine concentration with great finesse. A name worth remembering.

Château Cantenac-Brown
3e Cru Classé. Owner: **AXA Millésimes.** Administrator: **Jean-Michel Cazes. 32ha. 12,500 cases. CS 65%, Mer 25%, CF 10%.** Second labels: **Châteaux Canuet (Margaux) and Lamartine (Bordeaux Supérieur).**

The English name Brown derives from John Lewis Brown, a Bordeaux merchant of English origin and an artist famous for his animal pictures. He was also responsible for the unusual château, described as being in the 'Renaissance Anglaise' style. It now belongs to La Compagnie AXA, who also own Pichon-Baron and who have at their disposal the talents of Jean-Michel Cazes of Lynch-Bages fame.

Cantenac-Brown today does not enjoy the reputation (or sell for the price) it once did. The wine is more tannic with less finesse than the best Cantenacs and has a certain coarseness. Efforts are being made by the new owners to improve matters.

Château Dauzac
5e Cru Classé. Owner: **MAIF. 45ha. 29,000 cases. CS 57%,**

Mer 36%, CF 4%, PV 3%. Second labels: **Châteaux Labarde and La Bastide.**
Until recently this property in Labarde had suffered a long period of neglect and obscurity. The restoration began when W A B Miailhe from neighbouring Siran bought the vineyard in 1964. The Chatellier family from Champagne took over in 1978 and made considerable investments in both vineyards and installations before selling to an insurance group, MAIF, in 1989. Since then even further improvements have been made.

The wines have a certain coarseness but show signs of improvement. A property to watch.

Château Desmirail
3e Cru Classé. Owner: **Lucien Lurton. 18ha. 4,000 cases. CS 80%, Mer 10%, CF 9%, PV 1%.**
This famous old growth has been resurrected by Lucien Lurton, vineyard owner extraordinary of Margaux (*see* Brane-Cantenac, Durfort-Vivens etc). The wines are perfumed, soft and elegant in spite of the high proportion of Cabernet Sauvignon. Some outstanding wines were produced in '83, '85, '86 and '88. This is a *cru* rapidly establishing a reputation for itself.

Château Deyrem-Valentin
Cru Bourgeois 1932. Owner: **Jean Sorge. 10ha. 5,000 cases. CS 45%, Mer 45%, CF 5%, PV 5%.**
This small property is situated in the best part of Soussans, and neighbours include Lascombes, Malescot and the two Labégorces. It has belonged to the present family since 1928, and Jean Sorge is very much a working resident proprietor.

The wines have the bouquet and finesse associated with the *appellation* but are rather light in body.

Château Durfort-Vivens
2e Cru Classé. Owner: **Lucien Lurton. 25ha. 5,500 cases. CS 82%, CF 10%, Mer 8%.** Second label: **Domaine de Cure-Bourse.**
The names come from the Comtes Durfort de Duras, who were the proprietors from the 15th century until the Revolution of 1789; Vivens was added in 1824. As is often the way in Bordeaux, the

Vivens and the Durfort families were actually related. From 1937 until 1961 it was under the same ownership as Château Margaux, it was then sold to its present owner. The château itself is still inhabited by Bernard Ginestet, son of the former owner of Château Margaux.

The contrast between Durfort and Brane-Cantenac is always an interesting one. Durfort is always firmer and more tannic but usually has less finesse and charm. In recent vintages, however, the wines have more richness and fruit to match their tannin. Especially successful years are '75, '78, '81, '82, '83, '85, '86, '88, and '89.

Château Ferrière
3e Cru Classé. Owners: **Mme André Durand-Feuillerat (héritiers). 5ha. 4,500 cases. CS 47%, Mer 33%, PV 12%, CF 8%.**
This small growth has been farmed by Château Lascombes on behalf of its owners since 1960. A small quantity of wine is thus declared under this name at each vintage, but effectively the wine has lost its separate identity.

The wines are pleasantly light and soft, but hardly deserving of Troisième Cru Classé status any more. Mostly sold in France.

Château Giscours
3e Cru Classé. Owner: **GFA du Château Giscours.**
Administrator: **Pierre Tari. 81ha. 29,500 cases. CS 75%, Mer 20%, CF 3%, PV 2%.**
Since its acquisition by the Tari family in 1952, much time and money has been invested in this property to restore it to its former glory. Now it is one of the largest and most important properties in the Margaux *appellation*, as well as one of the most consistent.

The wines of Giscours are deep-coloured with a pronounced bouquet combining richness and fruit, while the wine itself is very fruity, vigorous and full-bodied. If not as stylish as the wines of Cantenac and Margaux, the wine clearly has breed. Because of their power, these wines require eight to ten years' ageing in the best vintages before being anywhere near their best. But the delicious 1980 was excellent at four years old. Later in the 1980s the wines have been more marked by a certain coarse-grained power than by the finesse of the past.

Château La Gurgue
Cru Bourgeois Supérieur 1932. Owner: **SC du Château La Gurgue.** Administrator: **Mme Bernadette Villars. 12ha. 5,000 cases. CS 70%, Mer 25%, PV 5%.**
A very well-placed vineyard, together with Desmirail it is the closest neighbour to Château Margaux on its western boundary. There was a change of ownership in 1978 and the new investment, together with the undoubted flair of Bernadette Villars (*see* Chasse-Spleen and Haut-Bages-Libéral), has resulted in a marked improvement in the wines. '81, '82, '83, '85, and '86 are all great successes.

This is the delicate, perfumed type of Margaux, with style and breed, nice fruit, not a lot of body but plenty of flavour and refinement. Certainly a wine to watch and follow.

Château d'Issan
3e Cru Classé. Owner: **Mme Emmanuel Cruse. 32ha. 14,000 cases. CS 75%, Mer 25%.**
Regum mensis arisque deorum ('for the tables of kings and the high altar of the gods') says the inscription over the gateway at d'Issan. This is one of the oldest properties and the most splendid château in the whole Médoc, with its beautiful early 17th-century château sitting within the moat of its mediaeval predecessor.

After a long period of neglect, d'Issan was bought by the Cruse family in 1945 and both château and vineyard have been painstakingly restored to their former glory. Formerly this was a Cruse (*négociant*) exclusivity; now it is sold on the market, and there have been marked improvements in the wine in recent years. This is a wine of great individuality, combining a power and richness rare in Cantenac with great breed and a lovely perfume. The '73 must be one of the most delightful wines of the vintage. Outstanding wines were also made in '70, '79, '81, '82, '83, '85 and '86. This is very much a château on the up – and already offers remarkable value for money.

Château Kirwan
3e Cru Classé. Owner: **Schröder & Schÿler. 34ha. 16,000 cases. CS 40%, Mer 30%, CF 20%, PV 10%.**
Château Kirwan is named after an Irishman from Galway who lost his head in the French Revolution. It now belongs to the Bordeaux

firm of Schröder & Schÿler, who bottled the wines in their Bordeaux cellars until 1966, 1967 being the first vintage to be château-bottled.

A great deal of work and investment has gone into improving the quality of Kirwan. New wood was used in the barrel-ageing for the first time in 1978. The recent vintages are deep-coloured, powerful, concentrated wines which are beginning to attract more favourable comments again. Personally I find them still a little short on Margaux charm with a tendency to dryness.

Château Labégorce
Cru Bourgeois Supérieur 1932. Owner: **Hubert Perrodo. 29ha. 11,000 cases. CS 55%, Mer 40%, CF 5%.**
This is certainly one of the best unclassified wines of Margaux, together with its close neighbour Labégorce Zédé. The vineyards are well placed in Margaux and Soussans, and the château has nothing bourgeois about it. The wines have Margaux finesse and delicacy. The property changed hands in 1989, when the Condom family, owners since 1965, sold to an oil tycoon who is also a wine-lover. He has already made a marked improvement. The distribution is in the hands of Dourthe Frères.

Château Labégorce Zédé
Cru Bourgeois Supérieur 1932. GFA Labégorce Zédé. Administrator: **Luc Thienpont. 27ha. 9,500 cases. CS 50%, Mer 35%, CF 10%, PV 5%.** Second label: **Château de l'Amiral.**
For some years the wines of Labégorce Zédé took second place to those of its neighbour Labégorce. Now, since Luc Thienpont took over in 1979, standards have improved and fine wines are being made. The emphasis is on finesse and breed with a superbly perfumed bouquet, and this is one of the best unclassified wines of the *appellation*. Although the *appellation* is Margaux, the greater proportion of the vineyard area lies in Soussans.

Château Lascombes
2e Cru Classé. Owner: **Bass-Charrington.** Administrator: **Michael Baily Gibson. 94ha. 35,000 cases. CS 65%, Mer 30%, CF 3%, PV 2%.** Second label: **Château Segonnes.**

Historically Lascombes was a small property until its purchase in 1951 by Alexis Lichine and an American syndicate, who subsequently sold to the giant UK brewery group Bass–Charrington in 1971. In the past 20 years its vineyards and production have been greatly increased and this is now one of the largest properties in the Médoc.

In recent years however, there have been some disappointing wines made here, lacking the style and breed of which this growth is capable. Its results in blind tastings tend to confirm this, though there are some signs of improvement. Certainly a stricter selection is necessary if wines comparable to other Deuxièmes Crus are to be made again regularly, and the recent launching of a new second label is a positive sign of this. The '86 and '89 are encouraging signs for the future.

Just under half the output of this château is of rosé.

Château Malescot-St-Exupéry
3e Cru Classé. Owner: **Roger Zuger. 34ha. 15,000 cases. CS 50%, Mer 35%, CF 10%, PV 5%.** Second labels: **Château de Loyac, Domaine du Balardin.**
Since acquiring the property in 1955 from the English firm of W H Chaplin, the Zuger family have done much to rebuild this *cru* which had greatly declined in size and standing. The charming château, now restored and lived in again, stands in the centre of the village of Margaux, while the vineyards are in Margaux (adjoining Château Margaux) and in Soussans.

The reputation of Malescot is now restored. The wines have a fine bouquet and finesse, but I find a harshness and sometimes a certain edginess which detracts from the final impression. However, recent vintages show a marked improvement.

Château Margaux
ler Cru Classé. Owner: **SC du Château Margaux (Mentzelopoulos family).** Administrator: **Paul Pontallier. 87ha. Red: 29,000 cases; CS 75%, Mer 20%, PV and CF 5%. White: 3,300 cases; Sauv 100%.** Secondary labels: **Pavillon Blanc and Pavillon Rouge du Château Margaux.**
This château has had its ups and downs, but new heights of quality and consistency have been achieved since the Mentzelopoulos

Harvesting the grapes by hand at Château Margaux

family acquired the property in 1977. A new underground cellar has been built, the château and gardens restored to their former glory, and much work has been done to improve the vineyard.

At its best Margaux is one of the most sumptuous and sensual wines of the Médoc, with all the perfume and finesse of a fine Margaux, as found in its neighbours, but allied to more body and remarkable character and individuality. After producing some great vintages in '45, '47, '49, '50 and '53, its wines became less outstanding and less consistent, although the '66 stands out in this lean period. Now, from '78 to '90 it has consistently produced wines which are each among the outstanding examples of their respective vintages.

A second wine, Pavillon Rouge du Château Margaux, is made as a result of the stricter selection now practised. The first vintage was '79. The wines are lighter than the Grand Vin, but have breed and charm and are ready to drink much earlier.

An excellent white wine, Pavillon Blanc du Château Margaux, made only from Sauvignon grapes from a vineyard in Soussans, is a wine of real distinction. Its bouquet and breed are remarkable, but so, unfortunately, is the price!

Château Marquis-d'Alesme-Becker
3e Cru Classé. Owner: **Jean-Claude Zuger. 10ha. 4,150 cases. CS 30%, Mer 30%, CF 30%, PV 10%.**
This small and little-known Cru Classé was owned by the English firm of W H Chaplin and run partly with Malescot. The present proprietor is the brother of Roger Zuger at Malescot and the château is the original building of Château Desmirail. The vineyards are in Soussans and Margaux.

With its small production and history of obscurity it remains a wine that is hard to find. But I have found it possessed of elegant, stylish fruit with a firm backbone. It needs time to develop.

Château Marquis-de-Terme
4e Cru Classe. Owner: **Famille Sénéclauze. 35ha. 12,000 cases. CS 45%, Mer 35%, CF 15%, PV 5%.**
A good proportion of this wine is sold direct on the French market, with the result that it is not so widely known on export markets as its size would lead one to suppose. Much work has recently been done to make good deficiencies in the *chai*, which is now modern and well equipped. The vineyard is very well kept. The yields, however, are high.

I have found this wine to have charm and a certain easy appeal, without being among the best of Margaux in terms of finesse or originality. The vintages of the 1980s, however, have marked a clear advance in quality.

Château Marsac-Séguineau
Cru Bourgeois 1932. Owner: **SC du Château Marsac-**

Séguineau. Administrator: **Jean-Pierre Angliviel de la Beaudelle. 10ha. 5,000 cases. Mer 60%, CS 28%, CF 12%.** Second label: **Château Gravières-de-Marsac.**
This is a full-flavoured, supple wine which nevertheless lasts well. The vineyard is in Soussans. The wines are exclusively distributed by the *négociants* Mestrezat, who are also in effect the owners, and who have done much to reorganize the vineyards since taking over.

Château Martinens
Cru Bourgeois Supérieur 1932. Owners: **Simone Dulos and Jean-Pierre Seynat-Dulos. 31ha. 8,300 cases. Mer 40%, CS 30%, PV 20%, PV 10%.** Second label: **Château Bois du Monteil.**
The pleasing château at Martinens was built in 1767 by three women from London, Ann, Jane and Mary White. But they sold after only nine years. The present owners have run the property since 1945. It lies in Cantenac and enjoys an excellent reputation for stylish, attractive wines.

Château Monbrison
Cru Bourgeois. Owners: **Elizabeth Davis & Sons. 14ha. 5,500 cases. CS 45%, Mer 35%, CF 15%, PV 5%.** Second label: **Château Cordat.**
Davis sounds English but is in fact American. The property was bought in 1921 by Robert Meacham-Davis, an American commissioner in the Red Cross, and the present proprietor is his daughter. She is now assisted by her three sons Bruno, Jean-Luc and Laurent Vonderheyden.
I have found the wine to be most attractive, well structured with plenty of fruit and balancing tannin. This is now one of the most sought-after unclassified wines of the *appellation*, and although very good before, it has been outstanding since 1985.

Château Montbrun
Cru Bourgeois 1932. Owner: **J Lebègue & Co.**
Administrators: **Jacques and Alain de Coninck. 8ha. 3,500 cases. Mer 75%, CS and CF 25%.**
This small but well-placed vineyard in Cantenac was once part of Château Palmer. With its high proportion of Merlot, it produces

rich, full-bodied wines, appropriate for a property run by men from the Libournais. It is distributed by the *négociants* J Lebègue & Co – now unconnected with the English firm of the same name.

Château Palmer
3e Cru Classé. Owner: **SC du Château Palmer.**
Administrator: **B Bouteiller. 45ha. 12,500 cases. CS 55%, Mer 40%, CF 3%, PV 2%.**
Named after a British general who fought under Wellington, Palmer is now owned by Dutch and British proprietors (Mähler-Besse and Peter Sichel). The château lies in the hamlet of Issan, and most of its vineyards were once part of Château d'Issan's domaine. The charming château itself was built in the years 1857–60 when the property was owned by the Péreire family.

The reputation of Palmer has soared in the past 20 years. This was one of the first of the 'Super-Seconds', a reputation which effectively dates from the superlative '61. The Chardon family (father Pierre and sons Claude and Yves) have had much to do with the quality and consistency of this splendid wine. The wine is characterized by an opulence and richness that are almost burgundian in the best years, yet this is combined with real finesse and breed. In recent years '70, '71, '75, '76, '78, '79 and '81 were all great successes. The '82 lacks the richness and concentration of the best '82s and cannot be compared with the '61 but is nevertheless a fine and attractive wine. The '83 is reckoned more successful, and is followed by the '85, '86, '88, '89 and '90, all of which are also very fine.

Château Paveil-de-Luze
Cru Bourgeois. Owner: **GFA du Château Paveil.**
Administrator: **Baron Geoffroy de Luze. 30ha. 7,000 cases. CS and CF 75%, Mer 25%.** Second label: **Château de-la-Coste.**
A fine vineyard on deep, well-drained gravel in Soussans with a charming château in the chartreuse style, Paveil has belonged to the de Luze family for over a century. The wines were always sound but often rather anonymous, and bottled in de Luze's cellars in Bordeaux. Now the de Luze family have parted company with the firm that bears their name and the wine is château-bottled and

seems to be improving. At its best this is a wine of some style and distinction, with lots of charm and breed rather than body. A wine to watch.

Château Pontac-Lynch
Cru Bourgeois Supérieur 1932. Owner: **GFA du Château Pontac-Lynch.** Administrator: **Serge Bondon. 10ha. 3,300 cases. CS and CF 57%, Mer 39%, PV 4%.** Second label: **Ch Puy Lesplanques.**
A little-known *cru* today, bearing two famous names; Pontac-Lynch apparently sold for higher prices in the mid-18th century than its famous neighbours which are today classified. The wines have been winning medals recently and should be worth looking out for.

Château Pouget
4e Cru Classé. Owner: **GFA des Châteaux Boyd-Cantenac et Pouget.** Administrator: **Pierre Guillemet. 11ha. 4,700 cases. CS 66%, Mer 30%, CF 4%.**
Under the same ownership as Château Boyd-Cantenac. Until the 1982 vintage both wines were made here and Pouget was treated as the second wine of Boyd-Cantenac; since 1983 however, the wines have had quite separate facilities. Pouget is exclusively distributed by Maison Dubos Frères of Bordeaux.

The wines are well made, rich and supple in style, and certainly worthy of Cru Classé status; '70, '71, '75, '78 and '79 were all very successful years. In the 1980s the wines have tended to become more tannic, but coarser in style.

Château Prieuré-Lichine
4e Cru Classé. Owner: **Sacha Lichine. 60ha. 25,000 cases. CS 55%, Mer 33%, PV 6%, CF 6%.** Second label: **Château de Clairefort.**
The property has been restored and the vineyard enlarged and reconstructed since it was bought by Alexis Lichine in 1952. This charming château in Cantenac, formerly the Priory, was Alexis Lichine's European home until his death in 1989. His son Sacha has now ably taken up the reins.

The quality and reputation of this *cru* have deservedly grown in recent years. The wines are full-bodied and rich, and a very consistent standard is maintained. Here they think that their fine '82 is surpassed by their '83. Other vintages that have particularly impressed me are '70, '76, '78, '79, '81, '85, '86, '88 and '89.

Château Rausan-Ségla
2e Cru Classé. Owner: **Walker Family Trust. 47ha. 13,000 cases. CS 66%, Mer 34%.**
This is one of the oldest and most famous *crus* in Margaux, but unfortunately its wines for some years failed to match their high classification. Having belonged to the Cruse family for several generations, it was bought by the Liverpool firm of John Holt (now part of Lonrho) in 1960, since when it has been managed and marketed by the famous *négociant* Louis Eschenauer. In 1989 Eschenauer and the château were sold to Brent Walker, who resold Eschenauer, but is still looking for a suitable buyer for Rausan.

In theory this is a long-lasting wine which develops great finesse; in practice too many vintages have been austere and charmless. The '82 marked the beginning of a substantial improvement, with the '85 possibly even better. '88, '89 and '90 have proved to be outstanding, challenging Palmer's position as the best wines in the *appellation* after Margaux.

Château Rauzan-Gassies
2e Cru Classé. Owner: **Mme Paul Quié et J-M Quié. 30ha. 8,300 cases. CS 40%, Mer 39%, CF 20%, PV 1%.** Second label: **Enclos de Moncabon.**
Until the French Revolution of 1789, this was part of the same property as Rausan-Ségla. There is no château. Since 1943 it has belonged to the Quié family and in the past some great wines were made. In recent years, however, the wines have been consistent but not top flight. The style of the wine is more powerful and richer than many Margaux, more in the character of Cantenac, with delicacy and charm developing in bottle. Recently efforts have been made to modernize and improve matters here, so the wines should be worth watching.

Château Siran
Cru Bourgeois Supérieur 1932. Owner: **William-Alain B**

Miailhe. 35ha. 12,500 cases. CS 50%, Mer 25%, PV 15%, CF 10%. Second labels: **Châteaux Bellegarde and St-Jacques.**
This is something of a show-place for a Cru Bourgeois, but then the proprietor Alain Miailhe is convinced that it should be a Cru Classé and is eloquent on this topic. There is a heliport here, an anti-nuclear shelter well stocked with the best vintages, and a park famous for its cyclamens.

The wines have a charming bouquet and have become noticeably richer and fuller in flavour since around 1970. There is some point of comparison with nearby Giscours, and the wines have more charm and breed than their other classified neighbour Dauzac.

Château Tayac
Cru Bourgeois. Owner: **André Favin. 34ha. 15,000 cases. CS 65%, Mer 25%, CF 5%, PV 5%.**
This is the largest of the Crus Bourgeois of Margaux, lying in Soussans. Its good reputation is the work of the present proprietor, André Favin, who inherited the property in 1960. The wines are perfumed and robust with something agreeably rustic in their make-up.

Château du Tertre
5e Cru Classé. Owner: **Philippe Capbern Gasqueton. 48ha. 14,000 cases. CS 80%, CF 10%, Mer 10%.**
The word *tertre* means a knoll, a piece of high ground, and Château du Tertre is a splendidly situated vineyard on the highest ground in the Margaux *appellation*, in Arsac. The soil is classically pebbly. Since taking over the property in 1961, Philippe Gasqueton (of Château Calon-Segur) has steadily restored the vineyard, buildings, and now the château itself.

I believe that this is the most underrated of the Crus Classés. The wines have beautifully vivid fruit and considerable finesse, breed and charm. The record for consistency is also impressive. The '80, for instance, is really fine and has more concentration than many wines of this vintage. The '82, '83 and '85 were also outstanding successes.

Château La Tour-de-Bessan
Owner: **Lucien Lurton. 15ha. 8,300 cases. CS 80%, Mer 20%.**
The *tour* is a ruined watch-tower of the 15th century dating from the last years of English rule. The vineyard in Soussans is the humblest part of Lucien Lurton's Margaux empire, and produces light, supple wines with breed and charm. A chance to buy a Lurton Margaux at a more modest price.

Château La Tour-de-Mons
Cru Bourgeois Supérieur 1932. Owner: **Clauzel-Binaud-Crochet.** Administrator: **Bertrand Clauzel. 35ha. 15,000 cases. CS 45%, Mer 40%, CF 10%, PV 5%.**
A very old property in Soussans with a long-standing reputation. Until recently the families that own it also owned Château Cantemerle. For some time La Tour-de-Mons has been spoken of as a candidate for classification.

Unfortunately the distribution of this wine was for many years a monopoly of the old house of H O Beyermann and, as their fortune declined, so this excellent wine was not as widely sold as it deserved to be. Fortunately, with the sale of Cantemerle, there has been some much-needed investment in the property, and a marked improvement in the wines during the 1980s has resulted. '82, '83, '85 and '86 show what this *cru* can do. The wines are wonderfully scented, combining vigour, tannin and real breed with plenty of charm. These are long-lived wines, of growing distinction.

Moulis

This is the smallest of the six communal *appellations*, but there are more outstanding Crus Bourgeois here than in Listrac. The area under vine has increased by as much as 47 percent in the last decade but is still only a modest 502 hectares. The vineyards lie northwest of Margaux and directly west of Arcins. The wines are powerful and rich, the best having fruit and finesse as well; they are long-keeping and of marked attractiveness.

Château Anthonic
Cru Bourgeois Supérieur. Owner: **Pierre Cordonnier.**
18ha. 8,000 cases. CS 65%, Mer 30%, PV 5%.
This *cru* has carried its present name only since 1922. It appeared in
the first edition of Cocks & Féret in 1850 under the name of Puy de
Minjon, and changed names once more between then and 1922.
The château is on the outskirts of the village of Moulis, and the
vineyards are some of the oldest in the commune.

Recently the vineyards have been in the throes of reconstruction. When I tasted the 1981 vintage in 1984, I found it deep-
coloured with well-projected fruit on the nose, but tasting slightly
stalky like a wine with too much *vin de presse*, although the structure
was good and it obviously needed time to develop. Certainly a
good solid wine, but not in the front rank of Moulis.

Château Bel-Air-Lagrave
Cru Bourgeois 1932. Owner: **Mme Jeanne Bacquey. 15ha.**
5,500 cases. CS 60%, Mer 36%, PV 4%.
This vineyard is on the gravelly ridges of Grand Poujeaux, certainly
the best sector of the Moulis vineyards. It has been in the same
family for 150 years. The owners believe in hard pruning and low
yields to produce the best quality.

The wines are clearly carefully made. Their charm and fruit is
emphasized, and they are softer and more refined than many from
this *appellation*, with individuality and a definite finesse and balance
that firmly removes them from any suggestion of the rustic. Very
attractive wines were made here in the vintages of '79 and '81. A
wine to watch.

Château Biston-Brillette
Cru Bourgeois 1932. Owner: **Michel Barbarin. 20ha. 8,000**
cases. CS 55%, Mer 40%, PV 5%.
An old-fashioned and rather rustic label hardly does justice to the
excellent wines now being made here. Typically Moulis with its
dense texture, there is also a hint of complexity about its spicy
concentrated fruit which lifts it from the general run of wines from
this *appellation*. The emphasis on fruit and balance makes this a wine
which can be enjoyed young, without sacrificing its keeping
qualities.

Château Branas-Grand-Poujeaux
Owner: **Jacques de Pourquéry. 6ha. 4,000 cases. CS 60%, Mer 35%, PV 5%.**
A small property with a well-placed vineyard and a most enthusiastic owner determined to make fine wines. In a blind tasting of '81 Moulis wines held in 1984 I placed this wine on the same level as some Crus Bourgeois Exceptionnels. At this stage the wine had both charm and a fine middle flavour and richness, with real style and breed. All the wine is aged in casks, of which a third are new each year. A wine to watch, if you can find it!

Château Brillette
Cru Grand Bourgeois. Owner: **SC du Château Brillette.**
Administrator: **Mme Berthault. 40ha. 15,000 cases. CS 50%, Mer 40%, PV 10%.**
When Raymond Berthault bought this property in 1976 it had greatly declined and there was much work to be done. The new proprietor was the owner of Viniprix and Euromarche, and Brillette was to be a hobby. Bertrand Bouteiller (Château Lanessan) now acts as *régisseur* and has had the benefit of Professor Peynaud's advice. One third new wood is used each year.

Unfortunately Raymond Berthault died in 1981, but his widow and son-in-law continue along the lines already laid down. This was always a good solid Moulis; now it looks like moving into the leading category.

Château Chasse-Spleen
Cru Grand Bourgeois Exceptionnel. Owner: **SC du Château Chasse-Spleen.** Administrator: **Mme Bernadette Villars. 75ha. 23,000 cases. CS 60%, Mer 35%, PV 3%, CF 2%.** Second label: **L'Ermitage de Chasse-Spleen. 5,000 cases.**
Chasse-Spleen has for long been recognized as not only the leading *cru* of Moulis, but as deserving of Cru Classé status. From the First World War until 1976 it belonged to the Lahary family and was very well run. Its present owners include a bank, but the most important partner is the Société Bernard Taillan whose director is the dynamic Jacques Merlaut. His daughter, a qualified oenologist, manages the property. The curious name Chasse-Spleen is attributed to a quip of Lord Byron's to the effect that the wine chased

away 'spleen' (ill humour or melancholy).

The wines often have an initial toughness, even coarseness, but this is quickly dispelled and the true character of the wine emerges. In mature vintages the wines quickly develop an almost opulent fullness of fruit on the nose, a lovely flavour with concentration, structure and real breed. It is extremely consistent and makes delicious bottles in lesser years. The '75 is a long-term *vin de garde*. The '78 is very fine and the '79 most attractive. '82 and '83 are a fine pair, showing the contrasting merits of these vintages. '85 is an approachable wine for its year and '86, '88 and '89 are all powerful tannic wines for long ageing. This is a wine which does not take as long to mature as you might think, it keeps well and seldom disappoints.

Château La Closerie-Grand-Poujeaux
Cru Bourgeois 1932. Owner: **GFA Le Grand Poujeaux.** Administrator: **Jeanne Bacque. 4ha. 3,500 cases. CS 65%, Mer 30%, PV 5%.**
This small vineyard was the creation of a former *régisseur* of Chasse-Spleen. Since 1941 it has belonged to the Donat family. For many years the redoubtable Mlle Donat ran the property and was one of the great characters of Moulis. Since 1984 Mme Bacquey has been in charge. Everything is done in a very traditional way, and long-lived, solid wines are the result, with the emphasis on body and richness, rather in the same style as Dutruch.

Château Duplessis-Fabre
Cru Bourgeois. Owner: **SC du Château Fourcas-Dupré.** Administrator: **Patrice Pagès. 14ha. 5,500 cases. Mer 45%, CS 42%, CF 8%, PV 4%, Mal 1%.**
This property belongs to the Pagès family, who have also made such an excellent job of running Château Fourcas-Dupré in recent years. Powerful assertive wines with just enough *souplesse* are made here, they are of middle-of-the-road character, good and honest.

Château Duplessis (Hauchecorne)
Cru Grand Bourgeois. Owner: **SC des Grands Crus Réunis.** Administrator: **Lucien Lurton. 17·5ha. 8,000 cases. CS 65%,**

Mer 20%, Mal 10%, PV 5%.
The wine of this château has for some time been labelled simply as
Duplessis. It is now proposed that the word 'Hauchecorne' should
be added to the label in smaller letters to avoid confusion with the
nearby Duplessis-Fabre.

The wines here are rich and supple and are made for reasonably
early drinking. Since Lucien Lurton took over the management in
1983, there have been signs of some impressive wines, with a more
marked character.

Château Dutruch-Grand-Poujeaux
Cru Grand Bourgeois Exceptionnel. Owner: **François
Cordonnier. 25ha. 12,000 cases. CS and CF 50%, Mer 42%,
PV 8%.**
The wines of Dutruch have long enjoyed a deserved reputation for
quality and consistency. The present owner, a relative of M
Lambert, took over in 1967.

In the 1960s I noted that the wines here were characterized by
their body and richness, and this is still the case. Both '79 and '81
were most successful, and an attractive '80 was also made. These are
wines which repay keeping.

Château Gressier-Grand-Poujeaux
Cru Bourgeois Supérieur 1932. Owner: **Héritiers de Saint-
Affrique.** Administrator: **Bertrand de Marcellus. 18ha. 9,000
cases. CS 50%, Mer 40%, CF 10%.**
This fine old property has been in the hands of the same family since
1724, and the family arms of the Saint-Affriqués gives the label a
very distinctive look.

Improvements and modernizations have been made in recent
years, and new oak is now used in the maturation process. The
wines have always had more fruit and finesse than those of many
neighbouring properties, and have maintained a consistent standard
over many years. The '79, '81, '82 and '85 were all excellent and
among the best wines in the commune.

Château Lestage-Darquier
Cru Bourgeois Supérieur 1932. Owner: **François Bernard.
4ha. 1,800 cases. CS 50%, Mer 40%, CF 10%.**

With such a small production it is hardly surprising that this wine is little known. The vineyard is well placed on the gravelly ridges of Grand Poujeaux and has belonged to the Bernard family for several generations. I have found the wines very deep-coloured with a bouquet dense with rich fruit and with a distinctive, assertive flavour, tannic and with the promise of something quite fine when mature.

Château Maucaillou
Cru Bourgeois. Owner: **Famille Dourthe. 55ha. 19,000 cases. CS 45%, Mer 35%, CF 15%, PV 5%.**
Maucaillou is the pride of the Dourthe family. They no longer control the *négociant* firm which bears their name, but they have kept this château, where the business started. Three-quarters of the vintage is aged in new oak, unusual for a non-classified growth, and there is a very modern stainless steel installation for the fermentation.

In a blind tasting of '79 Moulis wines held in 1984 I placed Maucaillou first, while the '82, '83 and '85 are also very successful vintages. The wines combine the power of Moulis with a really beautiful flavour, real breed and charm. This is a *cru* which often competes well in blind tastings with the Crus Classés.

Château Mauvesin
Cru Bourgeois Supérieur. Owners: **Vicomte & Vicomtesse de Baritault du Carpia. 53ha. 21,000 cases. CS 50%, Mer 50%. (7ha under AC Haut-Médoc producing 3,780 cases.)**
Lying in the south of the *appellation*, this is the largest property in Moulis. Records show that it belonged to the de Foix family – who also owned Château d'Issan – until 1647, when it was bought by Pierre Le Blanc, *conseiller du roi* at the Parliament of Bordeaux. It was the Le Blanc family who built the large Victorian château that stands on the property today. The wines of Mauvesin are light, soft and quite elegant, their easy fruit encouraging early drinking.

Château Moulin-à-Vent
Cru Grand Bourgeois. Owner: **Dominique Hessel. 24ha. 10,000 cases. CS 65%, Mer 30%, PV 5%.** Second label:

Moulin-de-St-Vincent. 4,500 cases.
Moulin-à-Vent may seem an odd name for a Bordeaux château, but
in the Middle Ages mixed agriculture was the norm in the Médoc,
and many ruined mills can still be found. Since buying the property
in 1977, Dominique Hessel has made many improvements,
enlarging the vineyard and maturing the wine in casks instead of
vats.

The wines have a fine flavour and are rich and vigorous,
developing a complex bouquet with bottle-age. This now deserves
to be numbered with the leading *crus* of Moulis.

Moulin-de-St-Vincent, the second label, used to be an exclusivity of Ginestet. Under the present management a deliciously
fruity, early-maturing wine is being produced.

Château Moulis
Cru Bourgeois Supérieur. Owner: **Jacques Darricarrère.**
12ha. 4,500 cases. CS 60%, Mer 40%.
In the last century this was a vast estate with around 100 hectares.
Now it is a modest one with vineyards grouped around the château
just outside the village of Moulis. There is a modern stainless steel
installation for vinification, and the wines are matured in wood. All
the wine is château-bottled.

Château Pomeys
Cru Bourgeois Supérieur 1932. Owner: **Xavier Barennes.**
8ha. 2,500 cases. CS 67%, Mer 33%.
This small property has now been in the same family for seven
generations. It is very traditionally run and its wines have a good
reputation.

Château Poujeaux
Cru Grand Bourgeois Exceptionnel. Owners: **François &
Philippe Theil. 52ha. 25,000 cases. CS 48%, Mer 37%, CF
9%, PV 6%.** Second label: **Château La Salle-de-Poujeaux.**
Though Moulis is the name of the *appellation*, the commune of
Poujeaux is where most of the best *crus* are, and there are none better
than Château Poujeaux itself. A third of the wine is put in new oak,
and everything here is meticulously carried out.

The wines are deep-coloured with an arresting bouquet –

sometimes there are overtones of tobacco and a flavour which is stylish and fine although tannic and powerful. This is a long-lived wine which deserves long maturing in the best vintages, and is certainly always one of the best wines in the *appellation*. In comparison with its rival Chasse-Spleen, Poujeaux tends to be more fleshy and fruity, but is equally deserving of Cru Classé status. The 1980s have been an impressive period here, with '82, '83, '85, '86, '88 and '89 all being outstanding vintages. Unusually for a wine of this class it is sold entirely direct and not through the Bordeaux trade.

Château Ruat-Petit-Poujeaux
Cru Bourgeois 1932. Owner: **Pierre Goffre-Viaud. 15ha.**
5,000 cases. CS and CF 65%, Mer 35%. Second label:
Château Ruat.
Petit Poujeaux is a hamlet just outside Moulis and well away from Grand Poujeaux. Ruat was the name of a pre-Revolution property, dispersed during the Revolution, but patiently pieced together again after the present proprietor's great-grandfather had bought the domaine in 1871. The wines have charm, fruit and typical Moulis richness and solidity, with a tendency to evolve more quickly than many wines of this *appellation*. This is good middle-of-the-road wine.

Listrac

Listrac and its neighbour Moulis differ in important respects from the other four commune *appellations*. They contain no Crus Classés, and do not border the river, where the best *crus* are, but are on a plateau inland. But both produce excellent wines whose distinctive characteristics are increasingly appreciated.

The area under vine here increased by 45 percent between 1972 and 1986. The wines were often considered to be tough and astringent, but are today markedly less rustic, quite powerful but with finesse and fruit.

Château La Bécade
Cru Bourgeois. Owner: **Jean-Pierre Théron. 23ha. 13,000**

cases. CS 75%, Mer 25%.
This is a well-placed vineyard lying to the northeast of Listrac on the road between St-Julien and Margaux. Its well-made, typical wines have won a number of medals in recent years. No wood is used in the maturing, and this makes the wines ready to drink young.

Château Cap-Leon-Veyrin
Cru Bourgeois 1932. Owner: **Alain Meyre. 16ha. 7,500 cases. Mer 60%, CS 40%.**
This is an amalgamation of two vineyards dating from 1908. The wines are matured in cask, including a proportion of new oak. These are powerful, long-lived wines that repay keeping, yet can also be enjoyed young. Also, as the notices on the Bordeaux-Lesparre road point out, the property offers farm holidays, so that visitors can actually stay on the domaine and enjoy traditional Médocain hospitality.

Château Clarke
Cru Bourgeois. Owner: **Baron Edmond de Rothschild. 135ha. 56,000 cases. CS 52%, Mer 43%, CF 4%, PV 1%.**
Second labels: **Châteaux Malmaison and Peyre-Lebade.**
This must be one of the most remarkable new developments in the Médoc. Baron Edmond de Rothschild has undertaken a long-term expansion scheme, introducing the most modern installations, and vineyard plantings that will take some years to realize. What has been done makes this *cru* worthy of a Cru Classé.

Prior to the '82 vintage I found the wines rather lean, austere, and marked by new wood. The '82 looked to point to an improvement, but then rather reverted to type; the '85 looked much more promising but at present the wines seem to be ageing rather quickly. An attractive rosé is also made here. There are good facilities for receiving visitors between June and September.

Château Ducluzeau
Cru Bourgeois 1932. Owner: **Mme Jean-Eugène Borie. 4ha. 1,650 cases. Mer 90%, CS 10%.**
In 1850 Charles Cocks listed this château as the second *cru* of Listrac. Since then it has decreased in size and importance, but nevertheless

produces some very fine wines. The wines of Ducluzeau are uncharacteristic of the region in that they come from vineyards planted with 90 percent Merlot. They are matured in cask for six months and château-bottled. Ideal luncheon wines, they are perfumed and have plenty of fruit. The '79 and the delicious '84 were ready for drinking early; other vintages such as the '83 needed longer to develop.

Château Fonréaud
Cru Bourgeois. Owner: **Héritiers Chanfreau.**
Administrators: **Mme Leo Chanfreau and M Jean Chanfreau.**
20,500 cases. CS 66%, Mer 31%, PV 3%.
The château here is something of a landmark on the main Lesparre road south of Listrac. Part of the crop is aged in vat, and part in cask. The wines tend to be elegant, attractive, fruity and easy to drink when young.

Château Fourcas-Dupré
Cru Grand Bourgeois Exceptionnel. Owner: **SC du**
Château Fourcas-Dupré. Administrator: **Patrice Pagès.**
44ha. 22,000 cases. CS 50%, Mer 38%, CF 10%, PV 2%.
Guy Pagès lived at and managed this château from 1967 until his untimely death in 1985. During this time he established high standards and made many improvements. He is succeeded by his son Patrice, already well versed in the affairs of the property. There are both stainless steel and concrete vats for fermentation, and casks from leading Crus Classés are used for ageing.

The wines of Fourcas-Dupré are very perfumed, quite tannic and powerful in the best years but supple and attractive in lesser ones. The comparison with the neighbouring Fourcas-Hosten is interesting, especially as Patrice Pagès has assisted in the running of the latter for several years. I found them closest in quality in the excellent '78. There is a tendency for the Hosten wines to have more depth and richness, especially noticeable in vintages like '79 and even '80.

Château Fourcas-Hosten
Cru Grand Bourgeois Exceptionnel. Owner: **SC du**
Château Fourcas-Hosten. Administrators: **Bertrand de**

Rivoyre, Patrice Pagès and Philip Poivers. 46ha. 20,000 cases. CS 48%, Mer 39%, CF 13%.
Until 1972 this château belonged to the Saint-Affriques of Gressier, and the wines were made and kept there. It now belongs to a syndicate of French, Danes and Americans. The *chai* and *cuvier* have been reconstructed. Some new wood is now used for ageing, and the vineyard has been gradually enlarged.

The wines of Fourcas-Hosten have exceptional colour and are notable for their power and richness, with a very assertive character but more fruit combined with tannin than the other *crus* of Listrac. This is a very consistent wine now. The '78 is outstanding, with '82 very enjoyable, '83 at its best, '85 exceptional, and '86 very concentrated.

Cave Coopérative Grand Listrac
Owner: **Coopérative. 160ha. 66,650 cases. Mer 60%, CS and CF 30%, PV 10%.**
This cooperative has long enjoyed an excellent reputation, especially in France, where Grand Listrac was for many years the best buy on the French Railways. Today there are 70 members. Three Listrac properties are sold under their château names: Capdet, Clos du Fourcas and Vieux Moulis, as are two Moulis wines: Guitignan and Bouqueyran.

Château Lafon
Cru Grand Bourgeois. Owner: **Jean-Pierre Théron.**
Administrator: **Serge Lavandier. 9ha. 5,000 cases. CS 60%, Mer 40%.**
The property is run jointly with the proprietors of another Listrac *cru*, La Bécade. When he bought it in the late 1960s Jean-Pierre Théron found no more than a dilapidated ruin. Everything had to be restored and the vineyard reconstructed and enlarged.

The wines are kept only in vat, seeing no wood at all, and this makes them ready to drink early. These are pleasant, commercial wines.

Château Lestage
Cru Bourgeois Supérieur. Owner: **Héritiers Chanfreau.**
Administrators: **Mme Leo Chanfreau and M Jean Chanfreau.**

52ha. 25,000 cases. Mer 52%, CS and CF 46%, PV 2%.
Under the same ownership and management as Château Fonréaud. The château here is a large, ornate, 19th-century mansion. Most of the wines are aged in vat rather than cask, which tends to produce supple, early-maturing wines. I have usually found this wine quite tannic though and sometimes a little dry. It certainly needs bottle-age in the better years.

Château Saransot-Dupré
Cru Bourgeois Supérieur 1932. Owner: **Yves Raymond.**
14ha. 6,250 cases. Red: Mer 55%, CS 40%, CF 5%; White: Sém 50%, Sauv 40%, Musc 10%.
Yves Raymond is the third generation of his family to own this *cru* although the family have lived in Listrac for 300 years. The property totals 225 hectares, including woods and pasture. A flock of sheep is kept to provide all the manure necessary for the vineyard.

   The wines have a reputation for being rich and supple. A small quantity of white AC Bordeaux is also made.

St-Julien

This is the commune with the highest proportion of Crus Classés. The increase in the area under vine was only 15 percent here in the years 1981–88. The soils have more clay than Margaux, and there is quite a difference between the vineyards near the Gironde and those further inland, where more fleshy wines are made. These are wines of great character and originality, with more body and vivid fruit than those of Margaux. They match the best Pauillacs for longevity.

Château Beychevelle
4e Cru Classé. Owner: **SC du Château Beychevelle.**
Administrator: **Maurice Ruelle. 72ha. 25,000 cases. CS 60%, Mer 28%, CF 8%, PV 4%.** Second label: **L'Amiral de Beychevelle.**
This is one of the most beautiful châteaux in the Médoc and in the summer months it is set off by a superb bank of flowers at its

roadside entrance. When it belonged to the Duc d'Epernon, who was an admiral of France at the end of the 16th century, ships passing by on the Gironde were required to lower their sails as a salute. Thus Beychevelle is a corruption of *baisse-voile*, meaning 'lower-sail'. In 1984 the Achille Fould family, then the proprietors, sold part of this holding to the GMF, the French Civil Servants' Pension fund. The GMF subsequently bought the remainder of the shares, later selling 40 percent of them to Suntory (*see* Château Lagrange). All this has resulted in some much-needed investment and a clear raising of standards.

At its best Beychevelle is a glorious example of everything that makes the wines of St-Julien so attractive: a bouquet of great elegance and immediate impact together with a ripe, fresh flavour that asks to be drunk from an early age, although the harmony of the wine also ensures good keeping.

In recent years the '75, '78, '79, '81, '82, '83, '85, '86, '88 and '89 are all most successful. There has in the past been some inconsistency, and lesser years in particular were unreliable, but recent improvements should lead to more consistency in future.

Château Branaire-Ducru
4e Cru Classé. Owner: **SA du Château Branaire-Ducru.**
Administrator: **Pierre Tari. 48ha. 20,000 cases. CS 60%, Mer 20%, CF 15%, PV 5%.**
The extremely simple, classical façade of the château here faces Beychevelle but can easily be missed as it stands well back from the road. It would be a pity to miss the wine though. Most of the vineyards lie further inland than those of Beychevelle and Ducru-Beaucaillou, and the wines have less finesse but more body and are not without breed. Jean-Michel Tapie ran the property, which his father had bought in 1952, with distinction until he sold his 50 percent holding to Sucrière de Toury, a leading French sugar refinery. The other 50 percent is still held by the Taris of Giscours, who inherited via Jean-Michel's sister.

The wines have a very marked character which often comes through in blind tastings. The bouquet is noticeably powerful with an almost Pauillac assertiveness and a distinct chocolate character in the fat years. The wine has a lot of body and fruit and is extremely supple, so that it is often possible to enjoy a Branaire when other wines are still not ready. This is a consistent wine, and excellent examples were made in '75, '76, '78, '79, '81, '82, '83, '85, '86, '88 and '89.

Certainly this is a wine to follow in terms of value for money. It is not yet an 'investment' wine, but is one of exceptional attractiveness.

Château La Bridane
Cru Bourgeois. Owner: **Pierre Saintout. 15ha. 8,000 cases. CS 55%, Mer 45%.**
This is one of the relatively new Crus Bourgeois in St-Julien though it has long enjoyed a good reputation. Much of the wine is exported. Changes occured in the 1980s when the Cabernet Franc was eliminated and the Merlot increased. This is good, attractive St-Julien at an accessible price.

Château Ducru-Beaucaillou
2e Cru Classé. Owner: **Jean-Eugène Borie. 49ha. 17,000 cases. CS 65%, Mer 25%, CF 5%, PV 5%.** Second label: **Château La Croix.**
This château acquired its name and reputation in the first part of the 19th century when it belonged to the Ducru family. Beaucaillou referred to the name of the vineyard itself. The distinctive château, with its massive Victorian towers and simple, classical façade between them, has been made familiar by the distinctive yellow-brown label. Unusually for Bordeaux, the *chais* are situated beneath the building. The reputation of the *cru* today is the work of Jean-Eugène Borie, a resident proprietor who is one of the most widely respected winemakers in the Médoc. Ducru-Beaucaillou was recently the first of the Médoc Crus Classés on the open market to break away from the pack and establish a higher price for itself than the other Second Growths, thus creating the 'Super-Seconds' (Palmer had achieved a higher price earlier but was available only through the two *négociant* owners, Mähler-Besse and Sichel).

The wines here have long had elegance, lightness and breed (Jean-Eugène Borie's first great vintage was 1953). In recent years they have acquired a little more firmness and richness, especially in the best vintages, although the beauty of flavour and finesse are still the hallmark, rather than the power one finds in Léoville-Las-

Cases. In recent years, '78, '81, '82, '83, '85, '86, '88 and '89 all produced classic examples, with '80 and '84 providing attractive, early-drinking wines.

Château du Glana
Cru Grand Bourgeois Exceptionnel. Owner: **Gabriel Meffre. 45ha. 17,000 cases. CS 68%, Mer 30%, CF 2%.**
Château du Glana is not one of the more romantic wines of the Médoc. Strictly speaking it has no château, and the ugly little red-brick villa that appears on the label is not now part of the property. More obvious is the massive and very functional *chai* sitting amidst the vineyards nearby, close to Gloria and Ducru-Beaucaillou. This and Gloria are the two largest Cru Bourgeois of St-Julien.

The reputation of du Glana has in the past been rather mixed. I can only speak about recent vintages, and have found the wine well made, easy, fruity and delicious. Glana is commercial in the good sense, it provides just the sort of wine, with the character of the *appellation*, that the wine-lover of today looks for and can enjoy without long keeping.

Château Gloria
Cru Bourgeois. Owner: **Héritiers de Henri Martin. 48ha. 20,800 cases. CS 65%, Mer 25%, CF 5%, PV 5%.** Second labels: **Châteaux Haut Beychevelle-Gloria and Peymartin.**
Gloria is the life work of Henri Martin, one of the great figures of the Médoc. As *Grand Maître* of the Commanderie du Bontemps he did much to promote the Médoc in general over many years. His son-in-law, Jean-Louis Triaud, who has succeeded him, had already in effect been running the property for some time. The vineyard has been put together in one generation from bits and pieces of Cru Classé vineyards only. For this reason it has not joined the Syndicat des Crus Bourgeois and sells for the same price as some Fifth Growths.

The wine is generous and supple, with breed and fullness and richness of flavour. It is noted for its consistency. The problem is that it is almost certainly not as good as the classified growths of St-Julien, although superior to some lesser Margaux and Pauillac classifieds, and of course it is more expensive than most Crus Bourgeois.

Château Gruaud-Larose
2e Cru Classé. Owner: **Cordier family. 82ha. 35,000 cases. CS 62%, Mer 25%, CF 9%, PV 4%.** Second label: **Sarget du Gruaud-Larose.**

Léoville-Las-Cases and Ducru-Beaucaillou are the archetypal St-Juliens of the riverside vineyards; Gruaud-Larose is the classic example of a St-Julien from the plateau that lies between the riverside properties and St-Laurent. This very large estate was created in the 18th century, divided in the 19th and then reunited by the Cordiers in 1934. Together with nearby Talbot, this property is their showplace and indeed the flagship of this leading *négociant* house.

As with some other Crus Classés sold as *négoce* exclusivities, Gruaud sells at a more modest price than it would on the open market. It would be a mistake to allow this to influence assessment of the intrinsic merits of this outstanding *cru*, for Gruaud is certainly worthy of being placed beside Las-Cases and Beaucaillou as a 'Super-Second', in quality if not in price.

The wines here have great concentration and richness and have been decidedly tannic in the past few years but with maturity they acquire a soft, velvety texture with great breed and charm. Very fine wines were made in '75, '76, '78, '79, '81, '82, '83, '85, '86, '88 and '89. The '80 was slower in developing than most of the wines of its vintage and the '87 looks to be very similar.

The new second wine is well worth looking out for. It is packed with fruit and can of course be drunk earlier than the Grand Vin, but still has plenty of structure.

Château Hortevie
Cru Bourgeois. Owner: **Henri Pradère. 3·5ha. 1,500 cases. CS and CF 70%, Mer 25%, PV 5%.**

This very small vineyard is a good example of the remarkable quality of the *terroir* of St-Julien. In competent hands it cannot avoid producing a wine of charm and breed. The vineyard lies behind the village of Beychevelle, and its proprietor, who is also the co-owner of Terrey-Gros-Caillou, runs the property jointly. This is a wine of real quality.

Château Lagrange

3e Cru Classé. Owner: **Château Lagrange SARL.**
Administrator: **Marcel Ducasse. 113ha. 19,000 cases. CS
66%, Mer 27%, PV 7%.** Second label: **Les Fiefs-de-
Lagrange.**

In 1983 Lagrange was sold to the giant Japanese firm of distillers and
wine merchants, Suntory, and so became the first Bordeaux Cru
Classé to be bought by a Japanese company. The vineyard here is
very well placed on the plateau of St-Julien behind Gruaud-Larose.
One of its attractions for the new owners was the considerable
potential for increasing the vineyard area; expansions and improvements complete, this has now increased from 49 hectares to 113
hectares. The buildings, including the château, have been completely overhauled, the 19th century *chai* restored and two new ones
built to cope with the anticipated increase in production. Marcel
Ducasse was brought in by the new owners to manage the property
and Michel Delon of Léoville-Las-Cases acts as consultant.

There was a time when the wines at Lagrange were tough and
coarse in style, but matters have been improving, even in the 1960s,
and the '78 had real St-Julien fruit and charm. So all the evidence
was there to suggest that something well above the rather modest
reputation of recent years was possible. The '82, made by the old
owners but sold by the new ones, is an excellent example of the
vintage, with a scent of prunes and great depth of flavour and fruit,
tannin and complexity; while the '83 has a lot of character and
finesse with real depth of flavour. It was at this stage that the second
wine was first introduced. For the delicious '85, the crop was split
60–40 between the *grand vin* and Les Fiefs. Very impressive wines
followed in '86, even '87, '88 and '89. The Les Fiefs is proving a
particularly attractive and stylish second wine.

Château Lalande-Borie

Cru Bourgeois Supérieur. Owner: **Jean-Eugène Borie.
18ha. 8,000 cases. CS 65%, Mer 25%, CF 10%.**

This *cru* has been created by Jean-Eugène Borie, owner of Ducru-
Beaucaillou, from a vineyard that was formerly part of Lagrange.
The new vineyard was planted only in 1970 but is now making very
stylish and elegant wines with charming fruit and medium weight.
The first important vintage was the '79, and since then there has

been a steady improvement.

This wine offers an excellent opportunity for sampling Jean-Eugène Borie's deft hand with St-Julien at a modest price.

Château Langoa-Barton
3e Cru Classé. Owner: **Société Fermière. 20ha. 8,000 cases. CS 70%, Mer 15%, PV 8%, CF 7%.**
This château has the distinction of having belonged to the same family since 1821, longer than any other Cru Classé. When Hugh Barton acquired the property it was known as Pontet-Langlois. It will come as no surprise to anyone familiar with the vagaries of French spelling of proper names to know that Langlois has become Langoa. The 18th-century château is one of the finest in the Médoc, not as well placed as Beychevelle but not far behind it in pure architectural terms. The wines of Langoa and the Barton portion of Léoville were not château-bottled until 1969, but were removed to Barton & Guestier's Bordeaux cellars for bottling.

The wines of Langoa accurately reflect their classification. Usually ready to drink earlier than those of Léoville-Barton, they have a classic St-Julien character but are generally lighter in texture, less tannic but with lots of elegance, fruit and charm – and real breed. Every now and then it produces something surprising, as with the unusually good '74 or the '71 which seems even better than the Léoville. A relationship not dissimilar to that between Gruaud-Larose and Talbot. The vintages here follow those of Léoville-Barton very closely, with a superb '78, an elegant if lightweight '79, a good '80, and with marvellous wines in '81, '82, '83, '85, '86, '88 and '89.

Château Léoville-Barton
2e Cru Classé. Owner: **Société Fermière. 39ha. 16,000 cases. CS 70%, Mer 15%, PV 8%, CF 7%.**
Like its neighbour Poyferré, Léoville-Barton was, until the 1820s, a part of the enormous estate of the Marquis de Las-Cases. In 1826 Hugh Barton, who had already bought Langoa only five years before, acquired what was then a quarter share of the original Las-Cases estate and used the cellars of Langoa for making and housing the produce of his new acquisition. 160 years later the Barton family still own the property with Anthony Barton having recently taken

on the burden of management from his uncle Ronald, who lived in the château until his death in 1986.

Léoville-Barton, under Ronald Barton's long stewardship, remained a very traditionally made wine. The wines are finely perfumed, very powerful and rich in tannin at first, then developing that beautiful fruit and richness of flavour that are hallmarks of the best St-Juliens. The style tends towards more richness than Las-Cases, but with a shade less elegance. There were some inconsistencies in the 1970s, with neither '73 nor '79 being as good as the general level of those vintages, though '75, '76 and '78 are years to look for. But since then, with stricter selection now evident, very good results were obtained in '80, and outstanding wines were made in '81, '82, '83, '85, '86, '88 and '89. With the marked improvement at Léoville-Poyferré from 1980 onwards, it is going to be especially interesting in the future to compare the three Léovilles again.

Château Léoville-Las-Cases
2e Cru Classé. Owner: **SC du Château Léoville-Las-Cases.** Administrator: **Michel Delon. 97ha. 30,000 cases. CS 65%, Mer 18%, CF 14%, PV 3%.** Second label: **Clos du Marquis.** Third label: **Domaine de Bigarnon.**
The label of this wine states 'Grand Vin de Léoville du Marquis de Las-Cases' – no mention of château – and serves to remind us that this is the residue of what was in the 18th century the most important estate not only in St-Julien but also in the Médoc. With its magnificent *clos* adjoining Latour on a gravel ridge within sight of the Gironde, Las-Cases represents half the original estate and runs from the village of St-Julien to Latour. The original château, standing at the southern entrance to the village, is actually divided between Las-Cases and Poyferré, with the Las-Cases portion on the left.

In 1900 the manager – the famous viticulturalist Théophile Skawinski – was given one share in the Société Civile and today his descendants are the majority shareholders! On his retirement in 1930 he was succeeded by his son-in-law André Delon, grandfather of the present administrator Michel Delon. In the 1960s the reputation of Las-Cases recovered from a poor patch, the result of extensive replanting after the Second World War. During the

1970s its reputation soared to fresh heights, so that today Las-Cases is once more regarded as the leading wine in St-Julien.

In style it is firmer and slower to mature than other St-Juliens. Recently the wines seem to have filled out and are now not only elegant but also very concentrated and powerful. The bouquet is especially characteristic, reserved at first but slowly evolving to become elegant and firm. Great wines were made in '78, '79, '81, '82, '83, '85, '86, '88 and '89, all true *vins de garde*. The '80 was slower in developing than most, but the '84 and the '87 especially, are much better than most wines from these vintages. Las-Cases is certainly now one of the stars of the 'Super-Seconds'.

The Clos-du-Marquis is one of the best and most consistent of the second wines.

Château Léoville-Poyferré
2e Cru Classé. Owner: **Cuvelier family.** Administrator: **Didier Cuvelier. 77ha. 30,000 cases. CS 65%, Mer 25%, PV 8%, CF 2%.** Second label: **Château Moulin-Riche.**

Like Léoville-Barton, Léoville-Poyferré originally represented a quarter portion of the Las-Cases estate, acquired by the Baron de Poyferré by marriage to a Las-Cases. Unlike the other two Léovilles, Poyferré has not had the same continuity of ownership since that time and its fortunes have been more varied. At its best it has produced wines as fine as Las-Cases, as in '28 and '29. But at that time, although under different ownerships, both were managed by Théophile Skawinski. Now, after a period of inconsistency, a member of the younger generation of the Cuvelier family has assumed responsibility, and the results are beginning to show. First of all the *cuvier* was completely modernized in 1980, then more new wood was introduced and a capable new *maître de chai*, with the reassuringly Médocain name of Dourthe, took over.

The 1980 vintage is the watershed here: not obviously a great vintage but elegant and fine – good by the general standard of the year. The '81 has a fine flavour, with structure, fruit, elegance and breed. The '82 is a glorious example of this exceptional year, a great bottle in the making, while the '83 has length, concentration and harmony. The '85 is a beauty, '86 is more powerful and tannic, while '88 and '89 promise to be outstanding. Although good wines were made before this (a particular favourite of mine being the delicious '73) the *cru* was not reaching the heights of which it is capable. Now the future looks exciting.

Château St-Pierre
4e Cru Classé. Owners: **Héritiers de Henri Martin. 17ha. 4,600 cases. CS 70%, Mer 20%, CF 10%.**
This property has certainly had a very chequered history. The name derives from a Monsieur St-Pierre who acquired the property in 1767. Then in 1832 it was divided between different branches of the family, and the suffixes Bontemps-Dubarry and Sevaistre appeared. Although reunited by its Belgian owners after the Second World War, parts of the vineyard had been sold off, notably to Gloria and du Glana. Then in 1982 Henri Martin of Gloria bought the château – now beautifully restored – and most of the vineyard. The original Sevaistre *chai* was bought by Jean-Eugène Borie for his property Lalande-Borie, while St-Pierre is now housed in the same *chai* as Gloria, itself originally the St-Pierre-Bontemps *chai*, which Henri Martin had originally bought without the name.

St-Pierre had made elegant, perfumed, stylish and typically St-Julien wines for some years, but Henri Martin and his son-in-law Jean-Louis Triaud (now wholly in charge since Henri Martin's death in 1991) lifted it to higher plains. From '82 onwards lovely wines of great breed have been produced, very clearly superior to Gloria.

Château Talbot
4e Cru Classé. Owner: **Jean Cordier. 101ha. Red: 40,000 cases. CS 71%, Mer 20%, CF 5%, PV 4%. White: 2,500 cases.** Second labels: **Connétable Talbot, Caillou Blanc du Château Talbot (Bordeaux Blanc AC).**
It is Talbot's misfortune that it is always obliged to stand in the shadow of Gruaud-Larose. The name commemorates the Earl of Shrewsbury who was killed commanding the English forces at Castillon la Bataille in 1453, although it seems doubtful that he ever actually owned the estate. As with all Cordier properties, Talbot is beautifully kept and very well equipped.

Talbot has long been noted for its consistency. The wines generally have less tannin and concentration than those of Gruaud-Larose, and are ready to be drunk sooner, but they also keep very well. The charm of Talbot is its harmony. The wines are beautifully perfumed and have great St-Julien refinement in their fruit. There is a fine '75 which still needs time. '76 is another attractive wine for drinking now. The '78 is a more long-term wine though the '79 is already drinkable. '80 is delicious (I prefer it at present to the Gruaud). The '81 has developed well and has great finesse. Not surprisingly '82 and '83 are superb. The opulent, rich '85 strongly contrasts with the dense tannic '86, the '87 will be a good follow-up to the '80, and '88, '89 and '90 are certainly a great trio. Because of Cordier's pricing policy Talbot is always marvellous value for money, especially if bought early.

The new second wine, Connetable Talbot, is really delightful, ideal for early drinking, with lots of vivid St-Julien fruit. The white wine is pleasant, fresh and clean, but nothing more.

Château Terrey-Gros-Caillou
Cru Bourgeois. Owners: **André Fort & Henri Pradère.**
15ha. 8,000 cases. CS and CF 65%, Mer 30%, PV 5%.
Ever since I came across this *cru* for the first time – it was the '60 vintage – I have been greatly impressed by the real breed and finesse of this wine. Certainly it is one of the very best of the Cru Bourgeois in St-Julien. The vineyard is in several parcels, the most important of which is behind the village of Beychevelle – where the *chai* is – and adjoining Talbot and Léoville-Barton. Another is next to Gruaud-Larose, and yet another adjoins Beychevelle and Ducru-Beaucaillou. A very fine '83 here epitomized the virtues of this wine, with its very vivid St-Julien fruit on the nose and its lovely flavour, combining richness and exceptional breed. This is due not only to good vineyards but also to fine winemaking. Certainly this is a wine to look for if you enjoy St-Julien but do not want to pay Cru Classé prices all the time.

Pauillac

The name of Pauillac is assured from the reflected glory of its three First Growths: Lafite-Rothschild, Mouton-Rothschild and Latour. The area covered by the Crus Classés here is greater than in any other *appellation*, even though it has only 18 in contrast with 21 in

Margaux. The area under vine increased by 15 percent in the years 1981–88.

It is here that the Cabernet Sauvignon achieves its most characteristic results, producing that marked blackcurrant style for which it is justly famous. The wines are the most powerful, in terms of bouquet, body and flavour, of all Médocs. The best *crus* combine this with a finesse that develops with ageing, but some lesser *crus* have a certain coarseness.

Château d'Armailhac

5e Cru Classé. Owner: **Baron Philippe de Rothschild SA. 51ha. 18,000 cases. CS 40%, Mer 30%, CF 28%, PV 2%.**
No leading Bordeaux château has experienced so many changes of name. Acquired by the late Baron Philippe de Rothschild in 1933, it retained its original name of Mouton d'Armailhac until 1956 when it became Mouton Baron Philippe, then in 1975 the Baron changed to Baronne to commemorate Baron Philippe's second wife. Finally in 1991 his daughter and sole heir, Philippine de Rothschild, decided that the names Mouton Rothschild, Mouton Cadet, and the company name Baron Philippe de Rothschild SA, were all too confusing, and that this old property deserved a distinctive personality of its own. So we shall now have to get used to Château d'Amailhac, which first saw the light of day with the lovely '89 vintage.

Situated just a few hundred yards from the front gate of Mouton-Rothschild, this château is a curious unfinished building, its classical portico sliced down the middle as if it were a piece of cake. Although only a stone's throw away from the great Mouton, it is run entirely separately but with equal care. The wines are true Pauillacs in style, though less rich and opulent than those of their big brother. In the most successful years the wines do have a very good concentration, but in some lesser ones they can be slightly mean and dull. As one would expect, they are nearer in style to their other neighbour, Pontet-Canet, than to the great Premier Cru.

Château Batailley

5e Cru Classé. Owner: **Emile Castéja. 50ha. 22,000 cases. CS 70%, Mer 24%, CF 4%, PV 2%.**
The early reputation and classification of Batailley date from the

period of Guestier's ownership. Now another *négociant*, Emile Castéja of Borie-Manoux, is in charge. There is sometimes a tendency to undervalue châteaux that are not sold through the Bordeaux market, especially if, in their pricing policy, they are more concerned with offering continuity to their customers than looking over their shoulders at what their neighbours are doing. The real worth of Batailley should not be underrated on account of its relatively modest price.

Interestingly, all of the present vineyard is on land classified in 1855. It lies at the back of Pauillac on the road to St-Laurent. The wines here are very consistent, solid and dependable. In the past Batailley occasionally produced something memorable ('53, '61, and '64 are examples). Otherwise it was sound but unexciting. Now the wines consistently have more fruit and concentration, as well as being more stylish. Years to look out for are '75, '76, '78, '79, '81, '82, '83, '85 and '88.

Château Clerc–Milon
5e Cru Classé. Owner: **Baron Philippe de Rothschild SA. 28ha. 12,000 cases. CS 51%, Mer 33%, CF 13%, PV 3%.**
This rather neglected property was bought by Baron Philippe de Rothschild in 1970. The vineyard is well placed between the road and the river, north of Pauillac and close to both Mouton and Lafite. Milon is the name of the small village where the property lies, and Clerc was the name of the proprietor at the time of the 1855 classification.

There was much to be done in the vineyard and for this reason it took time to turn the quality of the wine around. The turning point came with the 1981 vintage, when for the first time the wine surpassed Mouton Baronne Philippe (*see* d'Armailhac) in breed and harmonious fruit. After this, the most successful years have been '82, '85, '86 and '89.

Château Colombier-Monpelou
Cru Grand Bourgeois. Owner: **Bernard Jugla. 15ha. 7,000 cases. CS 68%, Mer 18%, CF 6%, PV 5%, Mal 3%.** Second label: **Grand Canyon.**
For many years this was the best wine to come out of the Pauillac cooperative. Then in 1970 it was bought by Bernard Jugla,

proprietor of the adjoining Château Pédesclaux. Because Colombier parted company with its château and *chai* in 1939 (these now serve as the headquarters of La Baronnie, *négociant* company of Baron Philippe de Rothschild) a completely new installation had to be built. The wines are fermented in metal vats and aged in casks of which a third are new each year. This is good, honest Pauillac that enjoys a growing reputation. The wines have a certain elegance and suppleness, with pleasing fruit.

Château La Couronne
Cru Bourgeois Supérieur Exceptionnel 1932. Owner: **Mme des Brest-Borie. 4ha. 1,750 cases. CS 70%, Mer 30%.**
This very small vineyard was created in 1879 by Armand Lalande, who was then owner of Léoville-Poyferré and Brane-Cantenac. It lies in the south of Pauillac, inland from the Pichons and Batailley. Since 1952 it has been managed by Jean-Eugène Borie of Ducru-Beaucaillou on behalf of his sister.

The wines are true Pauillacs but their aggressiveness is quickly shed as they develop excellent fruit. They are very harmonious and supple wines that maintain a consistent standard comparable to many Cinquièmes Crus Classés.

Château Croizet-Bages
5e Cru Classé. Owner: **Mme L Quié.** Administrator: **Jean-Michel Quié. 22ha. 8,500 cases. CS 37%, CF 30%, Mer 30%, PV and Mal 3%.**
This *cru* was created by the brothers Croizet in the 18th century. Its *chai* and *cuvier* are in the little hamlet of Bages, close to its more famous neighbour Lynch-Bages, on high ground in the south of Pauillac. It has belonged to the Quié family since 1930 and is now administered by Jean-Michel Quié, son of Mme Quié. There is no château.

The wines are attractively robust, full-flavoured Pauillacs, that mellow fairly quickly, yet in my experience still keep very well. If they seldom reach the heights, they also rarely disappoint. This is a *cru* which deserves its classification.

Château Duhart-Milon-Rothschild
4e Cru Classé. Owner: **Domaines Barons de Rothschild.**

50ha. 12,500 cases. CS 57%, Mer 21%, CF 20%, PV 2%.
Second label: **Moulin-de-Duhart.**

When the Rothschilds of Lafite bought the neighbouring vineyard of Duhart-Milon in 1962 it was in a sorry state, with only 16 hectares of vineyards in production and a high proportion of Petit Verdot. The wines were often undistinguished. It takes a long time to see the results when a vineyard has to be almost entirely reconstituted, but good results are now emerging and Duhart is again taking its place as a leading Pauillac.

The vineyard lies mostly on the plateau of the Carruades, and the *chai* and *cuvier* are in Pauillac. There is no château.

By the early 1970s a wine of elegance and charm was being produced – not a heavyweight, but rather in the mould of Haut-Batailley. For me the vineyard really came of age with its '78, a wine of immense breed, elegance and outstanding length. The '79 is more powerful and richer, the '80 is a lightweight charmer, the '81, '83 and '85 are all very elegant middleweight wines, while the '82, a true wine of the year, has massive fruit but is complex and fine. The '86 has extra concentration and opulence; '88, '89 and '90 also have great promise.

This is a wine that certainly deserves to be placed among the leading Pauillacs today and has truly realized its potential again.

Château La Fleur-Milon
Cru Grand Bourgeois. Owner: **Héritiers Gimenez.**
Administrator: **Claude Mirande. 13ha. 6,600 cases. CS 65%, Mer 25%, PV 10%.**

The vineyards of this *cru* are indeed well placed. Its *chai* is in the village of Le Pougalet (there is no château), and the various small plots of vineyard adjoin Mouton-Rothschild, Lafite-Rothschild, Duhart-Milon and Pontet-Canet. But this promising position is not reflected in the wine. The present owner has been in charge since 1955, a real working proprietor whose wines are still racked from cask to cask. I find the wine very artisanal, rather coarse and tough, with the sort of stalkiness that suggests too much *vin de presse*.

Château Fonbadet
Cru Bourgeois Supérieur 1932. Owner: **Pierre Peyronie.**
15ha. 6,500 cases. CS 60%, Mer 19%, CF 15%, Mal 4%, PV

2%. Second labels: **Châteaux Haut-Pauillac, Padarnac, Tour-du-Roc-Milon and Montgrand-Milon.**
This charming 18th-century château lies to the south of the village of St-Lambert, just past the two Pichons as you drive from Bordeaux. The trees in its park stand out like an oasis in the sea of vines. The present owner is very much the working, resident proprietor.

The proportion of new casks used is 25 percent. This is a sound, classic Pauillac, which often does very well in blind tastings and fully deserves its excellent reputation. Contributing factors include the very old vines and meticulous care in the winemaking.

Château Grand-Puy-Ducasse
5e Cru Classé. Owner: **SC du Château.** Administrator: **Jean-Pierre Angliviel de la Beaumelle. 37ha. 11,660 cases. CS 62%, Mer 38%.** Second label: **Artiges-Arnaud.**
Until the present proprietors bought it in 1971, Grand-Puy-Ducasse was a very small vineyard of only ten hectares, adjoining Mouton and Pontet-Canet. The new owners bought two additional vineyards, one adjoining Batailley and Grand-Puy-Lacoste on the plateau behind Pauillac, the other adjoining the two Pichons, so that it now has vineyards in all three main sectors of Pauillac. The château is a pleasing neo-classical building on the quayside near the centre of the village of Pauillac. For many years it also served as the Maison du Vin.

The new regime here seems to be producing fine results. The wines are classic Cabernet Sauvignon blackcurrant Pauillacs, but the structure is supple, rich and harmonious. The '75, for instance, was splendid. Since then the best years have been '79, '81, '82, '85, '86, '88 and '89. The wines are now very consistent. This is another example of a *cru* that, because it is marketed exclusively by a *négociant* (Mestrezat) at very reasonable prices, can be underrated. It is an excellent buy for the consumer.

Château Grand-Puy-Lacoste
5e Cru Classé. Owner: **Borie family.** Administrators: **Jean-Eugène Borie & Xavier Borie. 45ha. 12,000 cases. CS 70%, Mer 25%, CF 5%.** Second label: **Lacoste-Borie.**
This *cru* has long had an excellent reputation for constantly

producing typically robust and fine Pauillacs. Raymond Dupin was owner here from 1932 until extreme old age caused him to sell to the Borie family in 1978. If some things had begun to slip in his last few years this should not detract from his achievements. The Bories decided to replace the old *cuvier* with stainless steel after the 1980 vintage, and the dilapidated château has been tastefully renovated.

Most of the vineyard is in one piece in front of the château on the plateau of Bages and is of the highest quality. The consistency and excellence of the wines reflect this. These wines are really powerful and often rather tannic and tough at first. The Bories are still making very concentrated wines, but are trying to emphasize the fruit a little more. With the '81 vintage the wines seemed to acquire an extra dimension. '82, '83, '85 (which was exceptional), '86, '88 and '89, all produced very fine wines which have further advanced the reputation of this increasingly fashionable and sought-after *cru*.

Château Haut-Bages-Libéral
5e Cru Classé. Owner: **SC du Château.** Administrator: **Bernadette Villars. 26ha. 12,500 cases. CS 75%, Mer 25%.**
This *cru* has had a chequered history. When it was bought by the Cruses in 1960 it lost part of its vineyard to Pontet-Canet and its wines were Bordeaux-bottled in the Cruses' cellars. With the introduction of compulsory château-bottling for the Crus Classés in 1972 and the sale of Pontet-Canet, the Cruses were obliged to build a new installation for handling the wines. In 1983 they sold to a company that also runs Chasse-Spleen and La Gurgue, and has made important investments to bring the property and vineyards up to standard. So the future looks much brighter.

The vineyard, as the name suggests, is on the plateau of Bages and adjoins Latour, Lynch-Bages, and Pichon-Longueville Baron. The other part of the name has no political connotations but was the name of its 19th-century owner at the time of the classification.

In the last years of the Cruse management there were improvements in the wine, which was rich with good fruit; the '76 and '82 vintages were particularly good. Mme Villars (*see* Chasse-Spleen) soon made her mark though and after a good '85, the '86 was even better, followed by equally impressive wines in '88 and '89. The future seems assured.

Château Haut-Bages-Monpelou
Cru Bourgeois. Owner: **Emile Castéja. 10ha. 4,100 cases. CS and CF 60%, Mer 40%.**
One of the lesser lights of the Borie-Manoux stable. The vineyard was once part of Duhart-Milon. The wines are full-bodied but elegant and drinkable relatively young. This is pleasant, dependable, easy-to-drink wine at a modest price.

Château Haut-Batailley
5e Cru Classé. Owner: **Mme des Brest-Borie.** Administrator: **Jean-Eugène Borie. 20ha. 7,500 cases. CS 65%, Mer 25%, CF 10%.** Second label: **Château La Tour-d'Aspic.**
When the Borie family bought Batailley in 1942 they divided it between the two brothers: Marcel, who was the *négociant*, and François, who bought Ducru-Beaucaillou. Haut-Batailley is much the smaller part. Its vineyard had to be replanted and took time to mature. There is no château, as the house stayed with the main part of the property, and the wine is vinified at La Couronne.

There is a marked contrast in styles between Haut-Batailley and Batailley, with the former producing wines of less weight but real elegance. If one compares Haut-Batailley with Grand-Puy-Lacoste one sees the same sort of contrast. Grand-Puy and Batailley are more assertively, even aggressively Pauillac. Haut-Batailley is extremely consistent, the beautifully balanced fruit and mature tannins making it drinkable relatively young but still able to age attractively.

Château Lafite-Rothschild
1er Cru Classé. Owner: **Domaine Rothschild. 90ha. 17,000 cases. CS 70%, Mer 15%, CF 13%, PV 2%.** Second label: **Les Carruades.**
Lafite has experienced something of a renaissance in recent years. In the 1960s and early 1970s there were far too many disappointments for a wine of Lafite's standing. In 1974 a new era began with the appointment of a younger generation of the family, in the person of Baron Eric de Rothschild, as the member responsible for Lafite. Then in 1975 Professor Peynaud was called in to advise and Jean Crété was subsequently appointed *régisseur*, with his invaluable experience under Paul Delon at Léoville-Las-Cases behind him.

The combination of these changes has been most beneficial for Lafite and shows up vividly in the glass. Jean Crété retired in 1983 and was followed by Gilbert Rokvam. Further changes occurred and the old practice of keeping the wine in cask for three years, irrespective of the character of the vintage, has been abandoned. In 1987 a new second-year cash cellar in an innovative circular design was finished, and in the following year a new *cuvier* of stainless steel vats was introduced, to supplement but not to replace the traditional oak ones.

The features that one notices about recent Lafite vintages, compared with those of previous years, are their depth of colour, richness and concentration of flavour. The most outstanding recent vintages here are '76, '79, '82, '85, '86, '88, '89 and '90. '78 is light, delicious for drinking now, '81 is a small classic, '83 is surprisingly tannic and will need more time than most wines of this year, while '84 is one of the best wines of this uneven vintage; '87 is light but delicious for early drinking. Since 1985 there has been much stricter selection with more wine being set aside for the Carruades label, which, as a result, is much improved.

To drink a bottle of Lafite should be one of the ultimate experiences for any wine-lover, and it is good to know that in future there should be no disappointments.

Château Latour

1er Cru Classé. Owner: **Allied-Lyons.** Administrator: **Christian Le Sommer. 61ha. 16,600 cases. CS 80%, Mer 15%, CF 4%, PV 1%.** Second label: **Les Forts de Latour (10,000 cases).**

In 1963 the Pearson group bought a majority share-holding in Latour, with Harveys of Bristol taking a 25 percent holding. Harveys later became part of Allied-Lyons, who in 1989 also acquired Pearson's share of the property. Jean-Paul Gardère as administrator was the dominant influence on the wines of Latour from his appointment in 1963 until his retirement in 1987.

Latour has produced monumental wines for generations. The modernization of the *cuvier* and improvements in the vineyard have simply tended to make the wines more accessible. But retrospective tastings show that Latour has lost none of its legendary character-istics: its great depth of colour, classic Cabernet nose and remarkable concentration of fruit and tannin. Admirers of Latour often used to bemoan the fact that they doubted they would live long enough to enjoy the most recent vintages. After the legendary '61, the great vintages were '62 and '66, with '64 and '67 above average for these years. In the 1970s the outstanding wine is '75, followed in quality by '70 and '78, with an exceptional '73 and a good '76. Of the 1980s, the '81 is probably one of the best wines of its year, the '82 is a great classic, '86, '88 and '89 are outstanding and long-maturing, while '85 is lovely and more quickly maturing.

Les Forts de Latour is produced partly from vineyards whose produce never goes into the *grand vin* and partly from the younger vines of Latour. There is a shorter fermentation, and the wine has the characteristics of Latour but with less concentration, so it develops more quickly. The wine was not placed on the market until ready to drink but in 1991 a break with this tradition was made when the '90 was offered *en primeur*.

Château Lynch-Bages
5e Cru Classé. Owner: **Cazes family.** Administrator: **Jean-Michel Cazes. 85ha. 35,000 cases. CS 75%, Mer 15%, CF 10%.** Second label: **Château Haut-Bages-Averous (7,000 cases).**

Lynch-Bages is a wine that arouses markedly varying opinions among claret-lovers. Some admire it unreservedly; others call it the poor man's Mouton or claim that it lacks finesse and breed. Objectively this is a marvellously attractive, almost plummy, Pauillac with a really concentrated blackcurrant bouquet and flavour. At the same time it is less tannic and aggressive than many Pauillacs, with an emphasis on fruit and suppleness. This *cru* also has a fine record for making good wines in lesser vintages.

The château, which is the home of Jean-Michel Cazes, who now runs Lynch-Bages, stands on the edge of the plateau of Bages, commanding views across the Gironde with the vineyards behind it. In recent years there has been an impressive programme of enlarging and modernizing both *cuvier* and *chai*. Certainly standards have never been higher than they are today. Recent outstanding years have been '75, '78, '81, '82, '83, '85, '86, '88, '89 and '90.

Haut-Bages-Averous is something of a cross-breed. There are

five hectares of good Cru Bourgeois, the produce of which is assembled with those vats of Lynch-Bages that have been eliminated from the *grand vin*. The result is a light, deliciously fruity and easy-to-drink wine.

Château Lynch-Moussas
5e Cru Classé. Owner: **Emile Castéja. 33ha. 12,500 cases. CS 70%, Mer 30%.**
This *cru* has belonged to the Castéja family for many years and there were many members of the family involved until Emile Castéja was able to buy out the others in 1969. At that time the production had fallen to less than 2,000 cases and the property was in a very run-down condition. Emile Castéja, who is also responsible for all Borie-Manoux's properties (*see* Batailley etc), has had to rebuild and re-equip the *cuvées* and *chais* and replant the vineyard.

The vineyard adjoins Batailley and is the most westerly of all Pauillac *crus*. Part of the vineyard lies near the hamlet of Moussas, the rest near Duhart-Milon and Lafite to the north and near Pichon and Latour to the south.

Before the restoration this was a pleasant but rather light wine, without much distinction. An indication of the progress now being made came at a recent blind tasting of 1980 Crus Classés, where it did better than several better-known Pauillacs. I was struck by the aromatic, rather minty bouquet, and by the attractively fruity flavour and interesting individuality, an achievement in a small year such as '80. Since then the wines have been richer and more consistent than before and are sold at Cru Bourgeois prices, so are excellent value.

Château Mouton-Baronne-Philippe
(*see* Château d'Armailhac)

Château Mouton-Rothschild
1er Cru Classé 1973. Owner: **Baron Philippe de Rothschild SA. 75ha. 25,000 cases. CS 80%, CF 10%, Mer 8%, PV 2%.**
The Mouton-Rothschild we know today is the life's work of one man – Baron Philippe, who, from the day he took charge in 1923, until his death in 1988, set about making something special of it. He was the first to introduce compulsory château-bottling, along with the other First Growths, though at this time Mouton itself was not a First. He hit upon the idea of having an artist design an original work for each year's label, something that has happened every year since 1945. Finally he cut through the petty jealousies of Bordeaux to see Mouton proclaimed an official Premier Cru Classé in 1973. In his last years, he persuaded his only child, Philippine, to become involved, and she now ably fills her father's place.

The wines of Mouton are quintessential Pauillacs, curiously closer in style to Latour, on the other side of the commune, than to its near neighbour and long-time rival, Lafite. There is a similar concentrated blackcurrant bouquet and flavour, combined with a richness and opulence that disguise the tannin more than at Latour. In recent years, the great vintages have been '75, '78, '82, '83, '85, '86, '88, '89 and '90.

Château Pédesclaux
5e Cru Classé. Owner: **Jugla family.** Administrator: **Bernard Jugla. 18ha. 8,300 cases. CS 70%, Mer 20%, CF 5%, PV 5%.**
This is one of the more obscure of the Crus Classés. Its vineyards

and *chais* are just to the north of the village of Pauillac, near to Pontet-Canet. The name comes from a *courtier* (wine-broker) who was proprietor at the time of the 1855 classification. It was bought by the Jugla family in 1950, and the facilities have been improved and the production increased under their management. Belgium is the principal export market.

The reputation of Pédesclaux is for making solid, honourable Pauillacs rather than exciting ones – but following a new collaboration with Dourthe, there has been a marked improvement in quality beginning with the 1985 vintage.

Château Pibran
Cru Bourgeois. Owner: **AXA Millésimes.** Administrator: **J-M Cazes. 9·5ha. 4,000 cases. CS and CF 60%, Mer 24%, CF 11%, PV 5%.**
This *cru* lies just outside Pauillac to the northwest of and adjoining Pontet-Canet. It belonged to the Billa family from 1941 to 1987, and they established a good reputation for the wine. Now under Jean-Michel Cazes' supervision and part of the new AXA empire, attractively fruity, assertive wines are being made.

Château Pichon-Longueville Baron
2e Cru Classé. Owner: **AXA Millésimes.** Administrator: **J-M Cazes. 50ha. 14,000 cases. CS 75%, Mer 25%.**
The château here is a notable landmark on the *route des châteaux*, with its slender turrets and high-pitched roof giving it a fairly-tale look. In 1855 the property was undivided and, apart from Mouton (now elevated to Premier Cru status), was the only Pauillac in the Deuxième Cru category. The vineyard is superbly situated, adjoining Latour. The new owners have restored the château, which has been little more than a shell since the war, and have also built a new *chai* and *cuvier*, whose size and extent are rather too dominating for their surroundings.

There was a time when Pichon-Baron (as it is usually called to distinguish it from the neighbouring Comtesse) was normally the better of the two wines but the 1960s and especially the 1970s were disappointing times under the previous management. Since AXA bought the property in 1987, Jean-Michel Cazes has quickly turned things round again and produced classic wines in '88, '89 and '90.

2

This is quintessential Pauillac, compared to the more feminine character of Comtesse across the road.

Château Pichon-Longueville Comtesse-de-Lalande
2e Cru Classé. Owner: **Mme H de Lencquesaing. 60ha. 2,000 cases. CS 46%, Mer 34%, CF 12%, PV 8%.** Second label: **Réserve de la Comtesse.**

Unlike its neighbour, the Baron, Pichon-Comtesse has a charming château which is now lived in for much of the time by the present owner and administrator, Mme de Lencquesaing. It was her father, Edouard Miailhe, who originally acquired the property in 1926. He made various improvements, notably a partly submerged *chai* with a terrace above giving a splendid view of Château Latour and the Gironde. But it is really since his daughter took over in 1978 that the reputation of Pichon-Comtesse has soared into the top category of Second Growths. A new *cuvier* was ready for the reception of the 1980 vintage, further extensions have been made to the *chai*, and the facilities for receiving guests and providing tastings have been much improved. Also important has been the role of Monsieur Godin, who became *chef de culture* in 1970 and then *régisseur* in 1975. He is one of the new breed of Bordeaux managers who combine a modern technical training with an inbred feel for the *métier*.

The wines here have always had great finesse and breed. The fact that part of the vineyard lies in St-Julien helps to give the wine a special character, more opulent and feminine than a Pauillac, yet richer than a St-Julien. The introduction of the Réserve de la Comtesse has led to a more rigorous selection and a corresponding rise in quality. Outstanding wines have been made in '78, '79, '81, '82, '83, '85, '86, '88, '89, and '90, while '80, '84 and '87 have produced wines above the general level of these years.

Château Pontet-Canet
5e Cru Classé. Owner: **Guy Tesseron. 7ha. 30,000 cases. CS 68%, Mer 20%, CF 12%.** Second label: **Les Hauts de Pontet.**

This large property lies north of Pauillac and adjoins Mouton-Rothschild. For many years it was the pride of the Cruse family, who sold it in 1975 to Guy Tesseron, member of a well-known Cognac family who married a Cruse. The château and the fine *chai* and underground cellar, a feature found in few properties in the

Médoc, are most impressive. Unfortunately, during the latter years of the Cruse regime the reputation of Pontet-Canet declined. The wine was bottled in their Bordeaux cellars and not at the château. Now all the wine is château-bottled.

Under the new ownership the fortunes of Pontet-Canet might have been expected to improve but so far progress has been less than rapid. Often these powerful tannic wines seem to lack breed, and sometimes they seem dry and austere. Alfred Tesseron has made a determined effort to improve matters though and has had the benefit of Emile Peynaud's advice. The introduction of the new second label in 1982 has resulted in a stricter selection. The best recent vintages have been '75, '81, '82, '85 and '86.

Cave Coopérative La Rose Pauillac
Owner: **Groupement des Propriétaires-Viticulteurs de Pauillac. 110ha. 52,000 cases. CS and CF 45%, Mer 40%, PV 15%.**
This cooperative, founded during the crisis years of 1933, marked the beginning of the cooperative movement in the Médoc. At its inception there were just 52 members. Today there are 125, cultivating 110 hectares of vineyards. Most of the wine is sold under the label of La Rose Pauillac, but Château Haut-Milon and Château Haut-St-Lambert make their own declaration. Château Le Fournas-Bernadotte is also vinified at the cooperative, the *élevage* being carried out by the proprietor.

This cooperative enjoys a reputation for producing good, solid Pauillacs which are fruity and not too tannic or austere.

St-Estèphe

In many ways a transitional area between the two parts of Médoc. The wines exhibit a wide range of qualities from the breed and power of the leading *cru*, Cos-d'Estournel, to some rather lean, austere wines with a distinct *goût de terroir*. But improved methods of vinification have rendered many wines less rustic than they were. There has been little change in the area under vine, which has increased only slightly in the past 15 years.

Château Andron-Blanquet
Cru Grand Bourgeois Exceptionnel. Owner: **Domaine Audoy.** Administrator: **Bernard Audoy. 16ha. 9,000 cases. CS 40%, Mer 30%, CF 30%.** Second labels: **Château St-Roch, Blanquet.**

Since 1971 Andron-Blanquet has been under the same ownership and direction as Cos-Labory, whose vineyards it adjoins at some points. This wine has that strong *goût de terroir* found in some St-Estèphes, especially when young, but it is matched by sufficient fruit and richness to become a pleasing wine with quite a strong flavour. A wine of character – if you like the character!

Château Beau-Site
Cru Grand Bourgeois Exceptionnel. Owner: **Emile Castéja. 32ha. 20,000 cases. CS 63%, Mer 28%, CF 6%, PV 3%.**

The name means 'beautiful spot', and the view from the small courtyard in front of the château and *chai* explains why it was chosen. The village of St-Corbian, where it is situated, is on high ground and there is a splendid prospect across the vineyards of Calon-Ségur and towards the Gironde. The property is owned by the Castéja family and the wines are distributed exclusively by the Bordeaux *négociants* Borie-Manoux.

The wines, like many St-Estèphes, have quite a strong flavour at first but soon develop the richness to produce harmonious and pleasing wines. Sometimes there can be a touch of austerity about the finish, but this usually rounds off with ageing. I have found the most impressive of recent vintages to be '78, '81, '82, '83, '85, '88 and '89. This is a good Cru Bourgeois.

Château Beau-Site-Haut-Vignoble
Cru Bourgeois 1932. Owner: **Jean-Louis Braquessac. 20ha. 8,000 cases. CS 60%, Mer 30%, PV 10%.**

Beau-Site-Haut Vignoble is in St-Corbian, the same village as Beau-Site. This wine is distinctly more artisanal and although carefully made it is not in the same class as its neighbour. There is a lack of richness combined with toughness, giving a certain leanness and other features characteristic of many lesser St-Estèphes. Nevertheless, this is an honourable wine, typical of its region.

Château Calon-Ségur
3e Cru Classé. Owners: **Capbern-Gasqueton and Peyrelongue families.** Administrator: **Philippe Gasqueton.**
94ha. 20,800 cases. CS 65%, Mer 20%, CF 15%. Second label:
Marquis de Ségur.
This is the oldest of the leading St-Estèphe *crus*. In the 12th century it was given to a bishop of Portiers, Monseigneur de Calon, while in the 18th century it belonged to the famous Marquis de Ségur, who was proprietor of Lafite and Latour. He is supposed to have said that, although he made his wine at Lafite, his heart was at Calon – hence the heart-shaped device seen on the label and in many places at the property. Since the death of his uncle in 1962, Philippe Gasqueton has run the property and maintained the wine's reputation for consistency. In 1984 a large new underground cellar was completed. It is L-shaped and runs along two sides of the *chai*, 60 metres long on one side and 50 metres on the other. The beautiful old wooden *cuvier* is still preserved but has not been used since 1973. The new stainless steel *cuvées* are of 100 hectolitres each – this size representing half a day's picking – enabling control and selection.

This is a wine which seldom comes top in comparative tastings of cask samples of Cru Classé St-Estèphes, but then often does better in bottle. The wines are noticeably softer and fruitier, and more generous than Cos or Montrose, but less fine perhaps. In a blind tasting in Paris in 1976 for *La Nouvelle Guide de Gault-Millau*, Calon received the highest average mark of a group of leading Cru Classés. The vintages tasted were '66, '70, '71 and '73. Of the recent vintages the '78, '79 and '81 are all good and there is a delicious early-drinking '80. The '82 is among the leading wines of the vintage and '83 is soft and forward though rather overproduced. '85 is a little untypical but impressive and '88 and '89 are classic Calons. Calon was always a great favourite in England, but in recent years its reputation has been rather eclipsed. Perhaps it has just not made the headlines, but all the evidence points to this being just the sort of wine one wants – easy to drink yet lasting well, with plenty of character, and not over-expensive.

Château Capbern-Gasqueton
Cru Grand Bourgeois Exceptionnel. Owner: **Capbern-Gasqueton family.** Administrator: **Philippe Gasqueton.**

30ha. 10,000 cases. CS 60%, Mer 25%, CF 15%. Second label: **Le Grand Village Capbern (exclusively distributed by Dourthe).**

The château is a solid mansion in the centre of St-Estèphe. The vineyard is in two parts, one adjoining Calon-Ségur, the other near Meyney. The château is the home of Philippe Gasqueton and his family, and has been for many generations. All the wine is matured in casks but no new wood is used.

As at Calon-Ségur, Philippe Gasqueton succeeds in emphasizing the fruit and avoiding the harshness often associated with St-Estèphe. The '79 made here is rather light-structured but with well-balanced fruit and a pleasing flavour; a very attractive '83 was made, with lots of fruit and ripeness but also plenty of character.

Château Chambert-Marbuzet
Cru Bourgeois 1932. Owner: **SC du Château (H Duboscq & Fils). 16ha. 5,800 cases. CS 70%, Mer 30%.**
Another outpost of the Duboscq empire around Marbuzet (*see* Haut-Marbuzet). The wine is very well made and most attractive, even when young, yet clearly has the ability to age well. I have found it scented and packed with fruit, well supported by ripe tannin, with an attractive flavour.

Château La Commanderie
Cru Bourgeois 1932. Owner: **Gabriel Meffre. 16ha. 6,000 cases. CS 60%, Mer 40%.**
This is a northerly outpost of Gabriel Meffre's empire. At one time all the wines were made at du Glana; now they have their own *chai*. The name goes back to the Middle Ages when this was a *commanderie* of the Knights Templar. It is situated in the southern part of the commune, between Marbuzet and Leyssac. The wine is exclusively distributed by Dourthe and Kressmann, depending on the market.

Château Cos-d'Estournel
2e Cru Classé. Owner: **Domaines Prats.** Administrator: **Bruno Prats. 54ha. 18,000 cases. CS 60%, Mer 40%.** Second label: **Château de Marbuzet.**
Cos is a landmark familiar to all who travel the *route des châteaux* on

The striking *chai* of Château Cos-d'Estournel

account of its pagoda-like façade, strikingly placed on a hill overlooking Lafite. This building is in fact the *chai*, for there is no château. The present ownership dates back to 1919 when it was bought by Fernand Ginestet, the grandfather of Bruno Prats. The latter has been in charge here since 1971. Cos has usually been considered as the leading *cru* of St-Estèphe and certainly develops more finesse and breed in bottle than any other, as well as being very long-lived. There was a period in the 1960s when it was less convincing, but since Bruno Prats assumed the direction, Cos has become established as one of the leading Deuxièmes Crus Classés once more.

When this wine is in cask it is always most impressive, concentrated and tannic but finely balanced with great breed. There is often a dull patch in the early years in bottle, but then the fruit, balance and breed come into their own. This is a most rewarding wine to keep. Fine and often exceptional wines were made in '78, '79, '81, '82, '83, '85, '86, '88, '89 and '90.

Château Cos-Labory
5e Cru Classé. Owner: **Domaine Audoy.** Administrator:

Bernard Audoy. 18ha. 10,000 cases. CS 50%, Mer 30%, CF 10%, PV 10%.
The style of the wines here is light and elegant, and they mature rather quickly. There is certainly more refinement here than is usual in St-Estèphe, but not the weight and character of the leading growths. The '86, however, marked the beginning of more concentrated and impressive wines. This is now definitely a wine on the move.

Château Coutelin-Merville
Cru Grand Bourgeois. Owner: **Guy Estager et Fils.**
Administrator: **Bernard Estager. 20ha. 10,000 cases. CS and CF 43%, Mer 40%, PV 17%.**
Until 1972 this property was run jointly with Château Hanteillan in Cissac, whose vineyards it adjoins. But then inheritance problems forced the sale of the Cissac property, and this *cru* now stands on its own. The wines are matured in cask and no new oak is used; they have power and good structure and require bottle-ageing to round off and give of their best.

Château Le Crock
Cru Grand Bourgeois Exceptionnel. Owner: **Cuvelier family.** Administrator: **Didier Cuvelier. 31ha. 15,500 cases. CS 65%, Mer 35%.**
Since 1903 Le Crock has belonged to the Cuvelier family, who also now own Léoville-Poyferré. This property is now managed by the enthusiastic Didier Cuvelier who is assisted by Francis Dourthe, the Poyferré *maître de chai*.
  I do not know what the wines were like in the past, but recently they have been most impressive. They are scented, powerful and complex on the nose, with a marked and agreeable personality, rich, with structure and depth on the palate. In a blind tasting of '72 Crus Bourgeois in 1984 Le Crock was on the same level as Meyney. On this form it must be one of the leading Crus Bourgeois of St-Estèphe, a wine to look out for, especially since its revitalized management took charge.

Château Haut-Marbuzet
Cru Grand Bourgeois Exceptionnel. Owner: **SCV**

Duboscq. Administrator: **Henri Duboscq. 45ha. 22,500 cases. CS 50%, Mer 40%, CF 10%.**
In the last 20 years or so, Henri Duboscq has built up a formidable reputation for his wines. Situated around the village of Marbuzet, just to the south of Montrose, this was his starting point. Now he has added MacCarthy-Moula, Chambert-Marbuzet and Tour-de-Marbuzet to his empire.

One remarkable feature of this Cru Bourgeois is that all the wine is matured in new oak, something which even most Cru Classés do not attempt. One might expect this to result in austere, tannic wines, especially in St-Estèphe, yet in my experience the wines are outstandingly attractive. The colours are deep and dense, the nose rich and concentrated with fruit and well-married oak, the wine is very well balanced and stylish, with an outstanding flavour, possible to drink when relatively young and yet a good keeper. The consistency is also unusual; the '72 for example was one of the few wines from this vintage that one could drink with real pleasure.

Château Houissant
Cru Bourgeois Supérieur 1932. Owner: **Jean Ardouin. 20ha. 10,000 cases. CS 70%, Mer 30%.**
This *cru* is well situated on high ground inland from Montrose, in the southern sector of the *appellation*. The wines have long enjoyed a solid and consistent reputation. Not currently rated because it is not a member of the Syndicat, this is nevertheless a commendable Cru Bourgeois.

Château Laffitte–Carcasset
Cru Bourgeois 1932. Owner: **Vicomte Philippe de Padirac. 20ha. 8,000 cases. CS 65%, Mer 35%.** Second label: **Château La Vicomtesse.**
The name is not an attempt to ape the Premier Cru Classé but the name of an 18th-century owner. It is well placed, lying just past the Cave Coopérative as one travels north. The wines are carefully made, the emphasis being on finesse, although they also have plenty of body. This property is not a member of the Syndicat des Crus Bourgeois.

Château Lafon-Rochet
4e Cru Classé. Owner: **Guy Tesseron. 45ha. 12,000 cases. CS 80%, Mer 20%.**

Since Guy Tesseron (a Cognac *négociant* who married into the Cruse family) bought this *cru* in 1960, he has made great efforts to rebuild its reputation. There was much to be done, in the vineyard as well as the *chai*, and an entirely new château was built, designed in a suitably traditional mould. It is clearly visible from the road just past Cos d'Estournel on the *route des châteaux*.

I had felt by the mid-1970s that the wines were beginning to come of age and show clear improvements. However, looking back over regular tasting notes and seeing the results of some blind tastings in bottle, I find descriptions like 'austere', 'mean', 'dry finish' coming up with monotonous regularity. So what has gone wrong? One of the first things Guy Tesseron did here was to reduce drastically the Merlot content of the vineyard and increase the Cabernet Sauvignon to 80 percent. This compares to only 60 percent at Cos d'Estournel and Calon-Ségur, and 65 percent at Montrose. The reason why the proportions of Cabernet Sauvignon in St-Estèphe are significantly lower, even for Cru Classés, than in Pauillac, St-Julien or Margaux lies in the heavier soil with its high clay content. The Cabernet simply does not ripen as well on these soils and it is essential to plant Merlot in order to obtain balanced wines. It seems to me that at Lafon-Rochet they have treated the vineyard as if it were in Margaux and paid the penalty.

Château Lavillotte
Cru Bourgeois. Owner: **Jacques Pedro. 14ha. 5,800 cases. CS 75%, Mer 25%.**

This offers a good example of the vagaries of French spelling. When this *cru* hit the headlines by coming out above some Crus Classés in a Gault-Millau blind tasting, I rushed off to my Cocks & Féret to look it up, but there was no entry under this name. Later it transpired that it was entered as La Villotte! The château label spells the name as one word.

Jacques Pedro is a perfectionist, and this is reflected in his wines. They are matured in cask and not filtered, so decanting is essential, even for a vintage such as '78. It is not hard to see why this wine did so well in a blind tasting. It tends to be heavily perfumed and rich with distinctly minty overtones and real intensity. The flavour is fine and speaks of breed and complexity. I particularly like its attack and fruit upfront. Yet there is also finesse, with slightly less body than expected.

Château Lilian Ladoueys
Cru Bourgeois. Owners: **Christian & Lilian Thieblot. 50ha. 29,000 cases. CS 60%, Mer 40%.**
When the new owners bought this property in 1989, they rapidly transformed a rather run-down member of the cooperative into a Cru Bourgeois worthy of the name. The vineyard was increased from 20 hectares to its present size by some judicious purchases from neighbours, and a new *cuvier* and *chai* were constructed around the charming 'Directoire' chartreuse château, not far from Cos.

The first vintage to be bottled, '89, is impressively rich and spicy in character, with plenty of fruit and the charm of the year. This and an equally promising '90 suggest that this is a property of real potential.

Château MacCarthy
Cru Grand Bourgeois. Owner: **Henri Duboscq. 12ha. 5,000 cases. CS 65%, Mer 35%.**
As we know from the history of Lynch, Dillon and Kirwan, exiled Irishmen did well in Bordeaux in the 18th century, not to mention those like the Bartons who came of their own volition. The MacCarthys are not so famous, but they were people of consequence two centuries ago, and have left behind this small property and a street in Bordeaux to keep their name alive.

In 1988 Henri Duboscq (*see* Haut-Marbuzet) bought this property, so further increasing his holding around the village of Marbuzet. The vineyard has been joined to Chambert-Marbuzet and the name retained for the second label.

Château de Marbuzet
Cru Grand Bourgeois Exceptionnel. Owner: **Domaines Prats. 7ha. 10,000 cases. Mer 56%, CS 44%.**
The handsome château here is the home of the Prats family of Cos d'Estournel, which has no château of its own. The wine is vinified at Cos and is in fact treated as the second wine there. It is blended with

wine not suitable for inclusion in the *grand vin* of Cos, so, as at Haut-Bages-Averous and Lynch-Bages, is not quite a straight second wine. The result is a pleasing harmonious wine which ages more quickly than the Cos d'Estournel, and so fulfils a useful commercial purpose.

Cave Coopérative Marquis de St-Estèphe
Owner: **Société de Vinification de St-Estèphe. 205ha. 125,000 cases. CS 59%, Mer 29%, PV and CF 12%.**
The *cave* here was founded in 1934 by just 42 *viticulteurs*. Now there are over 200 'adherents', and this is one of the most up-to-date and best-run cooperatives in the Médoc, or anywhere else in the Gironde. Only grapes from the St-Estèphe *appellation* are received here. Apart from the wine sold under its own marque of Marquis de St-Estèphe, the wines of a number of other important properties are kept separately and bottled *à la propriété* to be sold under their own names. They are: de Mignot, Lille-Coutelin, Gireaud, Moutinot, L'Hôpital, Le Roc, Haut-Coteau, La Croix des Trois Soeurs, Palmier, Faget, Les Pradines, La Croix de Pez, Balangé, Ségur de Cabanac, Graves de Blanquet, Tour de Pez, Haut-Verdon, Ladouys, Les Combes, Violet, and Lartigue. Of course the quality of these wines varies according to the soil and the *cépages* planted, but all are carefully made. No wood is employed, and the wines normally show well after four to six years.

Château Meyney
Cru Grand Bourgeois Exceptionnel. Owner: **Domaines Cordier. 52ha. 29,000 cases. CS 58%, Mer 25%, PV 10%, CF 7%.** Second label: **Prieur du Château Meyney.**
St-Emilion abounds with old ecclesiastical buildings, or their remains, but they are rare in Médoc, and Meyney certainly has the best-preserved example. The present buildings, finely situated on a ridge with views across the Gironde, date from 1662–66. The large courtyard even today has a rather monastic atmosphere. The old name Prieuré des Couleys used, until recently, to appear on the label.

The wines balance fruit and tannin very judiciously; they are quite dense in texture and strong but always juicy in flavour. I find that they are normally at their best when on the young side, and that although they seem to have the structure for ageing, if kept too long they dry up and acquire a bitter finish. Of recent vintages '70 and '75 are at their peak, '78 was quite slow to develop, but '79 and '80 in their different ways represent Meyney at its most delicious and are for drinking now. '81, '82, '83, '85, '86 and '88 were all, in their different ways, great successes here. This is clearly one of the leading non-classified wines of St-Estèphe, in my judgement just behind de Pez and Phélan-Ségur as it lacks a little in breed.

Château Montrose
2e Cru Classé. Owner: **Jean-Louis Charmolüe. 68ha. 29,000 cases. CS 65%, Mer 25%, CF 10%.**
Disappointingly for the Scots, the name conceals no Scottish affiliation but refers to the old name for this vineyard, The Rose-Coloured Hill. This is the most recently planted of all the great Crus Classés, developed from completely uncultivated land, formerly part of Calon-Ségur, at the beginning of the 19th century. Like the neighbouring Meyney, it commands fine views of the Gironde from its ridge nearby. Montrose has belonged to the Charmolüe family since 1896 and is meticulously run by them. The present owner, Jean-Louis Charmolüe, is a resident working proprietor, like his much-respected mother before him. The *cuvier* is still completely traditional, with beautifully kept wooden vats, and this is very traditional wine. The only modern note is struck by a new *chai*.

I have always admired Montrose in cask. Although less marked by Cabernet Sauvignon than it used to be, it has a lovely clean, crisp, tannin flavour with new oak, tannin and fruit well matched. But this is not a wine to hurry over, and plenty of patience is required. The '78 is subtle and complex and the '79 opulent and powerful, well illustrating the contrast between these vintages. '82 is a great wine and the '83 is also a success, opulent with breed and power. '85 is more tannic than most wines of that year, while '86 is a massive wine and will need 15 to 20 years' maturation. '88 and '89 are classic, as is the '90, which looks like one of the outstanding wines of the vintage.

Château Morin
Cru Crand Bourgeois. Owners: **Marguerite & Maxime**

Sidaine. 10ha. 4,750 cases. CS 65%, Mer 35%.
This *cru* is just outside St-Corbian, in the northern sector of the
appellation, and has been in the same family for several generations.
It still uses a delightful old label, distinctly 19th century in
appearance, and the property is run on very traditional lines. The
strongly flavoured wines are however, reasonably supple and are of
good repute.

Château Les Ormes-de-Pez
Cru Grand Bourgeois. Owner: Cazes family. Administrator:
**Jean Michel Cazes. 32ha. 15,000 cases. CS 55%, Mer 35%,
CF 10%.**
The great gift for winemaking that the Cazes family has brought to
Lynch-Bages is also evident here. I have frequently been agreeably
surprised over the years by the consistently attractive wines made at
Les Ormes-de-Pez. Even in difficult years the wines are usually
supple and fruity, quite without the leanness or austerity of many
St-Estèphes. In 1981 new stainless steel fermentation vats were
installed here and a new ageing *chai* constructed. Previously the
wines had been kept at Lynch-Bages.
   The wines have plenty of concentration, but are very well
balanced with suppleness, fruit and plenty of character. Very good
wines were made in '78, '79, '81, '82 (especially promising and rich),
'83, '85, '86, '88 and '89. While Ormes-de-Pez sometimes lacks the
breed of its neighbour de Pez, it also seldom disappoints, and this
makes it one of the best and most reliable of the Crus Bourgeois of
St-Estèphe.

Château de Pez
**Cru Bourgeois Supérieur 1932. Owner: SC du Château
(Robert Dousson). 23·2ha. 14,500 cases. CS 70%, CF 15%,
Mer 15%.**
This is a very old property, and its grand twin-turreted château is
clearly visible from the *route des châteaux* as it winds through the
hamlet of the same name. It is situated just to the west of St-Estèphe.
Ever since Robert Dousson took over the management here for his
aunt in 1955 the reputation of this *cru* has grown, and for some years
now it has been regarded as a candidate for classification, and the
best non-classified *cru* in the commune.

The quality that de Pez has, and which is missing in most other Crus Bourgeois of the commune, is breed. This comes out very clearly in blind tastings. There is an attractive spiciness on the nose, together with elegance, charm, and a lot of fruit, while the flavour has good concentration and richness, with breed and balance. Some years can be a little lean, but the balance is preserved. Very fine wines were made in '75, '76, '78, '79, '82, '83, '85 and '86. Distribution worldwide is in the hands of Gilbey-Loudenne.

Château Phélan-Ségur
Cru Grand Bourgeois Exceptionnel. Owner: **Château Phélan-Ségur SA** (President: **Xavier Gardinier**). **70ha. 25,000 cases. CS 60%, Mer 30%, CF 10%.** Second label: **Frank Phélan. 8,330 cases.**
As with neighbours Meyney and Montrose, this is a château you will not see from the *route des châteaux*. The very handsome building is on the southern edge of St-Estèphe village on high ground with a fine view across the river. There is a massive *chai*. In 1985 the Delon family, who have owned the property since 1924, agreed to sell to Xavier Gardinier, the former President Director-General of Champagne Pommery.

At its best this *cru* can make very fine long-lasting wines which are rich and supple, with complexity and breed. In the latter days of the Delon ownership there was a lack of consistency and some poor wines were produced. In 1987, Xavier Gardinier impressed Bordeaux by announcing that he would take back all the '83 vintage and was not going to sell the '84 or '85 under the château label. Then, starting work with a clean slate, the château proceeded to make an excellent '87 (in the context of that year), followed by impressive wines in '88, '89 and '90. Phélan is once again challenging as one of the best unclassified wines of St-Estèphe.

Château Pomys
Cru Bourgeois Supérieur 1932. Owner: **SARL Arnaud. 6ha. 3,000 cases. CS 50%, Mer 30%, CF 20%.**
This is one of Pauillac's smaller estates, whose picturesque château is sadly now under separate ownership. The wines, often seen in England, are very reliable, attractive and well balanced.

Château Les Pradines
Owner: **Jean Gradit. 8ha. 3,500 cases. CS 60%, Mer 35%, CF 5%.**
Here is a good example of what vinification at a cooperative can achieve – the wines here are all bottled *à la propriété* and sold exclusively by Louis Dubroca. They have that positive, assertive character of St-Estèphe, but with very clean fruit and a complete absence of leanness. The wines see no wood, but need two to four years in bottle to give of their best. This is a very pleasing wine with plenty of agreeable character.

Château St-Estèphe
Cru Bourgeois 1932. Owner: **SARL Arnaud. 10ha. 4,400 cases. CS 55%, Mer 30%, CF 8%, Mal and PV 7%.**
This property is relatively new, dating from 1870. The house itself was acquired in 1950. It is owned by the Arnaud family, who also own Château Pomys but make their home at St-Estèphe. The wines lack the full-bodied character of Pomys but are sound and typical of the region.

Château Tour-des-Termes
Cru Bourgeois 1932. Owner: **Jean Anney. 26·5ha. 13,500 cases. CS 55%, Mer 35%, PV 10%.**
A good-sized property situated near the village of St-Corbian in the north of the *appellation*. The wines I have come across are well made, robust with plenty of character but also supple and quite fine. They are aged in cask. This is a wine of a good standard, not a member of the Syndicat des Crus Bourgeois.

Château Tronquoy-Lalande
Cru Grand Bourgeois. Owner: **Arlette Castéja. 16·5ha. 7,000 cases. Mer 50%, CS and CF 50%.**
I have always been attracted by the charming château here with its two distinctive towers at each end of a Chartreuse-style building. Lalande is the name of the place, Tronquoy that of an early 19th-century owner. At that time this *cru* was included in several unofficial classifications, but did not make the all-important one in 1855.

This is now a carefully managed property, for which Dourthe

have exclusive distribution rights and provide technical assistance. The wines are matured partly in *cuve* and partly in wood and are inclined to be tough and rustic when young, improving with time.

Haut-Médoc

The decline that this area suffered in the years of depression has now been triumphantly reversed. The area under vine nearly doubled between 1973 and 1988, a remarkable statistic.

This is *par excellence* the area of the Crus Bourgeois, which here accounts for 62% of the area in production and covers a greater area than in any other part of Médoc. Wines are produced in 15 very diverse communes but only in ten of these are more than 100 hectares planted, the most important are St-Seurin, St-Laurent, Cussac, St-Sauveur, Cissac and Vertheuil.

The styles of wine vary considerably, with the largest-producing northern communes making robust, full-flavoured wines, and softer, lighter ones being made in the south.

Château d'Agassac
Cru Grand Bourgeois Exceptionnel. Owner: **SC du Château.** Administrator: **Philippe Capbern Gasqueton. 35ha. 11,600 cases. CS 54%, Mer 40%. CF 6%.**
This is one of the few remaining examples of a genuine mediaeval fortress to survive in the Médoc. It is also the most important *cru* in Ludon, after La Lagune, and the only member there of the Syndicat des Crus Bourgeois. Since Philippe Gasqueton (*see* Calon Ségur, Capbern and du Tertre) took over 20 years ago, marked improvements have been made and the reputation of the wine has been much enhanced. The wine is matured in oak casks but no new wood is used. The yields are low, usually only around 30 hectolitres per hectare.

The wine has marked and attractive individuality; it is vividly perfumed, with a very special fruitiness and pronounced flavour. Much of the crop is traditionally exported to Holland. It is a pity this wine is not better known in England.

Château d'Arcins
Cru Bourgeois 1932. Owner: **SC du Château d'Arcins.**
82ha. 45,000 cases. CS 70%, Mer 30%.
The largest shareholders in the company running Château d'Arcins
are Castel Frères, who have in recent years invested much in the
development of this property which is the best in its commune. The
wines have many of the qualities of neighbouring growths
Margaux and Moulis, and are mostly sold in the north of France.

Château Arnauld
Owners: **M & Mme Maurice Roggy. 18ha. 9,000 cases. Mer
50%, CS 40%, CF 10%.**
Originally a priory, this property took its name from a *procureur* at
the court of the Parliament of Bordeaux – Pierre-Jacques Arnauld.
It was bought by the Roggy family in 1956. The vineyards were
replanted and improvements in vinification followed the marriages
of the two Roggy daughters to the Theil brothers of Château
Poujeaux. The '85 is an early developer, with fruit and charm; the
'88 is much more powerful. Certainly a wine to look out for.

Château d'Arsac
Cru Bourgeois Supérieur 1932. Owner: **Philippe Raoux.**
80ha. 26,600 cases. CS 62%, Mer 38%. Second labels:
Châteaux Ségur-d'Arsac and Le Monteil d'Arsac.
This *cru* is something of a curiosity, since it is the only one in Arsac
not to benefit from the Margaux AC (it carries the Haut-Médoc
AC). This is because at the time when the AC was being established
there were no vines planted and the proprietor did not bother to
apply for recognition. A start was made in reconstructing the
vineyard when it changed hands in 1959, but the real change came
when the present dynamic owner arrived in 1986. Since then the
massive *chai* has been restored, the *cuvier* modernized, and the
vineyard increased from only 11·5 hectares to its present 54
hectares. The new vinification facilities were fully operational for
the 1988 vintage. The amount of oak-ageing has been increased and
some new oak is now being used. With the excellent raw materials
available here, and the dedication and enthusiasm of the owner, the
future looks bright indeed. The proprietor hopes to be granted the
Margaux AC when the *appellation* is next reviewed.

Château Barreyres
Cru Bourgeois 1932. Owner: **SC du Château Barreyres.**
100ha. 48,000 cases. CS 70%, Mer 30%.
Castel Frères have, as at Château d'Arcins, invested much in this property, completing a new *cuvier* and *chai* in 1981 to enable improved vinification of this château's large output. The wines are attractive with pleasant fruit character but can be slightly coarse.

Château Beaumont
Cru Grand Bourgeois. Owner: **GMF.** Administrator:
Maurice Ruelle. 107ha. 66,700 cases. CS 62%, Mer 30%, CF 5%, PV 3%. Second labels: **Châteaux Moulin d'Arvigny and Les Tours-de-Beaumont.**
In marked contrast to those of their neighbour, Tour-du-Haut-Moulin, the wines of Beaumont tend to be light, fruity and ready to drink early. They are very perfumed, with well-integrated new oak, tannin and fruit, combining to make a very harmonious whole, most attractively flavoured. The '76 is fruity and light and I have also tasted a pleasant '79. The '82 is earlier drinking than most Médocs but is very attractive and the '83 is also very good. '85 is another attractive wine and only moderately oaked, '86 is the best Beaumont I have tasted to date.

The second wine, Château Moulin d'Arvigny, is a selection of about 25 percent of the production, mostly from young vines, and is designed for early drinking. The '82 is delicious and already drinkable.

Château Bel-Air
Owner: **Henri Martin. 35ha. 10,000 cases. CS 60%, Mer 40%.**
Henri Martin – owner of Château Gloria, and one of the Médoc's greatest personalities until his death in 1991 – bought this property in 1980. It is now managed by the highly capable Jean-Louis Triaud, Martin's son-in-law, who coordinates Bel-Air's three separate vineyards. I have tasted the '84 and found it to be dense for the year, with fruit and a good perfume. These are certainly wines to watch out for.

Château Belgrave
5e Cru Classé. Owner: **GFA.** Administrator: **Patrick Atteret. 55ha. 18,000 cases. CS 60%, Mer 35%, PV 5%.**
Until the CVBG group (Dourthe-Kressman) bought this property in 1979, it had suffered from under-investment and neglect for decades. It is hardly surprising then that the wine is little known and its reputation negligible. The vineyard, however, is well situated on gravelly ridges behind Lagrande, and certainly has the potential to do well. The new owners have recently been carrying out extensive improvements to the *chai*, and new casks are being used for maturation. Patrick Atteret, the chief oenologist at the CVBG (Consortium Vinicole de Bordeaux et de la Gironde), is responsible for the direction of this project.

Under this new regime there have been some much better wines, starting with the attractive '81. They are now well-made and solid, if lacking ultimate class.

Château Bel-Orme-Tronquoy-de-Lalande
Cru Grand Bourgeois. Owners: **Mme L Quié & Jean-Michel Quié. 26ha. 10,000 cases. Mer 45%, CS 30%, CF 20%, Mal 3%, PV 2%.**
Not to be confused with Tronquoy-Lalande in nearby St-Estèphe, this property once belonged to the Tronquoy family. The words *bel-orme* mean 'beautiful elm'. The wines here are powerful, solid and traditional, and they last marvellously, as was proven by some bottles from the 1920s that I sampled. They tend to lack the bouquet of wines from further south in the Médoc, but develop a warmth and richness of texture with age.

Château Le Bourdieu
Cru Bourgeois. Owner: **Monique Barbe. 30ha. 25,000 cases. CS 50%, Mer 30%, CF 20%.** Second labels: **Châteaux Victoria and Picourneau.**
Probably the best-reputed *cru* in Vertheuil today, the vineyards run from the village of that name to the boundary with St-Estèphe. The wine is matured in cask and well reflects Monique Barbe's careful winemaking, the results of which combine robustness with finesse. The style is that of a good, lush St-Estèphe.

Château du Breuil
Cru Bourgeois Supérieur. Owner: **Vialard family. 20ha.
11,600 cases. Mer 34%, CS 28%, CF 23%, PV 11%, Mal 4%.**
This is the oldest recorded property in the Médoc, records being
traceable through the barony of Breuil back to the sixth century.
The château is a mediaeval fortress, inhabited until 1861 but now
sadly deteriorated, though still majestic and imposing.

The current owners are the Vialard family who bought the
property in 1987; the *chai* and *cuvier* were in a very run-down state
at this stage and needed much care and attention. Although some
respectable wines were made before this, under the new ownership
the situation has been transformed, with the '88 (the second vintage
under the new management) being even better than Cissac. This
marks the beginning of a bright future for these wines.

Château Cambon-la-Pelouse
Cru Bourgeois Supérieur 1932. Owner: **Indivision Carrère
Fils Frère & Gendre. 60ha. 35,000 cases. Mer 50%, CS 25%,
CF 25%.**
The *cru* has recently been resurrected by an energetic family of
growers from St-Emilion, who also own Château Grand Barrail-
Lamarzelle Figeac.

The wines have real breed, with emphasis on elegant fruitiness.
They are soft and develop quickly for early drinking – no casks are
used for the maturation but this is a good example of how clean,
fresh and attractive such wines can be. At Cambon-la-Pelouse, this
approach clearly makes good commercial sense. Very good wines
were made in '81, '83 and '85, with the '82 producing something
extra. I noted a lovely scent of cherries and liquorice, a delicious
flavour, rich but also complex. This looks like a *cru* with an
interesting future.

Château de Camensac
5e Cru Classé. Owner: **Forner family. 65ha. 29,000 cases. CS
60%, CF 20%, Mer 20%.**
Like the other Crus Classés of St-Laurent, Camensac had sunk into
a state of complete obscurity and neglect when it was rescued by the
Forner brothers in 1965. Of Spanish origins (they produce a fine
Rioja) and new to Bordeaux, they sought the help of Professor

Emile Peynaud in rebuilding this *cru*. Much of the vineyard had to be replanted, and the *chai* and *cuvier* completely modernized and re-equipped.

In the early 1970s I noted that light-textured, fruity, harmonious wines were being made which were eminently drinkable. More recently the wines seem to have a stronger, coarser flavour, even when, as with the '82, there is a lot of richness and ripeness. In 1985 the '78 was still very tannic and coarse, solid, but without any highlights. Perhaps as the vines age the residual character of the soil is re-asserting itself for there is no reason to believe the wine is any less carefully made. Still a wine to watch.

Château Cantemerle
5e Cru Classé. Owner: **Société Assurances Mutuelles du Batîment et Travaux Publics.** Administrator: **Jean Cordier. 53ha. 20,000 cases. Mer 40%, CS 40%, CF 18%, PV 2%.**
This famous old property, after a period of decline, has now been rapidly restored to its former glory. It achieved a great and deserved reputation when Pierre Dubos was proprietor, a regime which lasted over 50 years and corresponded roughly with the first half of this century. Then came the division among a number of heirs – a constant problem in France – and the result was a lack of money and direction, so decline and decay set in. The turning point came in 1980 with the sale to a syndicate of which Domaines Cordier are part. Cordier are responsible for the management and marketing, their partners have provided the finance. The *cuvier* and *chai* have been modernized, with stainless steel fermentation vats taking the place of the old wooden ones.

The style of Cantemerle leans towards lightness and elegance combined with good richness in the middle flavour. With the *cuvier* being rebuilt at the time, I found the first vintage of the new regime disappointing and dull. The '81 was better but not special, but then in '82, '83 and '85 superb wines were made, with an opulence and richness only encountered in exceptional years. Unfortunately the '86 crop suffered from the effects of hail but in general the future looks bright indeed.

Canterayne
Owner: **Cave Coopérative de St–Sauveur. 113ha. 19,000**

cases. CS 60%, Mer 35%, CF, Mal and PV 5%.
There are 69 members of this cooperative, which was founded in 1934. It produces some 5,000 hectolitres of wine annually, which is well-made and expresses the firmness and solidity characteristic of the region's wines.

Château Caronne-Ste-Gemme
Cru Grand Bourgeois Exceptionnel. Owner: **Jean & François Nony-Borie. 45ha. 25,000 cases. CS 65%, Mer 35%.** Second label: **Château Labat.**
This very good *cru* is deservedly becoming much better known since François Nony-Borie became involved in the management in the early 1980s. The family has owned the property since 1900. The vineyards are separated from Camensac and the rest of St-Laurent by the Jalle du Nord, which divides St-Julien from Cussac, and the nearest vineyard is Lanessan in Cussac. So the situation of the vineyards is rather special.

My overall impression of the wines here is that they are very well made, have more style and breed than most St-Laurent wines, with nothing rustic about them. But there is a strong assertive character which comes through clearly, nicely balanced with fruit, and resulting in some complexity. The '78, '79, '80 and '81 are all good examples of these vintages and the '82 is excellent, with the concentration typical of the year. '83 is tannic but has plenty of fat, bigger than the '81 and finer perhaps than '79. '85 and '86 are both concentrated and attractive, with the '86 being slightly more powerful. This is really a top Cru Bourgeois, with excellent keeping qualities.

Château Charmail
Owner: **Roger Sèze. 20ha. 12,000 cases. Mer 50%, CS 45%, CF 5%.**
This property is excellently situated on the gravelly ridges of St-Seurin-de-Cadourne, near to the river. It was bought and restored in the 1970s by a Burgundian – Monsieur Laly – who came to the Médoc as he was unable to afford a vineyard in his home region. Roger Sèze, owner of Château Mayne-Vieil, took over in the early 1980s and is now producing wines that are rich, supple and charming, likely to improve as the vineyards mature.

Châtelleine
Owner: **Cave Coopérative de Vertheuil. 110ha. 16,000 cases. CS 50%, Mer 50%.**
The total annual output of the 70 members of this cooperative is 7,000 hectolitres. They are solid wines of good quality, some of which are marketed under their own château labels: Châteaux Ferré Portal, Fondeminjean, Julian, Laride, Miqueu and Tamière.

Château Cissac
Cru Grand Bourgeois Exceptionnel. Owner: **Vialard family. 50ha. 25,000 cases. CS 75%, Mer 20%, PV 5%.**
Cissac has been inseparably linked for over a generation with Louis Vialard, who comes from an old Médocain family. They have owned it since 1885, and Louis Vialard has lived here since 1940. Recently, extensive modernization has occurred and traditional methods – old vines, wooden fermenting vats and oak ageing casks (of which 50 percent are normally new) – have been supplemented with new vats of stainless steel.

In 1971 Louis Vialard made some important changes in his methods. He stopped adding *vin de presse*, using only the free-run juice; he began vintaging later, and he increased the proportion of Cabernet Franc at the expense of the Cabernet Sauvignon. In 1983 he gave a tasting of the vintages of the 1960s and 1970s to assess the results. For me the most noticeable difference was caused by the *vin de presse*, it gave the older vintages a background of flavour and complexity lacking in most of the younger wines; the exception being the '75, itself a year unusually rich in tannin and extract. In otherwise excellent years such as '76, '78 and '79, a certain leanness was perceptible. Of the more recent vintages, the '85 is full of charm and '86 is a real *vin de garde*. The Cabernet Franc at Cissac tended to lack body and colour, somewhat diluting the final blend, and this grape is no longer used. This is a fine *cru*, whose wines have real breed and elegance, and reward keeping.

Château Citran
Cru Grand Bourgeois Exceptionnel. Owner: **Société Touko Haus.** Administrator: **Keïchi Fujimoto. 22ha. 41,000 cases. Mer 60%, CS 35%, PV 5%.**
This is the most important *cru* in Avensan. Part of the vineyard lies

close to the village, but the oldest part is between the château and Paveil-de-Luze. When the Miailhe family bought the property in 1945 there was hardly any vineyard left. For many years, until 1980, Jean Miailhe of Château Coufran ran the property, he expanded the vineyards and established a fine reputation for the wine. He then handed over to his sister and brother-in-law, who sold to the present proprietors, the Japanese company Fujimoto, in 1986.

The wines now have a good reputation and I have found them to have an excellent bouquet with pronounced fruit. They have a good flavour and balance with a certain earthiness. From 1979 until the sale, the wines were less consistent and were dilute and dry in large vintages, especially '79 and '83. But the first efforts under the new regime, '88 and '89, together with an attractive new label, have been most rewarding.

Château Clément-Pichon
Owner: **Clément Fayat. 23ha. 9,000 cases. CS 60%, CF 10%, Mer 30%.**
Originally called Château Parempuyre, this property was owned by the Pichons until 1880. The subsequent owners built the flamboyant château that stands there today: it is of a similar romantic-Gothic style to Châteaux Lanessan and Fonréaud, which were designed by the same architect. Clément-Pichon is currently owned and lived in by Clément Fayat – it was he who changed the name. Fayat made his fortune building autoroutes and has invested some of it in replanting and creating a new drainage system in the vineyards. The *chai* has been similarly modernized and new vats installed enabling computer-controlled fermentation. The vineyards need more time to mature but the wines are already very pleasant, if light.

Château Coufran
Cru Crand Bourgeois. Owner: **SC du Château.**
Administrator: **Jean Miailhe. 64ha. 33,600 acres. Mer 85%, CS 10%, PV 5%.** Second label: **Château La Rose Maréchale.**
The very high proportion of Merlot here is unusual for the Médoc, even on these heavier soils. The result is an easy, supple, fruity wine for early drinking but without much style or personality and distinctly on the light side. This is good commercial claret though

and fulfils its declared purpose of producing easy-to-enjoy Médoc at a very reasonable price.

Château Dillon
Cru Bourgeois 1932. Owner: **Lycée Agricole de Bordeaux-Blanquefort. 38ha. 22,500 cases. Red: Mer, CS, CF and PV. White: Sauv and Sém.** Second label: **Château Linas (Bordeaux Blanc).**

This *cru* takes it name from an emigré Irishman who acquired the property in 1754. It has belonged to the Lycée Agricole since 1956, and they have made improvements in the *cuvier* in order to carry out temperature-controlled fermentation. At their best, the wines produced here are light and elegantly flavoured, but there have been lapses in consistency. Some good wines were made in the 1970s, especially the '70, '75 and '79. Since then a new parcel of young vines has been added and little or no selection has been practised: the wines have therefore taken a step backwards in quality. It remains to be seen what the future holds.

Château Fontesteau
Cru Grand Bourgeois. Owners: **Jean Renaud and Dominique Fouin. 11ha. 5,000 cases. Mer 40%, CS 30%, CF 30%.**

From 1939 until 1984 the owner of Fontesteau was René Eglise. Since 1984 it has been owned by Jean Renaud. The name comes from *fontaines d'eau*, because there are a number of old wells on the property. The wines are made quite traditionally, with fermentation in concrete vats and ageing in casks. I found the '79 vintage had a note of *goût de terroir*. It was already attractive and desirable at five years old, but rather lacked personality, which is unusual for the St-Sauveur commune. It will be interesting to see what the current owners achieve.

Château Grandis
Cru Bourgeois 1932. Owner: **GHF du Château Grandis. 7ha. 2,000 cases. CS 40%, CF 30%, Mer 30%.** Second label: **Murac-Mayor.**

Grandis was bought in 1857 by Armand Figerou and it remained in the family ever since; today it is run by François Vergez and Paul Figerou. The wines have the solidity typical of St-Seurin-de-Cadourne and are traditionally made, the '85 being ripe and powerful. Certainly a wine that repays keeping.

Château Hanteillan
Cru Grand Bourgeois. Owner: **SARL du Château Hanteillan.** Administrator: **Catherine Blasco. 83ha. 41,600 cases. CS 48%, Mer 42%, CF 6%, PV 4%.** Second label: **Château Larrivaux-Hanteillan.**
In 1972 this property was bought by a group of partners connected to France's largest construction company. The property used to share the same owners as Château Coutelin-Merville in St-Estèphe, and the vineyards adjoin one another. Despite Coutelin-Merville's superior *appellation*, I have found that Hanteillan today makes a more impressive wine. A high proportion of Merlot grown reflects the clay present in parts of the vineyard.

The rich, well-structured '79 showed how well the rather young vineyard is maturing as well as the careful selection which had been exercised in a year of high yield. This is a serious wine with some real breed and should be followed with interest as the vineyard matures.

Château Haut-Madrac
Owner: **Castéja family. 20ha. 5,500 cases. CS 70%, Mer 30%.**
Bought by Emile Castéja's father in 1919, this property adjoins the family's other property in Pauillac (Lynch-Moussas). It produces wines that are well-made, charming and good for early drinking. Even the '84 was pleasing, with the light, fresh and fruity characteristics typical of these wines.

Château La Lagune
3e Cru Classé. Owner: **SC Agricole.** Administrator: **Jean-Michel Ducellier. 55ha. 25,000 cases. CS 55%, CF 20%, Mer 20%, PV 5%.** Second label: **Château Ludon-Pomiès-Agassac.**
The restoration of La Lagune began when it was bought by Georges Brunet in 1957. This dynamic man replanted the vineyard and reconstructed the *chai*, where he installed a marvellous system

of stainless steel pipes to bring the new wine straight from the vats to the barrels and also to carry out racking entirely mechanically and without contact with the air. It was a revolutionary system when installed over 25 years ago, but no one else has yet copied it, which seems surprising. Unfortunately Burnet did too much too quickly and ran short of money so had to sell in 1961, having made the mistake of selling that great year *sur souche* (on the vine, before the harvest). It was bought by the champagne house of Ayala for whom Jean-Michel Ducellier is today the administrator. The *régisseuse* is the daughter of the redoubtable Madame Boyrie; she succeeded her mother when she died unexpectedly in 1986, and her meticulous hand creates some fine wines.

Now the vineyard has come of age a series of splendid wines have given La Lagune an enviable reputation. This is a wine of great elegance, very perfumed, usually rather marked by new wood at the start (100 percent new wood is usual here) but this is soon absorbed to give a very rich, supple flavour with great finesse. The '75, '76, '78, '79, '81, '82 and '83 are all great successes. The '80 has perhaps suffered slightly from the new wood policy and could have been better with less. A wine clearly of 2e Cru Classé standing.

Château de Lamarque
Cru Grand Bourgeois. Owner: **SC Gromand d'Evry.** Administrator: **Roger Gromand. 47ha. 25,000 cases. CS 50%, Mer 25%, CF 20%, PV 5%.** Second label: **Réserve du Marquis d'Evry.**

The château here is the best-preserved and most impressive fortress in the Médoc of those that survive from the English period in Aquitaine. Although parts of it date from the 11th and 12th centuries the main structure is 14th century with some 17th-century alterations. It lies between the *route des châteaux* and the ferry to Blaye, but is well-concealed amid the trees of its park. Until recently the wine of Lamarque was unknown, but reconstruction of vineyards and *chais* was undertaken in the 1960s and is now bearing fruit. Ownership of the château has passed down through inheritance since 1841 when it was acquired by the Comte de Fumel, passing via a daughter to the present owner Marie-Louise Burnet d'Evry, who married Roger Gromand. He is the driving force behind the renaissance of Lamarque, and with Professor Emile

Peynaud's constant advice and supervision he has again established a
reputation for the wines. The wine is matured in casks, a quarter of
which are new each year.

In the 1970s I found the wines light and agreeable in the good
vintages but without much personality. Then in the 1980s they
filled out and became more powerful and much richer. Clearly the
vineyard has come of age, and this is now a wine to watch.

Château Lamothe-Bergeron
Cru Bourgeois. Owner: **SC Grand-Puy-Ducasse. 60ha.
25,000 cases. CS 66%, Mer 30%, CF 4%.**
The name Lamothe-Bergeron comes from the word '*motte*' (a piece
of high ground) and from the name of a previous owner of the
château. This is a *cru* with a reputation for producing well-made,
reliable wines that are reasonably priced. Particularly attractive
vintages were the '79, '81, '82, '85, '86 and '87, with the '88 and '89
being even better.

Château Lamothe-Cissac
Owner: **SC du Château Lamothe.** Administrator: **Gabriel
Fabre. 47ha. 22,000 cases. CS 70%, Mer 26%, CF 2%,
PV 2%.**
This is a very old property: it was a *maison noble* in the 17th century
and evidence of Roman occupation has also been found here. The
château itself does not share this history and was built comparatively recently in 1912. Lamothe-Cissac was bought by the Fabre
family in 1964, in an extremely run-down state. Since then a new
cuvier, *chai* and underground cellar, have been built. 20 percent new
oak is used each year for maturation, and as the vineyards develop
some impressive wines are emerging. The '81, '83, '85, '86, '88 and
'89 are stylish, with solidity and fruit. They are mostly sold direct,
not via Bordeaux *négociants*.

Château Lanessan
Cru Bourgeois Supérieur 1932. Owner: **Bouteiller family.**
Administrator: **Hubert Bouteiller. 40ha. 16,700 cases. CS
75%, Mer 20%, CF and PV 5%.**
Since 1790 this property has effectively been in the same family, the
Delbos, whose name still appears on the label alongside that of

Bouteiller. It was handed from father to son until 1909, when the daughter of the last male Delbos inherited. She married Etienne Bouteiller. Hubert Bouteiller, the present member of the family in charge, has his home here. A feature of Lanessan unrelated to wine is the carriage museum, where the original stables and harness room are displayed together with a fine assortment of carriages.

The wines of Lanessan have a marked personality. There is a tendency to firmness at first, but in good years the wines have marvellous fruit and richness and considerable breed. They are also very consistent. There is a great capacity for ageing. I have tasted a number of old vintages going back to 1916, all of them well preserved and many outstanding. Even the '77 was good from this property and a useful and elegant '80 was also made. Recently '81, '82, '83, '85, '86, '88 and '89 were all excellent examples. This is a wine for those who love fine Médocs for their own sake and are not slaves to labels.

Château Larose-Trintaudon
Cru Grand Bourgeois. Owner: **Assurances Générales de France.** Administrator: **Elisée Forner. 172ha. 83,300 cases. CS 60%, Mer 25%, CF 15%.**
Bought and developed by the Forner family in the 1960s this is now the largest vineyard in the Médoc. Although the Forner family sold to the present owners at the end of 1986, Elisée Forner continues to manage the property, with his nephew in charge of sales and marketing. Mechanical harvesting is used, but all the wines are matured in casks of which 30 percent are new each year.

The aim is to produce fruity, light-textured wines which can be drunk young, and the '76 is a good example of this. I was surprised to find the '79 still rather aggressive at five years old, but the '83 is particularly good.

Chateau Lestage-Simon
Cru Bourgeois. Owner: **Charles Simon. 32ha. 16,600 cases. Mer 68%, CS 22%, CF 10%.**
The wines here are typical of St-Seurin: fine, robust and solid, with the Merlot giving fruit and suppleness. I was once given a bottle of the '29 by a former proprietor, and I found it had kept splendidly. Today's wines are made for earlier drinking but are none the worse

for that. They are widely distributed in good restaurants in France.
'81, '82, '83 and '85 are good examples.

Château Liversan
Cru Grand Bourgeois. Owner: **Prince Guy de Polignac. 48ha. 20,000 cases. CS 49%, Mer 38%, CF 10%, PV 3%.**
Since 1983 Liversan has been owned by the Polignacs, formerly the
principal shareholders of Champagne Pommery. They immediately installed a new *cuvier* with stainless steel fermentation vats.
The wines are now to be aged in oak with a good proportion of new
wood. The scented, opulent yet elegant '85 and the '86, for which
only 65 percent of the crop was included in the final *assemblage* and
only 25 percent of it was Merlot, show the potential of this *cru*.
With the dedication of the new owners to quality and plenty of
mature vines in the vineyard, this is one worth following, for it is
producing some of the best Cru Bourgeois wines among the inland
communes north of St-Laurent.

Château Magnol
Cru Bourgeois. Owners: **Barton & Guestier. 17ha. 6,250 cases. CS 75%, Mer 25%.**
This château does not have an extensive history: most of its
vineyards were planted within the last 40 years. Its current owners
are a subsidiary of the Seagram group. Vinification is carried out
with much care, using modern temperature-controlled stainless
steel vats and producing wines that are full-flavoured, rich and
supple. Wines to be drunk young.

Château Malescasse
Cru Bourgeois. Owner: **SCI Château Malescasse.**
Administrator: **Alfred Tesseron. 32ha. 16,000 cases. CS 70%, Mer 20%, CF 10%.**
A charming high-roofed château, dating from 1824, overlooks this
property which is situated on the gravelly ridges of the commune of
Lamarque. Its vineyards are some of the best in the area between
Margaux and St-Julien. During the years of recession the area under
vine had dwindled to only four hectares. Since 1970 a programme
of replanting has been under way, aimed at completion for 1992.
Restoration of the *chai* was carried out after Guy Tesseron bought

the property in 1978.

The style and solidity of these wines is particularly impressive for a vineyard which is not yet fully mature, the '79, '81, '85, '86, '88, '89 and '90 are all of a high standard, and sold at modest prices. A *cru* proving to be one of the *appellation*'s best buys.

Château de Malleret
Cru Grand Bourgeois. Owner: **SC du Château (Marquis du Vivier). 59ha. 25,000 cases. CS 70%, Mer 15%, CF 10%, PV 5%.** Second label: **Château Lemoine-Nexon.**
These wines are extremely scented and elegant, very fruity with real length of flavour and a quite seductive charm. Despite the high proportion of Cabernet Sauvignon and the small amount of Merlot, the character of the delightful '80 seems to suggest Merlot rather than Cabernet first, which again emphasizes the important role of the soil. Very good wines were also made in '79 and '81.

Château Le Meynieu
Cru Grand Bourgeois. Owner: **Jacques Pédro. 14ha. 6,700 cases. CS 70%, Mer 30%.**
The energetic and meticulous Jacques Pédro is mayor of Vertheuil as well as proprietor of this *cru* and those of Lavillotte and Domaine de la Ronceray. His aim is to make very typical Médocs with plenty of tannin but developing bouquet and finesse in bottle.

Cave Coopérative La Paroisse
Owner: **Union de Producteurs. 130ha. 61,000 cases.**
The cooperative was founded in 1935 and now has 60 adherents, it is considered the best coop in the Haut-Médoc *appellation*. Most of the wine is sold in bulk to *négociants* or under the La Paroisse brand, but a few property wines are kept separate: Château Quimper, Domaine du Haut et de Brion, Château Le Tralle, Domaine de Villa and Château Maurac.

These are solid, well-balanced wines which resemble the lesser St-Estèphes but usually have more flesh.

Château Peyrabon
Cru Grand Bourgeois. Owner: **Jacques Babeau. 53ha. 20,500 cases. CS 50%, Mer 27%, CF 23%.**

This distinctive twin-towered château has been owned by the Babeau family since 1958, they are proud to be able to say that Queen Victoria once attended a concert here. Prior to 1958 the wines of Peyrabon were relatively unknown as they were mostly sold privately; they now have a very good reputation and are classics of the northern Médoc, having a note of *terroir* on the finish. The wines come from extensive vineyards which were supplemented by land bought from Château Liversan in 1978. They are fermented in concrete vats and matured in wood, 25 percent of which is new.

Château Pontoise-Cabarrus
Cru Bourgeois. Owner: **SICA de Haut-Médoc.** Administrator: **F Tereygeol. 24ha. 15,000 cases. CS 60%, Mer 30%, CF 6%, PV 4%.**
A modest *cru bourgeois*, with an interesting history. Owned by the Cabarrus family during the Terror in Bordeaux, the daughter of the house, Thereza Cabarrus, saved many lives in her role as mistress of the notorious Tallien, a colourful character, she was later a witness at the wedding of Napoleon and Josephine.

The Tereygeols bought the château in 1960, and built up the seven-hectare property to its current size. They produce carefully made, solid wines with flavour, needing plenty of time to reveal their best characteristics.

Château Puy-Castéra
Cru Bourgeois. Owner: **Henri Marès. 25ha. 10,800 cases. CS 60%, Mer 30%, CF 8%, Mal 2%.**
Puy-Castéra was given a new lease of life in 1973 when it was bought by Henri Marès. At this stage the buildings were dilapidated and the vineyards had been returned to pasture. Replanting took place gradually: 25 hectares were in production by 1980, and winemaking was put into the hands of Bertrand de Rozières from Château Sestignan.

The vineyards are well sited and as they mature are yielding wines of increasing quality.

Château Ramage-la-Bâtisse
Cru Bourgeois. Owner: **SC du Château. 54ha. 20,800 cases.**

CS 55%, Mer 30%, PV 15%. Alternative label: **Château Tourteran.** Second label: **Château Dutellier.**
This is a combination of several properties which have been put together since 1961. The wines are very scented (I detected a smell of violets) and extremely fruity and easy to drink. It is easy to see why they have rapidly gained a reputation.

Château du Retout
Cru Bourgeois 1932. Owner: **Gérard Kopp. 25ha. 10,800 cases. CS 60%, Mer 20%, CF 10%, PV 7%, Mal 3%.**
An old mill tower (dating from 1395) stands on this property: it was used in the Seven Years War (1756–63) to look out for British ships advancing up the Gironde estuary. This is yet another example of a property where extensive restoration has been needed. Its wines are well made and sold at very reasonable prices. They are unusual in that they often comprise all of the five main grape varieties traditional to the Médoc.

Château Reysson
Cru Bourgeois. Owner: **Mercian Corporation.**
Administrator: **Jean-Pierre Angliviel de la Beaumelle. 66ha. 24,000 cases. CS 56%, Mer 44%.** Second label: **Château de l'Abbaye. 12,000 cases.**
Château Reysson was restored by the Mestrezat Group who bought it in 1972, subsequently selling to the Mercian Corporation (part of the Japanese Ajimoto group). They produce pleasant wines at reasonable prices, suitable for drinking young.

Chevaliers du Roi Soleil
Owners: **SICA des Viticulteurs de Fort-Médoc. 45ha. 27,500 cases. CS 50%, Mer 40%, CF 10%.** Other labels: **Fort-Médoc, Château Les Capérans, Château Eglise Vieille, Château les Jacquets, Château Le Neurin.**
Initially a small group of growers who pooled their efforts in 1966 to improve their output and to market it more efficiently. Today a *négociant*, Ginestet, is also involved with this group of producers, based in a very modern site complex, somewhat startling for the traveller in the Médoc countryside, intruding on the flat landscape en-route from Lamarque to Cussac. 22 members are now involved

in producing wines under the label 'Chevaliers du Roi Soleil', they are unlike cooperative wines in that they reflect the character and personality of their château origins.

Château Sénéjac
Cru Bourgeois Supérieur 1932. Owner: **Charles de Guigné. 18ha. 7,500 cases. CS 40%, Mer 30%, CF 24%, PV 6%.**
There is an international air about Sénéjac. The proprietor is an American citizen of French origin, and he is assisted by Jenny Bailey, an oenologist from New Zealand. The wines are good and have made progress recently. They are completely different from those of de Malleret, the other important *cru* of Pian. They are deep-coloured and perfumed, but classically austere and tannic. These wines are made to last and do last, as the older vintages show. They have a good following among many traditional English wine merchants and it is easy to see why.

Château Sociando-Mallet
Cru Grand Bourgeois. Owner: **Jean Gautreau. 30ha. 18,500 cases. CS 60%, Mer 30%, CF 10%.** Second label: **Château Lartigue-de-Brochon.**
The aim here is to produce very traditional Médocs. There is long vatting, for maximum extraction of colour and tannins, and maturing in casks, of which between a third and half are new – a very high proportion for a Cru Bourgeois. When young the wines are very taut and marked by new wood – at a stage when other wines are beginning to be drinkable. The '79 was like this in 1984. With patience the wines develop a fine flavour and character and during the 1980s they seem to have filled out and become much richer – '82, '83, '85 and '88 are especially impressive.

Château Soudars
Cru Bourgeois. Owner: **Eric Miailhe. 15ha. 10,000 cases. CS 60%, Mer 40%.**
Eric Miailhe cleared 2,500 tons of stones before planting his new vineyards here in 1973. The property is near to those owned by his father and grandfather – Verdignan and Coufran – but they were discouraged from using this land by the quantity of stones and boulders covering it. Miailhe's care and attention has produced

some very fine wines: the '82, '83, '85 and '86 are evidence enough
that this *cru* has a good future.

Château du Taillan
Cru Grand Bourgeois. Owner: **Henri-François Cruse. 20ha.
10,800 cases. Red: CS 54%, Mer 39%, CF 7%. White:
Château La Dame-Blanche. 6ha. 2,500 cases. Sauv 67%,
Col 33%.**
This property has belonged to the Cruses since 1896. The château
and the even older cellars are classified as historic monuments. The
wine is kept mostly in large wooden *foudres* of 80–170 hectolitres,
but 20 percent passes through new casks of the conventional size.

The aim here is to produce supple, easy-to-drink wines without
much tannin. The white wine, La Dame-Blanche, with its heavy
dose of Colombard, is rather different in character from the usual
Bordeaux Blanc, with much more obvious flowery fruit.

Chateau La Tour-Carnet
4e Cru Classé. Owner: **Mme Marie-Claire Pelegrin. 40ha.
18,000 cases. CS 33%, Mer 33%, CF 33%, PV 1%.**
Like so much else in St-Laurent, La Tour-Carnet was on its last legs
when Louis Lipschitz bought it in 1962. In the early days the
Ginestets gave technical assistance and sold the wine on an exclusive
basis. After Louis Lipschitz died his daughter and her husband
continued the work.

The wines are conscientiously made, and a third of the wood
used in making them is new. At their best they are vivid in colour,
very fruity and intense in flavour, but light. The '76 was attractive
but hardly of 4e Cru standing. I found the '80 austere and dry, with
a taste of iron – a disappointment for the year. Certainly a number
of unclassified wines are better than this.

Château Tour-du-Haut-Moulin
Cru Grand Bourgeois. Owner: **Laurent Poitou. 32ha.
12,000 cases. CS and CF 50%, Mer 45%, PV 5%.**
The vineyards of this *cru* lie beside those of Beaumont around the
village of Cussac, but the wines are very different. Laurent Poitou is
the fourth generation of his family to own this property, and he
makes fine traditional wines. They are aged in wood, of which 25

percent is new. The result is a wine of exceptional colour and rich in extract. Tannic and powerful but well-balanced, these wines have great character, and with ageing their very real breed emerges.

Château Tour-du-Mirail
Cru Bourgeois 1932. Owners: **Hélène & Danielle Vialard.**
18ha. 9,000 cases. CS 70%, Mer 25%, PV 5%.
This property has belonged to the daughters of Louis Vialard of neighbouring Château Cissac since 1970. Louis Vialard himself supervises the winemaking, but everything is quite separate from Cissac. Vinification is in stainless steel vats, and the wines are matured in cask. They have a lot of flavour and a well-projected and quite perfumed bouquet. At the same time they are fairly light in body and have a certain Cabernet Sauvignon 'edge'. Despite their firmness, I find these wines are at present more enjoyable when fairly young (five to seven years), before the fruit begins to fade. This is an honourable Cru Bourgeois, but at present lacks the style and charm of Cissac.

Château Verdignan
Cru Grand Bourgeois. Owner: **SC du Château.**
Administrator: **Jean Miailhe. 47ha. 30,000 cases. CS 55%,**
Mer 40%, CF 5%. Second label: **Château Plantey-de-la-**
Croix.
Coufran is the last château in the Haut-Médoc and this is the last but one – both are administered or owned by Jean Miailhe. Verdignan has an attractive château with a tall turret, easily visible from the road. When Jean Miailhe bought it in 1972 the reputation of Verdignan was not good. I remember wines of rather tough character during the 1960s. Now Jean's son Eric is in charge of the winemaking, as he is at Coufran. The wine is fermented in stainless steel and matured in cask, and as one would expect of a wine from St-Seurin, is solid and well-structured with a strong flavour, it also has lots of fruit, something that was lacking in the past.

Château de Villegeorge
Cru Bourgeois Supérieur Exceptionnel 1932. Owner:
Lucien Lurton. 12ha. 2,700 cases. Mer 60%, CS 30%,
CF 10%.

Villegeorge has long enjoyed a good reputation. It was one of only six Crus Bourgeois classified as *Exceptionnel* in 1932, and was again classified as *Exceptionnel* in 1966. However, Lucien Lurton took it out of the Syndicat after he bought it in 1973, so it did not feature in their 1978 classification. The soil here is extremely gravelly, resembling that of Margaux, and has been largely abandoned by *vignerons* in recent years, becoming prey to gravel merchants, so the countryside is now scarred with water-filled pits. Lucien Lurton is now engaged in a battle to prevent further spoiling of his land.

The fermentation is in stainless steel, and the wine is matured in cask with 25 percent new wood used. The vineyard here is particularly prone to frost damage which often causes low and irregular yields. The high proportion of Merlot is most unusual in the Médoc. The wines of Villegeorge have always been deep-coloured, with a very strong character, and they remain so under Lucien Lurton with the difference being that they are now rather more polished and less rustic than they sometimes were. Excellent wines were made in '79, '81, '82 and '83.

Médoc AC

The fortunes of this area have revived considerably in recent years. Between 1972 and 1988 the area under vine more than doubled to 3,709 hectares. Wine is now produced in 16 communes, of which the most important are Bégadan (by far the largest), St Yzans, Prignac, Ordonnac, St-Christoly, Blaignan and St-Germain-d'Esteuil.

Because of the heavier soils, even where there are good outcrops of gravel, more Merlot is found here than in the Haut-Médoc and there is therefore a lower proportion of Cabernet Sauvignon. The wines are pleasantly perfumed, especially when young, and develop quite a lot of finesse in bottle. They are mostly light in body but well flavoured. There are plenty of good Crus Bourgeois – nine were designated as Grands Bourgeois in 1978.

Cave Coopérative Bellevue
Owner: **Société Coopérative de Vinification d'Ordonnac. 225ha. 100,000 cases. Mer 50%, CS 45%, CF 5%.**

The cooperative at Ordonnac was founded in 1936 and has 75 members drawn from this commune and the neighbouring one of St-Germain d'Esteuil. The following individual *crus* are vinified here: Château de Brie, Château Belfort, Château Lagorce, Château Moulin-de-Buscateau, Château Moulin-de-la-Rivière, Château l'Oume-de-Pey, Château La Rose-Picot, Domaine du Grand-Bois and Château Les Graves. The coop is also a member of Uni-Médoc, the association of *caves coopératives* of Médoc, and supplies much wine in bulk for *négociants'* own brands as well as under its own marque of Pavillon de Bellevue. This is good, dependable Médoc.

Château de By
Cru Bourgeois. Owner: **J-C Baudon. 10ha. 4,500 cases. Mer 40%, CS 30%, PV 20%, CF 10%.**
Located on the ridge of By, between Bégadan and the Gironde, this *cru* is unusual in that a high percentage of Petit Verdot is grown, giving de By's wines a distinctive vivid colour. The proprietor, Monsieur Baudon, also believes in chaptalising as little as possible – another unusual factor – which lends the wines a refreshingly natural, crisp character. These are wines which develop quickly and are full of Médoc style, with finesse and plenty of individuality.

Château La Cardonne
Cru Grand Bourgeois. Owner: **Guy Charloux. 85ha. 35,000 cases. CS 72%, Mer 23%, CF and PV 5%.**
This large property, the most important in Blaignan, was acquired by Domaines Rothschild in 1973, since when the vineyard has been considerably expanded, the existing buildings restored and the equipment replaced. The vineyard is very well placed on the highest plateau of the region. The wines do not see wood at all, being entirely matured in vat prior to bottling. In 1990 the Rothschilds sold to the present owner, but they continue to manage the estate and sell the wine.

I have found the wines deep-coloured, very perfumed, very fruity, frank and fresh. This is archetypal Médoc, straightforward and easy to enjoy young. It has moved up a gear in recent years and now has more fruit and succulence, this is especially noticeable from the '88 vintage onwards.

Château Castéra
Cru Bourgeois. Owner: **Alexis Lichine & Co. 45ha. 15,000 cases. CS and CF 60%, Mer 40%.**
This is one of the principal *crus* of St-Germain-d'Esteuil. It is an old property which has links with the Black Prince, who beseiged the original château. Since 1973 it has belonged to Alexis Lichine & Co, the important Bordeaux *négociants* (now a subsidiary of Pernod-Ricard), who have enlarged the vineyard and modernized the *chai*. This is a good, solid, enjoyable Médoc, developing a mellow, fruity character, full and soft when quite young. Can be enjoyed from three years onwards.

Château La Clare
Cru Bourgeois. Owner: **Paul de Rozières. 20ha. 10,000 cases. CS 57%, Mer 36%, CF 7%.** Second labels: **Châteaux Laveline and du Gentilhomme.**
Situated on the ridge of By, 50 percent of La Clare's vineyards have been replanted by the present owners over the last 20 years. These are mostly mechanically harvested, but the older vines – some over 60 years old – are hand-picked. The Rozières, owners since 1969, originally came from Tunisia and have used their experience as vineyard owners there to advantage, producing the excellent vintages of '71, '73, '82, '83, '85 and '86, all of which are attractive and well made with spiciness, opulence and plummy fruit.

Cuvée de la Commanderie du Bontemps
The word *cuvée* here means a quantity of different wines blended together in a vat (*cuve*). The origin of this particular *cuvée* was that each member of the Bontemps used to donate one cask of its production and these were then assembled to make the *cuvée*. This meant that it was composed of wines from all over the Médoc and Haut-Médoc including both Crus Classés and Crus Bourgeois. Then, with the introduction of compulsory château-bottling for the Crus Classés in 1972, this was no longer possible, and it was eventually decided to set up the *commission de dégustation* to control, by means of both analyses and tasting, the selection of wines for a Cuvée du Bontemps. They appointed Jean-Paul Gardère to prepare the *cuvée*. He is not only a *courtier* of long standing and impeccable reputation, but was also from 1965 to 1987 the manager of Château

Latour. The Cuvée du Bontemps is commercialized through a house called Ulysses Cazabonne, once belonging to Monsieur Gardère but now owned by Allied-Lyons.

The wines of this *cuvée* are as one would expect, classic Médoc, with real depth of flavour and beautifully-balanced fruit and tannin. The component parts actually all come from the Haut-Médoc. A *cuvée* is not produced every year but only when it is considered that one of sufficient quality can be made. Recent vintages have been '78, '79, '81, '82, '83 and '85. All are fine examples of their respective years.

Château Greysac
Cru Grand Bourgeois. Owner: **Domaines Codem.** Administrator: **Philippe Dambrine. 60ha. 35,000 cases. CS and CF 60%, Mer 38%, PV 2%.**
Since the late Baron François de Gunzburg bought this château in 1973 its importance has increased considerably. Fermentation is in stainless steel *cuves* and the wine is aged in cask.

I have found the wines to have an expansive and almost opulent fruit flavour, with a rather overripe style in the best vintages. They can be drunk with great pleasure when three to four years old.

Château Laujac
Cru Grand Bourgeois. Owner: **Madame H Cruse. 30ha. 12,500 cases.**
A widely-known château belonging to the Cruse family, Laujac is situated on the Médoc's central plateau. It is a large property and used to produce much more wine, of higher repute than is now the case. These are lacking in much of their neighbours' character.

Château Livran
Cru Bourgeois. Owner: **Robert Godfin. 50ha. 20,000 cases. Mer 50%, CS 25%, CF 25%.** Second label: **Château La Rose-Goromey.**
Once owned by the de Goth family – one of whom became Pope Clement V in 1305 – this château's history is as impressive as its appearance. It was also owned by a London wine merchant – James Denman – until the Second World War. The present proprietor is its former manager. Pleasant well-made wines are produced.

Château Loudenne
Cru Grand Bourgeois. Owner: **W & A Gilbey Ltd. 50ha. Red: 15,000 cases; CS 53%, Mer 40%, CF 7%. White: 5,000 cases; Sauv 50%, Sém 50%.**
The wines of Loudenne tend to be lighter in colour, but with more perfume and finesse than most wines of the Médoc AC. There is a real elegance about them which becomes more noticeable as the wines mature in bottle.

The excellent white wine is fermented in stainless steel at between 17° and 20°C. It is delicious, perfumed and elegant soon after bottling in the spring, but the Sémillon lends the potential for ageing as well.

Château de Monthil
Cru Bourgeois. Owner: **Les Domaines Codem. 20ha. 8,000 cases. CS 30%, CF 30%, Mer 30%, Mal 5%, PV 5%.**
Les Domaines Codem also own Châteaux Greysac, Bégadan and Les Bertins in the same commune. Prior to their buying this property in 1986, the traditionally made wines were mostly sold to good restaurants within France. Now they are exported too, and with their fine reputation – placed fifth in Gault-Millau's 1982 tasting of Crus Bourgeois – they ought to do very well. Certainly a wine to look out for.

Château Les Ormes-Sorbet
Cru Grand Bourgeois. Owner: **Jean Boivert. 20ha. 10,000 cases. CS 65%, Mer 35%.**
The wines here are nicely perfumed and elegant, with a strong, assertive Cabernet flavour and plenty of structure. Like many wines in the Bas-Médoc, they have lots of flavour but not a lot of body. A classic '78 was produced and very good wines were made in '79, '81, '82 and '83 with more *goût de terroir* and body than usual.

Until 1985 about half the crop was sold to Schröder & Schÿler in bulk for their own bottling, the rest château-bottled. This is an excellent example of what the Bas-Médoc can do with care and dedication.

Château Patache-d'Aux
Cru Grand Bourgeois. Owner: **SC du Château.**

Administrator: **Claude Lapalu. 44ha. 28,300 cases. CS 68%, Mer 20%, CF 7%, PV 5%.**
This *cru* has had a good reputation for many years and belonged to the Delon family (*see* Léoville-Las-Cases and Potensac) until Claude Lapalu bought it in 1964. The actual château now belongs to the municipality. The fermentation is partly still in wooden *cuves* and partly in concrete and stainless steel vats, but all the wine is matured in cask.

The wines are finely perfumed, with clear overtones of violets and Cabernet, finely flavoured, fruity and supple, quite light in body but with a good backbone.

Château Plagnac
Cru Bourgeois. Owner: **Domaines Cordier. 30ha. 15,000 cases. CS 60%, Mer 40%.**
The present owners acquired this property in Bégadan in 1972 and have brought about many changes and improvements since then: the vineyards have been adapted for mechanical harvesting, stainless steel vats bought in for fermentation, and wooden casks for maturation. This progress is reflected by the emergence of some very impressive wines; the '81 and '82 were good, followed by the extremely attractive '84, '85 and '86.

Château Potensac
Cru Grand Bourgeois. Owner: **Mme Paul Delon.**
Administator: **Michel Delon. 50ha. 20,000 cases. CS 60%, Mer 25%, CF 15%.** Second labels: **Châteaux Gallais-Bellevue and Lassalle.**
There is a good gravelly outcrop at Potensac lying between St-Yzans and St-Germain-d'Esteuil, where the Delon family (*see* Léoville-Las-Cases) own three vineyards. Good wines have been made here for years, but in the last decade, under Michel Delon's management, they seem to have gone from strength to strength. The biggest vineyard is Potensac itself, then come Lassalle and Gallais-Bellevue, and the three are effectively run together. The *cuvier* has been re-equipped with stainless steel *cuves*, and the wines enjoy a long, slow fermentation, followed by ageing in casks of which 20 percent are new each year – with a further proportion from Léoville-Las-Cases.

The wines are characterized by their depth of colour and a nose full of vigour, very typical of the Médoc, often with spicy or floral overtones. They have a concentrated, complex and powerful flavour, and a rather angular structure. Usually five or six years are needed before these wines are at their best for drinking, and they last very well. '76 is an exceptional wine and '78 and '79 were also very good. '80 is good in its class and '81, '82, '83, '85, '86, '88 and '89 are also fine. This is certainly one of the best wines being made today in the Médoc AC.

Château Preuillac
Cru Bourgeois. Owner: **Raymond Bonet. 30ha. 16,500 cases. Mer 50%, CS 45%, CF 5%.**
Lesparre's most important *cru*, Preuillac is one of the best-kept properties in its commune. Vinification is still carried out using traditional methods, and due to the high proportion of Merlot involved the wines tend to be quite full-bodied. '82 was an especially good vintage here.

Château St-Bonnet
Cru Bourgeois 1978. Owner: **Michel Solivères. 35ha. 18,000 cases. CS 50%, Mer 50%.**
Some excellent wines are made in St-Christoly, and this is one of the most important *crus* there. It is a very traditional Médoc with a marked character. The wines are deep in colour with a distinctively spicy bouquet and a robust, powerful flavour where tannin and fruit are well balanced. There is a distinct *goût de terroir* which is arresting but attractive.

Cave Coopérative St-Jean
President: **René Chaumont. 567ha. 300,000 cases. Mer 50%, CS 24%, CF 24%, PV 2%.**
The Cave St-Jean, also referred to as the Cave Coopérative de Bégadan, is by far the largest cooperative in the Médoc AC. Its 170 members come not only from this commune but also from the neighbouring ones of Valeyrac and Civrac. It is also a member of Uni-Médoc, a group of four cooperatives which store and mature the wines of the region. The external buildings have a capacity of more than 60,000 hectolitres. The following châteaux vinify their

wines separately at the *cave*: Meilhan, Breuil-Renaissance, Le Barrail, Labadie, Pey-de-By, Lassus, Le Bernet, Le Monge, Bégadanet, Vimenay, Rose-du-Pont, Haut-Condisas.

The produce of this cooperative has a good reputation. Much of it is supplied to *négociants* for their own generic blends. These wines are characteristic and attractive Médocs.

Cave Coopérative St-Roch
Owner: **Societé Coopérative de Vinification de Queyrac. 125ha. 50,000 cases.**
This cooperative was founded in 1939 and now has 165 members, drawn from the communes of Queyrac, Gaillan, Jau-Dignac-et-Loirac, Vensac, Valeyrac and Vendays. Three individual *crus* are vinified here: Château Laubespin, Château Les Trois-Tétons and Château Pessange. The cooperative is a member of the Uni-Médoc, and, apart from its own marque of St-Roch, much of the wine is sold in bulk to *négociants* for their own blends, contributing to the good overall standard of generic Médoc.

Château St-Saturnin
Cru Bourgeois. Owner: **Adrien Tramier. 21ha. 10,000 cases. Mer 50%, CS 30%, CF 15%, PV 5%.**
Situated just outside Bégadan, St-Saturnin produces light, attractive wines that are suitable for drinking young. They see no wood during maturation but are nevertheless perfumed and fruity.

Cave Coopérative de St-Yzans-de-Médoc
Owner: **Société Coopérative. 200ha. 100,000 cases. Mer 55%, CS and CF 45%.**
The cooperative of St-Yzans has 120 members and was founded in 1934. The wines are sold under the name of St-Brice or in bulk to *négociants* for their own marques. The *cave* has a good reputation for making fine typical Médocs. Apart from those in St-Yzans itself, St-Brice also has members in Blaignan, Couquèques and St-Christoly. Two châteaux, Taffard and Tour-St-Vincent, vinify their grapes here.

Château Sestignan
Cru Bourgeois. Owner: **Bertrand de Rozières. 8·5ha. 5,000**

cases. CS 76%, Mer 22%, Mal 2%.
On the edge of the Bas-Médoc region, this château is surrounded by
alluvial *palus* and drainage ditches. Like Château de Monthil it rated
well in Gault-Millau's 1982 tasting of Crus Bourgeois, and was
placed fourth. It is therefore a *cru* to look out for; the '85 and '86 are
both excellent vintages.

Château Sigognac
Cru Grand Bourgeois. Owner: **SC Fermière.** Administrator:
**Mme Colette Bonny-Grasset. 44ha. 20,000 cases. CS 34%,
CF 33%, Mer 33%.**
A Roman villa once stood on this site, and some of the pottery
found here may be seen at the *mairie* (town hall) at St-Yzans. This
vineyard had been reduced to only four hectares of vines when Paul
Grasset bought it in 1964. It was then transformed, first by him and
then, after his death in 1968, by his wife, now married to M Bonny.
The fermentation is in concrete vats, and the wine is matured partly
in vat and partly in cask. The wine has a good colour and is full and
soft on the nose, with pleasant fruit and tannin on the palate, elegant
rather than powerful. If it lacks the finesse of its more illustrious
neighbour, Château Loudenne, it is nevertheless a very pleasant,
honourable Médoc of a good general standard.

Château Le Tertre-Caussan
Cru Bourgeois. Owner: **Guy Caussan. 11ha. 6,500 cases.
Mer 55%, CS 40%, CF 5%.**
Le Tertre-Caussan is in the village of Caussan itself and produces
attractive wines which have shown improvements through the
1980s. '82 and '85 are especially good vintages.

Château La Tour-de-By
Cru Grand Bourgeois. Owner: **SC (Cailloux, Lapalu,
Pagès).** Administrator: **Marc Pagès. 73ha. 46,000 cases. CS
58%, Mer 36%, CF 5%, PV 1%.** Second labels: **Châteaux La
Roque-de-By and Moulin-de-la-Roque.**
This fine *cru* is situated on one of the highest and very best gravelly
ridges in the whole of the Bas-Médoc. There is a very attractive
château, and parts of the other buildings are even older and also
very pleasing. The tower stands on high ground near the château,

and is actually an old lighthouse. Since buying the property in 1965, Marc Pagès and his partners have made many improvements. They have expanded the *chai* and put in some stainless steel, although the old wooden *cuves* are also retained. The wine is matured in cask with a small percentage of new oak. It is deeply coloured and finely scented, and the lively, sappy fruit is often reminiscent of violets. The flavour is very harmonious and attractive; it is also powerful, with real depth, and quite tannic. Other marked characteristics are elegance and length of flavour. This château certainly has a good claim to be considered as the finest wine of the Médoc *appellation*.

Château La Tour-Haut-Caussan
Cru Bourgeois. Owner: **Philippe Courrian. 10·5ha. 6,000 cases. CS 50%, Mer and Mal 50%.**
A windmill dating from 1734 stands on this property in Blaignan and is evidence of the polyculture that held sway before the 19th century in this part of the Médoc. The current owner comes from a family of true Médocains, whose history here is traceable back to 1615. He believes in traditional methods of viticulture, and vinification is carried out with the utmost care, using high temperatures for the fermentation of his Merlots and lower temperatures for the Cabernets. The wines are then blended and matured in oak, 25 percent of which is new. The results have been successful and won many awards, they are in high demand from good French restaurants, but are widely distributed in France and on the export markets.

Château La Tour-St-Bonnet
Cru Bourgeois. Owner: **Pierre Lafon. 41ha. 20,000 cases. Mer 50%, CS 28%, CF 22%.** Second label: **Château La–Fuie-St-Bonnet.**
This is the largest and probably the best known *cru* in St-Christoly. The vineyard is splendidly placed on the best gravelly ridges of the commune, with its distinctive tower among the vines. The wines, very typical of the Médoc, are highly coloured, vigorous and powerful. They require some ageing to show of their best.

Château La Valière
Cru Bourgeois. Owner: **Cailloux family. 15ha. 7,500 cases. CS 74%, Mer 25%, PV 1%.**
Situated on the famous gravelly ridges of St-Christoly, this château is one of the best in its commune, producing charmingly fruity wines with good solidity. The '79, '84 and '85 are the most successful of its recent vintages.

Vieux Château Landon
Cru Bourgeois. Owner: **Philippe Gillet. 35ha. 16,500 cases. CS 70%, Mer 25%, Mal 5%.**
This property has been in the same family for several generations. The present owner married his predecessor's daughter. It is one of a number of excellent *crus* in the commune of Bégadan and produces attractive wines with lots of fruit and plenty of Médocain character.

Cave Coopérative du Vieux-Clocher
Owner: **Uni-Médoc. 1,200ha.**
This is the newest of the Médoc cooperatives and is situated at Gaillan, two kilometres north of Lesparre. Founded in 1979, it is a grouping of the cooperatives of Bégadan, Ordonnac, Prignac and Queyrac, as well as amalgamating the old cooperatives of Prignac and Gaillan. The aim is to hold a maturing stock of around 2 million bottles. The wines are commercialized through the Union des Caves Coopératives Vinicoles Sovicop-Producta. The brand name is Préstige-Médoc. A good standard is maintained.

Caves Les Vieux Colombiers
Owner: **Uni-Médoc. 110,000 cases.**
This large cooperative is located in Prignac and collects the produce of 200 members in this commune and also those of Lesparre and St-Germain-d'Esteuil. It also produces two independent *crus* which are vinified separately: Château de Beusse and Château Lafon.

Graves

It is not easy to get to grips with this disparate region. Geographically, it is a continuation of the Médoc, but in the north many vineyards have disappeared beneath Bordeaux's urban sprawl, and further south one can travel for miles and see nothing but trees and believe one is already in Les Landes. This used to be a region of many mediocre whites and a few aristocratic reds, but this picture has changed significantly in the past 20 years. The changing pattern can be gauged to an extent from the following table comparing production figures for 1970 and 1989.

	1970	1989	Increase
Graves Rouge	40,958 hl	143,167 hl	+ 250%
Graves Blanc	10,095 hl	56,486 hl ⎫	
Graves Supérieures	45,558 hl	17,356 hl ⎭	+ 33%

This demonstrates the two important trends: from white to red, and from alcoholic whites (12 percent alcohol by volume minimum, plus some residual sugar) to dryer, lighter (11 percent) ones. The term Graves Supérieures here refers purely to the higher alcohol level, such wines usually have some residual sugar as well. The table also shows the revival in the district as a whole, with total production up 125 percent when these two large vintages 19 years apart are compared. Over a similar period, the areas under vine have developed as follows:

	1970	1988	Increase
Graves Rouge	1,172 ha	2,304 ha	+ 97%
Graves Blanc	1,486 ha	1,304 ha	− 12%
	2,658 ha	3,608 ha	

This shows that the expansion of the red vineyards has been only partly at the expense of the whites; yet, in spite of this, as we have seen already, white as well as red wine production has increased. Clearly new vineyards and better husbandry have brought much higher yields. The 1982 edition of Cocks & Féret's *Bordeaux et ses Vins* monitors the decline of the vineyards which have been caught up in the expansion of the town of Bordeaux. In the four

The Graves Region

Areas covered by the
appellations of Graves,
Cérons and Sauternes and
Barsac, showing the main
wine-producing
communes.

communes most affected, Gradignan, Mérignac, Pessac and Talence, there were 119 winemaking properties in 1908; by 1981 there were only nine. In the whole of Graves in 1981 there were 33 communes where some declarations under the Graves AC were being made (in several others entitled to the *appellation*, only Bordeaux or Bordeaux Supérieur was declared). Most of the wines are actually being made in eight communes: Léognan and Martillac in the north; Portets, Illats, Cérons, St-Pierre-de-Mons, Langon and Landiras in the south. Of these, Illats and Cérons produce both Cérons and Graves, though it seems that 80 percent of the white wines made in these communes are now declared as Graves, as are the reds, and the proportion is almost certainly rising.

There are plenty of hopeful signs that the region is beginning to come out of its long decline. There is the general improvement in the quality of dry white Graves through the use of cold-fermentation methods. The gospel preached by Professor Peynaud in the 1960s has been put into practice by men like André Lurton and Pierre Coste. André Lurton has reclaimed large tracts of abandoned vineyards in the best parts of the northern Graves. Pierre Coste has made many delicious and very inexpensive white and red wines in the southern Graves. And Peter Vinding-Diers has shown what the whole gamut of modern technology, including yeast selection, can do to transform wines coming from quite modest sites in the southern Graves.

There are differing views as to the best *encépagement* for white wines. Traditionally the Sauvignon and the Sémillon are blended. The Sauvignon gives the initial fruit, on the nose especially, and acidity, while the Sémillon provides the possibility of bottle-ageing, its bouquet gradually taking over as the Sauvignon begins to fade after one to two years in bottle. Sémillon also gives the wine body. However, in the search for freshness and fruit for early drinking, some properties have abandoned the Sémillon entirely. Such wines tend to lose their charm rather quickly and my impression is that many growers are now realizing that this grape has a role to play in giving balance.

The list of red wine available ranges from some of the greatest wines in Gironde (Haut-Brion, La Mission-Haut-Brion, Domaine de Chevalier, Haut-Bailly and Pape-Clément) to a host of very modestly priced and deliciously vivid wines of individuality. All have the Cabernet Sauvignon as their major grape variety, assisted by the Merlot and the Cabernet Franc.

It is taking time to bring the wine-drinker back to an appreciation of white Graves, so poor has its image been. But, as more and more fine wines come onto the market at very reasonable prices, their following is bound to grow. For the red wines, the special charm of those based on Cabernet, which are quite distinct in character from their Médocain cousins, is bound to win them more friends as they become more widely available.

On the quality front, the growers in the north have now won the right to the new *appellation* Pessac-Léognan, which came into force in 1987, with the 1986 vintage the first to bear the new title. It covers the communes of Cadaujac, Canéjean, Gradignan, Léognan, Martillac, Mérignac, St-Médard-d'Eyrans, Talence and Villenave-d'Ornon. André Lurton, who has done so much to revive the vineyards of this area, was the driving force behind this new *appellation*.

So the prospects of Graves taking a larger share of Bordeaux's prosperity in the future look bright. The worldwide demand for good dry white wines and the continuously growing market for middle-price red wines of quality must make Graves a happy hunting ground for wine-lovers.

Pessac-Léognan

Château Baret
Owners: **Héritiers A Ballande. Red: 7ha; 4,000 cases; CS 72%, Mer 25%, CF 3%. White: 6ha; 3,000 cases; Sém 65%, Sauv 32%, Musc 3%.**
Philippe Castéja has run this property since 1981, when he took over after the death of his father-in-law André Ballande. He commercializes the wines through the family's *négociant* house of Borie-Manoux. Although they have always had a very good reputation, there has been a marked improvement in vintages of recent years. The red wines are light but have depth and plenty of spicy fruit, the '83, '85 and '86 being especially attractive. The whites are stylish, classic wines, the '83, '84, '85, '86 and '87 all being good vintages.

Château Bouscaut
Cru Classé. Owner: **SA du Château Bouscaut (Lucien Lurton). Red: 39ha; 11,500 cases; Mer 48%, CS and CF 42%, Mal 10%. White: 7ha; 2,500 cases; Sém 56%, Sauv 44%.**

The only important *cru* in Cadaujac and the Graves Cru Classé closest to the Garonne. Between 1968 and 1980 an American syndicate led by Charles Wohlstetter rescued the property from neglect by installing up-to-date equipment and restoring the 18th-century château. During this period, Jean Delmas, *régisseur* of Haut-Brion, acted as *régisseur* here. In 1980 the Americans sold to Lucien Lurton, proprietor of Brane-Cantenac and Durfort-Vivens in Margaux as well as Climens in Barsac. The vineyards, which adjoin the Bordeaux-Toulouse road, are on gravelly ridges over lime-stone, perfect for natural drainage. Stainless steel vats are used for red and white wines, the latter fermented at 18–20°C (64–68°F). The reds are matured in casks of which a quarter are new, and the whites are also cask-aged, spending six months in wood.

I must confess to disappointment at the Bouscaut wines of recent vintages. The reds are relatively light in colour and body, supple and pleasant but lacking in personality or any real distinction, although there has been some improvement, notably with the '85. To put it in context, there are a number of Crus Bourgeois in the Médoc which make better wine.

The white wines often seem to lack breed and 'lift' or projection of flavour, though the '83 marked an improvement, and '85 and '88 were even better. It will be interesting to see if Lucien Lurton's flair can improve matters further.

Château Brown
Owner: **Jean-Claude Bonnel. 11ha. 3,750 cases. CS 60%, Mer 40%.**

This property takes its name from the family who owned Cantenac-Brown in the middle of the last century. Its vineyards are well situated on two gravel ridges in the commune of Léognan and most of them were replaced when the property was bought by André Bonnel in 1939. The wines are delicious, with plenty of spiciness and soft fruit, some have a definite tobacco aroma.

Château Carbonnieux
Cru Classé. Owner: **Société des Grandes Graves.**
Administrator: **Antony Perrin. Red: 50ha; 16,600 cases; CS
60%, Mer 30%, CF 7%, Mal 2%, PV 1%. White: 40ha.
15,000 cases; Sauv 60%, Sém 38%, Musc 2%.**
This famous old property first had vineyards in the 12th century,
and winemaking was revived by the Benedictine monks who took
over in 1741. Marc Perrin bought and restored it in 1956, and his
son now administers the estate. The white wine is fermented in
stainless steel and used to see no wood at all, but recently has been
put in new oak for about three months. The reds are matured in
cask, of which a quarter are new oak.

The more famous white Carbonnieux comes from the largest
vineyard of the Graves Crus Classés. The high proportion of
Sauvignon and early bottling mean that it is delicious when very
young (nine to 18 months), then often goes through a dull stage as
the primal Sauvignon fruit fades, only to emerge again as the
Sémillon begins to mature and flower (after about two and a half
years). In recent years this has been a most consistent wine, the best
of the Crus Classés available in commercial quantities.

The red wine has been rather rustic, and certainly not among the
top classified Graves, but determined efforts have been made in
recent vintages to improve the quality. The '80 is an attractive
example of its year and the '81, '82 and '83 are all good too, with the
'81 especially so in the context of the vintage.

Château Les Carmes–Haut–Brion
Owners: **Chantecaille family.** Administrator: **Philippe
Chantecaille. 3·5ha. 1,500 cases. Mer 50%, CF 40%,
CS 10%.**
The unusual combination of grape varieties grown at this property
yields wines that are concentrated with deep colour and tannin but
that are rather coarse. This may be due to the low percentage of
Cabernet Sauvignon in the blend.

Domaine de Chevalier
Cru Classé. Owner: **SC du Château.** Administrators: **Claude
Ricard & Olivier Bernard. Red: 15ha; 5,000 cases; CS 65%,**

Mer 30%, CF 5%. White: 3ha; 800 cases; Sauv 70%, Sém 30%.

From 1865 to 1983 Chevalier was the property of the Ricard family, and Claude Ricard owned it from 1948. He has been obliged to sell but the new owners, the Bernard family, have contracted him to manage the *cru* for a further five years and pass on his vast experience to Olivier Bernard, the member of the family deputed to look after the property. Here they ferment the red wine at a slightly higher temperature than is fashionable, 32°C (90°F), to facilitate the maximum tannin extraction from the grape skins. For the maturation in cask 50 percent new oak is used. The white wine fermentation takes place entirely in cask at a low temperature, it is then matured in oak (a small proportion of which is new) for 18 months – a traditional practice that was for a time abandoned elsewhere in Graves, but has now been revived.

The results of this meticulous winemaking are exceptional wines. The reds are deep in colour. The bouquet takes time to open out and is then complex, with overtones of tobacco, while the flavour is compact and well structured with great breed, power and length of flavour. This wine in some years can approach the quality of Haut-Brion and La Mission. It is also a slow-developer. '76 and '80 were charming examples of their years while outstanding wines were made in '78, '79, '81, '82, '83, '85, '86, '88 and '89.

The white wine has a different style from that of Laville or Haut-Brion, perhaps because of its cask-ageing. It is perfumed, firm and compact of flavour and only slowly opens out after six to eight years. It has extraordinary delicacy and finesse, and can improve and last for 15 to 20 years.

Château Couhins
Cru Classé. Owner: **Institut National de la Recherche Agronomique. Red: 7·5ha; 3,300 cases; CS 45%, Mer 34%, CF 18%, PV 3%. White: 2·4ha; 1,000 cases; Sauv 82%, Sém 18%.**

A curious situation exists at Couhins, which is now divided between the National Agricultural Research Institute (INRA), which owns the main part, and André Lurton, who has a smaller section (*see* Couhins-Lurton). For many years the Gasqueton and Hanappier families were owners and produced only white wines (this is the only property in Graves where only the white wine is classified). Then the INRA bought the property in 1968. It lies on an elevated site in Villenave-d'Ornon, with vineyards near the Garonne. This is a modern, low-temperature fermentation wine, and is fresh and elegant in style. Unfortunately, with the division of the property and the production of unclassified red wine, the small quantities available mean that this wine is hard to find.

Château Couhins-Lurton
Cru Classé. Owner: **André Lurton. White: 6ha; 2,000 cases; Sauv 100%.**
André Lurton began as *fermier* here in 1967, just before the INRA bought out Gasqueton-Hanappier, and made the wine for the whole of Couhins during most of the 1970s. The INRA then took a major part of the property into their own control and André Lurton was able to buy this part. The gravelly soil here has traces of clay in the subsoil and this gives body to the wine. Unlike the INRA part, which is classically planted with both Sémillon and Sauvignon, this vineyard is 100 percent Sauvignon. The fermentation takes place in new casks (since 1982) at 16–18°C (61–64°F), followed by ten months' ageing before bottling. The '82 was very attractive with real length of flavour and beautiful fruit when three years old. I would expect this wine to be at its most attractive at between two and four years due to the Sauvignon. There are now plans to plant Cabernet Sauvignon and Merlot to produce red wines, and the white vineyard, already extended from 1·5 hectares to 6 hectares, will be further extended.

Château du Cruzeau
Owner: **André Lurton. Red: 36ha; 15,000 cases; CS 60%, Mer 40%. White: 11ha; 3,500 cases; Sauv 90%, Sém 10%.**
Another outpost of André Lurton's viticultural empire, this is the most important *cru* in the commune of St-Médard-d'Eyrans and lies on the borders of this commune and Martillac. The property was acquired by André Lurton in 1973 and entirely replanted by 1974. The vineyard is on deep gravel. Harvesting of the red grapes is by machine, while the white are hand-picked. The red wine is vinified in lined cement tanks and stainless steel vats at 28–30°C (82–86°F) and then matured for a year in casks of which a third are new.

The white is vinified in stainless steel and glass-lined steel vats at 16–18°C (61–64°F) and sees no new wood before bottling.

The red wine is scented, full-bodied, fruited and supple, with the capacity for ageing while at the same time being pleasant to drink after about three or four years. The white has a subtle aroma of spring blossoms allied to a pleasant fruitiness of flavour. The '83 showed this to be a wine of considerable class and potential, and certainly worth looking out for.

Château Ferran
Owner: **Hervé Béraud-Sadreau. Red: 5ha; 1,650 cases; Mer 80%, CS 10%, CF 10%. White: 5·5ha; 2,000 cases; Sém 80%, Sauv 20%.**
This property takes its name from a member of the *Parlement de Bordeaux* – Robert de Ferrand – who was proprietor during the 17th century. In 1715 it changed hands and was run by the philosopher Montesquieu. Both the red and white wines produced here are long-lived and need time for their sound fruit characteristics to develop.

Château de Fieuzal
Cru Classé. Owner: **SA Château de Fieuzal.** Administrator: **Gérard Gribelin. 23ha. Red: 8,000 cases; CS 60%, Mer 30%, PV 5% and Mal 5%. White: 600 cases; Sauv 50%, Sém 50%.**
In 1945 a Swede, Erik Bocké, took over this property, then in a ruinous condition, and lovingly restored it. In 1974 the present proprietor took over and has continued developments in the same vein.

The red wines are fermented in lined steel vats equipped with an electronic temperature-control system, and are then matured in casks, of which 50 percent are new. They are well made, on the light side, but with elegance and a very marked and vivid fruity character. Since the '85 vintage there has been a marked filling-out, and recent wines show an extra dimension of concentration and depth of flavour that now puts them in contention with those of the leading *crus*, such as Haut-Bailly and Chevalier. The Graves character is there, but is not too obtrusive. The reputation of this wine has grown steadily in recent years. The change in the white wine has been even more dramatic. From 1985 onwards, the wines have been barrel-fermented under the supervision of Denis Dubordieu, the new white wine guru. They have become intensely scented and quite rich, and are now fetching some of the highest prices in Graves.

Château de France
Owner: **Bernard Thomassin. Red: 26ha; 13,000 cases; CS 50%, Mer 50%. White: 4ha; Sauv 50%, Sém 30%, Musc 20%.**
Situated just south of Léognan, this property was replanted and refurbished by Bernard Thomassin, who bought it in 1971. The white wine vineyards are still not mature but the reds are developing well, producing good vintages in '83 and '85. Certainly a property worth watching.

Château La Garde
Owner: **Maison Dourthe. Red: 41ha, 20,000 cases; CS 70%, Mer 30%. White: 6ha; 3,000 cases; Sauv 100%.**
After belonging to Louis Eschenauer since 1926, this *cru* was sold to Dourthe in 1990. A substantial programme of development has been undertaken here in recent years. Not only has the red wine vineyard been expanded, but an elegant pure Sauvignon white wine has now been introduced. The red wine is soft and rather light-textured but with plenty of flavour.

Château Haut-Bailly
Cru Classé. Owner: **SCI Sanders.** Administrator: **Jean Sanders. Red: 28ha; 12,000 cases; CS 60%, Mer 30%, CF 10%.** Second label: **La Parde de Haut-Bailly.**
Today Haut-Bailly is regarded as one of the best red Graves properties, just behind Chevalier, and on a level with Pape-Clément. The soil is abundant in gravel and pebbles, which are mixed with sand and clay.

The wine tends to be lighter in colour and texture than the other leading red Graves, but the great feature is its harmony. It has both richness and vinosity, reminiscent of La Mission but with less tannin and power; the bouquet is strikingly similar to Pape-Clément. Thus the wines often develop quickly at first, yet keep very well. The '78 is good but not up to top form owing to problems at the end of Daniel Sanders' administration, and this affected all the vintages after 1970 to a greater or lesser extent. A pleasant early-drinking '80 was made and there were great successes in '79, '81, '82, '83 and '85. Exceptionally concentrated wines were made in '86.

Château Haut-Bergey
Owner: **J Deschamps. 16ha. 7,000 cases. CS 70%, Mer 30%.**
The vineyards of Haut-Bergey are well situated near the commune of Léognan. They produce pleasant wines which have a very good reputation; they are aged in oak, a proportion of which is new.

Château Haut-Brion
1e Cru Classé 1855. Owner: **Domaine Clarence Dillon. Red: 43ha; 17,000 cases; CS 50%, Mer 35%, CF 15%. White: 3ha; 800 cases; Sém 55%, Sauv 45%.** Second label: **Château Bahans.**
Haut-Brion is the only wine outside the Médoc to feature in the 1855 classification of red wines. In 1935 it was acquired by Clarence Dillon, the American banker. Since 1979, Clarence Dillon's granddaughter Joan, the Duchesse de Mouchy, has been president of the company, with her husband as director-general. The much-respected Jean Delmas succeeded his father as *régisseur* in 1961. In 1960 this was the first of the great *crus* to install stainless steel fermentation vats.

The essence of the Haut-Brion style today can be summarized as elegance and harmony. The tannin, new oak (100 percent each year) and fruit seem to be in balance after the first few months. This can give the wine the appearance of being ready to drink very early. I remember my disbelief at the forwardness of the '75 in '79. But, while this wine is more forward and more enjoyable than most leading wines of '75, there is also no doubting its ability to age well. Of the '78 I have tasted some superb bottles but also some disappointing ones. It is hard to fathom the inconsistency. The great successes here in recent vintages are '75, '76, '79, '80, '81, '82, '83, '85, '86, '88, '89 and '90.

The very small quantity of white wine produced makes it a rarity, and most of it seems to go to the USA. It appears to show its charm more quickly than the Laville, though the wine seems to go through a period of change while ageing, as shown by the '78 and '79, neither of which showed well in May 1985 when the '76 was superb. The '83 was full of charm at this time, only a few months after bottling.

Château Larrivet-Haut-Brion
Owner: **Gerverson family.** Administrator: **Philippe Gerverson. Red: 32ha; 7,600 cases: CS 55%, Mer 45%. White: 9ha; 400 cases; Sauv 50%, Sém 35%, Musc 15%.**
A famous old property in the central sector of Léognan, adjoining Haut-Bailly. It was once called Haut-Brion-Larrivet, until a lawsuit from Haut-Brion compelled a change. The Guillemaud family owned the property from 1941 until they sold to the present owners in 1988.

This is a classic Graves, with a fine colour and a spicy, delicate bouquet. The wines have both finesse and the ability to age well. Usually they are as good or better than some of the red Crus Classés. The white wine, of which very little is made, has not been of the same standard, but with fermentation in cask from 1987, here too better things can be expected.

Château Laville-Haut-Brion
Cru Classé. Owner: **Domaine Clarence Dillon. White: 6ha; 2,000 cases; Sém 60%, Sauv 40%.**
The history of this tiny vineyard follows that of Château La Mission-Haut-Brion, where the wine is vinified, matured and bottled. The soil here is richer and less stony than that of La Mission or La Tour-Haut-Brion, and this contributes towards the wines' remarkable keeping powers. The vinification is in cask and not *cuve*, and takes place in an air-conditioned cellar. From 1961, the wines were bottled in the late spring, after the vintage, but for the '85 vintage Jean Delmas has reverted to a longer cask maturation, bottling in the March of the second winter.

This is, with Chevalier, the great example of classic white Graves. It is full-bodied with a complex flavour and character which evolves only gradually. These wines differ from year to year in weight and power, and therefore the speed at which they evolve varies. These are very long-lived wines: the '34 was still superb in 1989; and off vintages such as '65 are a delightful surprise. After some austere vintages from '78 to '83, the wines are now richer and more harmonious again; '84, '85, '86, '87, '88 and '89 were all excellent.

Château La Louvière
Owner: **André Lurton. Red: 37ha; 16,500 cases; CS 70%, Mer 20%, CF 10%. White: 18ha; 7,500 cases; Sauv 85%, Sém 15%.** Second labels: **Châteaux Cantebeau, Coucheray and Clos du Roi.**
This very old property, which is a historical monument, has been largely restored and reconstructed by the dynamic André Lurton, owner since 1965.

The white wine of Louvière has been notable for its outstanding finesse, delicacy and fruit since the 1970 vintage at least. It certainly deserves to be Cru Classé.

The red has made steady progress. The wines during the 1970s were vivid in colour, quite tannic but light-textured and with a tendency to be rather one-dimensional. However, the balance has recently improved. In '83, for example, the quality was very similar to Carbonnieux, with a perfumed bouquet, a tobacco aroma and a lovely flavour, while the '85 was better than a number of Crus Classés, and the '86, more tannic but also opulent, was perhaps even finer. This is now a wine on a par with those of Pessac-Léognan's leading *crus*.

Château Malartic-Lagravière
Cru Classé. Owner: **Champagne Laurent-Perrier & Co. 17ha. Red: 7,900 cases; CS 50%, CF 25%, Mer 25%. White: 1,000 cases; Sauv 100%.**
This is a very well-positioned vineyard on a high platform of gravelly soil, just southeast of the town of Léognan. Malartic, after remaining in the same family since 1850 (the Ricards – *see* Chevalier – then through marriage to Marlys), was sold in 1990 to the family champagne firm of Laurent-Perrier. Bruno Marly has stayed on to manage the property. The red and white wines are vinified in stainless steel vats, the white at a low temperature not exceeding 18°C (64°F). The red wines are matured in casks, of which a third are new, the white in one-year-old casks for about seven months.

The red wines have a very marked Graves character, without a lot of weight or flesh, but with a very clean, fresh flavour and good fruit. In recent years the leanness which afflicted some wines of the 1960s seems to have been overcome. They have a good backbone and age well. Charming light wines were produced in '76 and '80, while the '75, '78, '79, '81, '82, '83 and '85 were all very successful examples of their vintages. This is good Graves at the level of a Cinquième Cru Classé in the Médoc.

The white wine is one of the most attractive of white Graves with an outstanding bouquet and real individuality. With its 100 percent Sauvignon it develops quickly and for me is at its best in its youthful phase. A consistent wine from year to year.

Château La Mission-Haut-Brion
Cru Classé. Owner: **Domaine Clarence Dillon. Red: 17ha; 7,000 cases; CS 60%, Mer 35%, CF 5%.**

When the all-too-familiar problems of succession caused the Woltner heirs to put La Mission on the market in 1983 it was logical that their neighbours across the road at Haut-Brion should decide to buy. These two properties now constitute an oasis of vines surrounded by housing, much of it built on former vineyards between the two World Wars. Henri Woltner, who masterminded the vinification here from 1921 until his death in 1974, was responsible for installing between 1926 and 1950 a system of glass-lined steel vats to enable better control of the fermentation. La Mission was probably the first property in Bordeaux to ferment its red wines at around 28°C (82°F) as a consistent policy, and in 1987 the old *cuvier* was replaced by the latest in stainless steel models. The wine is matured in casks, of which half are new. The gravel in the vineyard is of exceptional depth and results in low yields and great concentration of flavour.

The wine of La Mission is rich and powerful, whereas that of Haut-Brion is all finesse and delicacy. Clearly La Mission is a Premier Cru in all but name. Its price has yearly been edging closer to that of the Premiers Crus Classés, and since it has belonged to Domaine Clarence Dillon, the opening price has on occasion been only 10 francs a bottle below that of the best of the Médoc. The quality and individuality of this wine is outstanding. Always deep in colour, it is rich and concentrated in flavour, without being uncomfortably tannic. It needs time to evolve and lasts well. It also has a wonderful record for successes in 'off' vintages. Classic wines were made in '75 and '76, and '78 and '79 were quite splendid. '80 was a fine vintage and those of '81, '82, '83, '85, '86, '88, '89 and '90 were all exceptional.

Château Olivier
Cru Classé. Owner: **Mme P de Bethmann.** Administrator: **Jean-Jacques de Bethmann. Red: 18ha; 8,500 cases; CS 65%, Mer 35%. White: 17ha; 9,000 cases; Sém 65%, Sauv 30%, Musc 5%.**
For over 70 years this famous old estate was farmed by Eschenauer, the *négociants*, and was their monopoly. Then in November 1981 the Bethmann family took the management back into their own hands and Jean-Jacques de Bethmann assumed the responsibility for running the property. The distribution remained in Eschenauer's hands until 1987, but for only part of the crop.

The vineyard was radically reconstructed in the early to mid-1970s with a view to increasing the size of the red vineyard, and ensuring that the various grape varieties were planted on the most favourable soils, much of the vineyard is therefore still immature. A wonderfully scented and complex '82 has been made. The '83 is leaner and the '84 is above average, '85 was better, but '86 seems too austere and tannic. The red is a wine to watch.

The white wine is what Olivier has always been known for. With the high proportion of Sémillon you must not expect the instant charm the Sauvignon gives in the first months of bottle-ageing, but the wines do become more interesting. The flavour is marked and individual with plenty of character. Again it will be interesting to see what difference the new management makes.

Château Le Pape
Owner: **GFA du Château Le Pape.** Administrator: **Antony Perrin. 5ha. 1,600 cases. Mer 95%, CS 5%.**
This property has a particularly attractive château, built in the style of the First Empire. Antony Perrin has been administrator for a comparatively short while and it will be interesting to see what changes he makes. An unusually small proportion of Cabernet Sauvignon is grown here, but the vines are young and the full impact of this *encépagement* is yet to be revealed.

Château Pape-Clément
Cru Classé. Owner: **Montagne family. 29ha. Red: 12,000 cases; CS 60%, Mer 40%. White: 100 cases; Sém 34%, Sauv 33%, Musc 33%.**
The vineyard here has the longest continuous history of any in Bordeaux, having been first planted in 1300. This is a red wine château, although a few cases of white are produced and are sometimes found in Bordeaux restaurants. The soil is sand and gravel and there are traces of iron. After traditional vinification, the wine is matured in casks of which 30 percent to 40 percent are new, according to the vintage.

The wines of Pape-Clément have a marvellous bouquet, intense with overtones of tobacco, and a supple, rich texture that enables them to be enjoyed relatively young. But after some wonderful vintages in the 1960s, Pape-Clément was disturbingly inconsistent for a number of years. After a good '75 came a string of small and often dilute wines. Even the '82 was a disappointment. But with the appointment of Bernard Pujols in 1985, and the completion of a new *cuvier* and re-equipped *chai*, Pape-Clément returned to its real form with the '85, and since then '86, '88, '89 and '90 have produced wines to set beside the great vintages of the 1960s. The last vintage I found really satisfactory in bottle was '78.

Château Picque-Caillou
Owner: **Alphonse Denis. 17·5ha. 7,500 cases. Mer 35%, CS 35%, CF 30%.**
This vineyard lies on gravelly and stony soil, surrounded by the sprawling suburbs of Bordeaux. The wines have a good reputation for being stylish, supple and full-flavoured. They usually evolve fairly quickly and also keep well. Wines of breed.

Château Pontac-Monplaisir
Owner: **Jean Maufras. Red: 8ha; 4,500 cases; CS 60%, Mer 40%. White: 6ha; 2,700 cases; Sauv 70%, Sém 30%.** Second label: **Château Limbourg.**
An old *cru*, dating back to the 1690s, this property is recorded on Cassini's map produced in the 18th century. The vineyards themselves are not the original ones as these were sold by the present owner and a supermarket now stands on their site. Much care and

attention has been put into the winemaking and the results are elegant, scented reds with the character and breed typical of Graves; the whites are very stylish with plenty of varietal Sémillon, the Limbourg whites having more Sauvignon character.

Château de Rochemorin
Owner: **André Lurton. Red: 45ha; 18,000 cases; CS 60%, Mer 40%. White: 12ha; 2,500 cases; Sauv 85%, Sém 15%.**
The name of this château is derived from 'Roche-Morine', indicating that it was a fortified place at the time of the Moorish incursions from Spain in the 7th and 8th centuries. The energetic André Lurton bought this old property in 1973 and began replanting the vineyards (which had been replaced by forest) in 1974. The vines are on deep gravel on the highest ridge of Martillac. As at other Lurton properties, harvesting is mechanical for the reds and manual for the whites. Fermentations are controlled at 28–30°C (82–86°F) for the reds and 16–18°C (61–64°F) for the whites. The reds are matured for a year in cask, with one-third new wood, but the whites see no wood at all.

The red wines already show quite a spicy, aromatic Graves bouquet allied to elegance and breed, and are lighter and more marked by new oak than nearby Cruzeau. Fine '81, '82 and '83 vintages have been made. The white wine is very different from that of Cruzeau. It has a less floral bouquet and more body, but is very elegant, with a finish that is flinty and drier than that of Cruzeau. Again, the white is more evolved than the red, but, as the vineyard develops and the reds acquire more depth and finish, they should become really interesting.

Château de Rouillac
Owner: **P Sarthou. 5ha. 1,650 cases. CS 85%, Mer 15%.**
Distinctive on two counts, first because it is the only *cru* left in the commune of Canéjean and secondly due to its attractive château, built by the architect Baron Haussmann in 1869. These days the Sarthous are using the most up-to-date equipment for vinification and the vineyards have recently been replanted. The wines produced since their first vintage in 1978 are well balanced and full of Graves character.

Château Le Sartre
Owner: **GFA du Château Le Sartre.** Administrator: **Antony Perrin.** Red: 10ha; 2,000 cases; CS 60%, Mer 40%. White: 5ha; 2,000 cases; Sauv 70%, Sém 30%.
The Perrin family had to rebuild this property completely when they bought it in 1981: it had been much neglected since 1914. It is now promising to yield some interesting wines.

Château Smith-Haut-Lafitte
Cru Classé. Owner: **Daniel Cathiard.** Red: 45ha; 25,000 cases; CS 63%, Mer 26%, CF 11%; White: 10ha; 4,000 cases; Sauv 100%.
A proprietor with the splendidly English name of George Smith bought this *cru* in 1720 and added his name to that of the place-name. The firm Louis Eschenauer, distributors since 1902, owned the property from 1958 until 1991 when they sold to the Cathiard family. In recent years there has been major investment here in the vineyards and buildings. In 1960 less than six hectares were planted, and no white wine was made. Now there are 51 hectares planted, 5·6 devoted to white wines. A large new underground cellar was built in 1974 to hold 2,000 casks, and all the vinification equipment was renewed. Half the red wine is matured in new oak.

The wines have a very pronounced character, aromatic and spicy. Until '83 there was no selection, so big vintages like '79 and '82 tend to be diffuse and quick-developing, although delicious. Now sturdier wines are being made which augur well for the future. The '84 is remarkably good for the year.

A very pleasant perfumed white Sauvignon is being made, which is ideal for early drinking.

Château La Tour-Haut-Brion
Cru Classé. Owner: **Domaine Clarence Dillon.** Red: 4ha; 1,500 cases; CS 70%, CF 15%, Mer 15%.
This is a small property, adjoining La Mission, that the Woltner brothers purchased in 1933. The wines have been vinified at La Mission since then, and under the Dewavrin administration (1975–83) were treated as second wines. One of Jean Delmas' first decisions was to restore its position as a *cru* in its own right. The result is still a very fine wine, certainly better than a number of the other Crus

Classés of Graves. It is full-bodied but less intense than La Mission, and matures very quickly. Excellent wines were made in '85, '86, '87, '88, '89 and '90.

Château La Tour-Martillac
Cru Classé. Owner: **Jean Kressmann. Red: 20ha; 8,500 cases; CS 60%, Mer 25%, CF 6%, Mal and PV 9%. White: 4·75ha; 1,500 cases; Sém 55%, Sauv 30%, other varieties 15%.** Second label: **Château La Grave-Martillac (red, 1,000 cases).**

The name comes from a 12th-century tower, once the staircase of a fort, the ruins of which were used in the building of today's farm two centuries ago.

In the 1870s, Edouard Kressmann, the founder of the famous old *négociant* house, obtained the exclusivity of this *cru*, and the family finally bought it in 1929. Ten hectares of pasture provides the estate with invaluable cattle manure for the vineyard. The grapes from the older vines are still fermented in the traditional wooden vats at 32–33°C (90–91°F), while the production from younger vines goes into lined steel vats which are water-cooled. Maturation is in casks of which a third are new. The second wine, Château La Grave-Martillac, is made from vines less than ten years old and *vin de presse*. It is not sold through the trade but only direct from the château. The white wine was vinified in stainless steel with automatic water-cooling until 1987, when, under Denis Dubordieu's supervision, fermentation in cask was introduced. This has given the wines an extra dimension and lifted them into the upper echelons of white Graves.

I have found the red wine has elegant fruit on the nose and a fine flavour with breed and length, but is rather light-textured. Although the character is different, the level of quality is similar to Malartic-Lagravière. The white wine is elegant and fresh with quite an original character. It has delicacy, real breed and a fine finish. This is high-class white Graves.

Southern Graves

Château d'Archambeau
Owner: **Jean-Philippe Dubourdieu. 25ha. Red: 6,600 cases; Mer 50%, CS 50%. White: 8,300 cases; Sém 55%, Sauv 40%, Musc 5%.** Second label: **Château Mourlet.**
The commune of Illats which adjoins Barsac, like those of Cérons and Podensac, can vinify its white wines either as Cérons or as Graves Supérieur. Here at d'Archambeau only very small quantities of Cérons are now made, and the emphasis is on classic dry Graves. The Dubourdieu family have a formidable reputation as winemakers in Barsac and Graves, and Jean-Philippe, nephew of Pierre Dubourdieu of Doisy-Daëne fame, is no exception. The white wines are cold-fermented in lined metal and stainless steel vats, and bottled in the spring. The combination of Sémillon and Sauvignon produces wines of elegance and depth of character that are delicious within months of bottling but also keep and mature well. The red wine is a more recent development, the first commercialized vintage from young vines being the '82. The wines have vivid fruit and immediate charm, and doubtless will take on more depth and complexity as the vineyard matures.

Château Ardennes
Owners: **François & Bertrand Dubrey. 20ha. Red: 7,000 cases; Mer 50%, CS 40%, CF 10%. White: 5,000 cases; Sém 60%, Sauv 40%.**
Both red and white wines are made at Château Ardennes, the red being rather better, with a violet perfume, good structure and the ability to age well (an unusual quality in wines of this area).

Château d'Arricaud
Owners: **M & Mme Albert Bouyx. 28ha. Red: 3,000 cases; CS 65%, Mer 30%, Mal 5%. White: 7,000 cases; Sém 70%, Sauv 25%, Musc 5%.**
An old property and the most important in the commune of Landiras, Château d'Arricaud was actually built by a former president of the *Parlement de Bordeaux*. Its wines are well-made, the reds ideal for young drinking with a delicious fruitiness and plenty of charm, the whites are elegant with good length.

Château Belon
Owner: **Jean Depiot. Red: 4ha; 3,000 cases; CS 50%, Mer 50%. White: 4ha; 2,500 cases; Sauv 45%, Sém 40%, Musc 15%.**
This property in St-Morillon has been owned by the Depiot family since 1800. The wines produced here tend to be rather coarse, but some of the reds have an attractive spiciness.

Château La Blancherie and Château La Blancherie-Peyret
Owner: **F-C Braud-Coussié. White: 11ha; 4,200 cases; Sém 55%, Sauv 35%, Musc 10%. Red: 9ha; 3,300 cases; CS 70%, Mer 30%.**
The commune of La Brède is famous for its château of the same name, where Montesquieu, the renowned 17th-century philosopher and historian, was born and lived. Today this is the most important wine-producing château of the commune. It also has a history of its own, for its proprietors at the time of the Revolution of 1789 were both guillotined! The white wines (sold under the La Blancherie label) are fermented at low temperatures, the reds (La Blancherie-Peyret) receive a long maceration and are aged in cask. The whites are fruity and vigorous in style. The reds have an arresting bouquet, redolent of tobacco and spice, and lots of flavour and character, but are supple and powerful at the same time, so that they can be drunk young yet can also age. This is an excellent *cru*, with well-made wines.

Château Brondelle
Owner: **Rolland Belloc. 20ha. Red: 5,000 cases; CS 60%, Mer 20%, CF 10%, Mal 10%. White: 3,000 cases; Sém 60%, Sauv 30%, Musc 10%.** Second label: **Château La Croix-Saint-Pey.**
Brondelle is located in Langon, one of the most important winemaking communes in Graves, where the growers have profited much from the work on clonal selection carried out by INRA. The wines produced at this property, both the red and white, are attractive and worth looking out for.

Château Cabannieux
Owner: **René Barrière, Dudignac family. 20ha. Red: 8,000**

cases; Mer 50%, CS 45%, CF 5%. White: 4,000 cases; Sém
80%, Sauv 20%.
This property is in the highest part of the commune of Portets on
well-drained, gravelly soil, with some traces of clay. It belongs to
the same owners as the well-respected *négociant* firm of A & R
Barrière. The red wines are given two to three weeks in contact
with the skins for maximum extraction. Part of the crop is put in
cask, and a small amount of new wood is used. For the white there is
a controlled low-temperature fermentation at below 20°C (68°F).
The aim is to produce red wines with a pronounced Graves
character, full-flavoured but soft and good for early drinking. The
white has a small percentage of Sauvignon to give the early
bouquet. Both enjoy a good reputation.

Château Cazebonne
Owner: **Marc Bridet. 13ha. Red: 2,700 cases; CS 50%, Mer
50%. White: 2,300 cases; Sauv 60%, Sém 40%.**
A property producing red wines with plenty of fruit and colour but
which are perhaps a bit firm. The whites are slightly more elegant
with a very pleasant crispness.

Château de Chantegrive
Owners: **Henri & Francoise Lévêque. Red: 40ha; 15,000
cases; CS 60%, Mer 40%. White: 47ha, 17,500 cases; Sém
50%, Sauv 30%, Musc 20%.** Second labels: **Châteaux Bon-
Dieu-des-Vignes, Mayne-Lévêque, Mayne-d'Anice.**
The Lévêques have steadily built up this property from modest
beginnings. When I first visited Chantegrive there were only 15
hectares of vines, now there are 60. The soil is white sand mixed
with quartz pebbles. The vinification is carefully controlled at low
temperatures for the whites. The reds are aged for six months in oak
vats, then for a year in casks, of which 20 percent are new oak, in an
underground cellar. The white wines are fresh, delicious, fruity,
aromatic and easy to drink, without being quite top class. The reds
are fruity and supple but with some depth as well, the sort of easy-
to-drink wines that deserve more attention than they get.

Château Chéret-Pitres
Owners: **M & Mme Jean Boulanger. 12ha. 7,000 cases. CS 50%, Mer 50%.**
The Boulangers produce only red wines at Chéret-Pitres, these though are most attractive, with plenty of distinctive Graves flavour. Their fruitiness makes them excellent for drinking young but some of the better vintages mature well and are worth keeping.

Château Chicane
Owner: **Coste family. 6ha. 3,000 cases. CS 70%, Mer 20%, CF 10%.**
Pierre Coste produces red wines for drinking young – at around two to four years old. They are light-bodied with a pleasing spicy nose and lots of fruit.

Château de Courbon
Owner: **Jean Saunders. 6·5ha. 3,000 cases. Sauv 60%, Sém 40%.**
Only white wines are vinified here; they are grown on soils of sand, gravel and clay, which, being relatively near to Sauternes, produce wines that are richer and more full-bodied than those of the northern Graves regions. The proportions of Sauvignon and Sémillon used ensure that the wines are supple and fruity but also have good keeping properties.

Château Coutet
Owners: **Marcel & Bertrand Baly. White: 38ha; 9,000 cases; Sém 80%, Sauv 15%, Musc 5%.**
The wines of the châteaux Coutet can be rather confusing. Dry wines made in Sauternes and Barsac are allowed only the Bordeaux Blanc AC and in 1977 the Baly family bought another château of the same name, the famous Barsac *cru* of Coutet, where they produce such wines. They are also proprietors in Pujols-sur-Civon, a commune with Sauternes and Barsac on three sides of it, and are selling their Pujols *cru*, formerly known as Reverdon, as 'Vin Sec du Château Coutet' with the Graves AC. These are wines produced using very cold fermentation, that I find rather disappointing at present. Having a strong aroma of gooseberries they are surprisingly skeletal for wines with so much Sémillon.

Château L'Etoile
Owner: **Domaines Latrille Bonnin. Red: 10ha; 6,000 cases; CS 60%, Mer 30%, CF 10%. White: 5ha; 3,000 cases; Sauv 50%, Sém 50%.**
At Château L'Etoile, vinification at high temperatures produces red wines which are rich in fruit and spice, balanced by body and tannin; they have plenty of ageing potential but are also delicious when young. The whites undergo cool fermentation and are macerated slightly prior to this to enhance the wine's bouquet and fruit character. They are also most attractive for drinking young.

Château Ferrande
Owner: **Héritiers H Delnaud.** Administrators: **Castel Frères. Red: 34ha; 15,000 cases; Mer 34%, CS 32%, CF 31%, Mal 3%. White: 9ha; 5,000 cases; Sém 62%, Sauv 38%.** Second label: **Château Lognac.**
This is the most important *cru* in the commune of Castres. Since the Delnaud family began their partnership here with Marc Teisseire in 1955 the vineyard has been much expanded and the facilities improved. Concrete and stainless steel vats are used for the vinification and the red wine is matured in cask, with 10 percent new oak.

I have found the red deep in colour with a lively and spicy bouquet with tobacco overtones. The flavour is frank and fresh, light-textured but full and fruity. This is a very enjoyable wine which can be drunk with pleasure when three to four years old – the '81 was perfect in '85.

The white has quite a pronounced Graves flavour. It is powerful and slightly earthy but fruity. It has its admirers, but for me it has less charm and breed than the red.

Château de Gaillat
Owner: **Coste family. 8ha. 4,000 cases. CS 60%, Mer 30%, Mal 10%.**
The care and attention Pierre Coste gives to vinification has resulted in some outstanding vintages. The wines are mostly early-bottled in order to retain as much fruit as possible; the '83 and '85 being evidence that these aims are achieved. These wines need to be drunk young.

Château du Grand Abord
Owner: **Marc Dugoua. Red: 18ha; 4,500 cases; Mer 90%, CS 10%. White: 3ha; 2,000 cases; Sém 90%, Sauv 10%.**
A property situated on the gravel soils of the plateau at Portets. The red wines are most attractive and for drinking young.

Domaine La Grave
Owner: **Peter Vinding-Diers. 7ha. Red: 3,000 cases; CS 50%, Mer 50%. White: 500 cases; Sém 100%.**
Peter Vinding-Diers acquired this property in 1980 and it was here that he produced his first wines. Both the reds and the whites are full in flavour, the reds tending to be rather tannic, but still having much elegance and a fine perfume.

Château Landiras
Owner: **Peter Vinding-Diers. (Vineyard currently being replanted.)**
The château's history can be traced back to 1173 and a castle once stood on this site, the ruins and moat still remain. The proprietor has built up a good reputation for himself in Graves in recent years (*see* Château Rahoul) and is at present expanding this ancient *cru* to its full 20-hectare AOC allocation. One of the first stages of reconstruction was to build a new *cuvier*. This was completed in time for the 1988 vintage and since then some stylish wines have been produced – the reds reflecting their Cabernet origins and the whites with plenty of classic Sémillon style and body.

Château Magence
Owner: **Dominique Guillot de Suduiraut. Red: 18ha; 5,800 cases; CS 41%, CF 32%, Mer 27%. White: 12ha; 10,000 cases; Sauv 64%, Sém 36%.**
One of the best-known properties in St-Pierre de Mons, the most important Graves commune lying to the southeast of Sauternes. It has been in the same family since 1800, in spite of which everything here is up to date. The fermentation is in stainless steel with careful temperature control. This was one of the early classic modern white Graves, at one time entirely Sauvignon, but now balanced with some Sémillon, producing wines of real finesse and style. The reds are also useful, supple as well as slightly tannic.

Château Magneau
Owner: **Henri Ardurats. Red: 6ha; 1,000 cases; Mer 50%, CS 35%, CF 15%. White: 20ha; 10,000 cases; Sauv 50%, Sém 30%, Musc 20%.** Second label: **Château Guirauton.**
The white wines produced at this *cru* in La Brède are particularly good: they lack the coarseness of some Graves wines and are stylish and well-made with plenty of fruit. The reds too are attractive and have a distinctly pungent aroma; mostly ready to drink when young. The Château Guirauton label is used only for white wines.

Château Millet
Owner: **de la Mette family. Red: 45ha; 25,000 cases; Mer 60%, CF 40%. White: 20ha; 9,000 cases; Sém 40%, Sauv 30%, Musc 30%.** Second label: **Château du Clos Renon.**
This is now the largest property in Portets, with a large château to go with it. The red wine, now more important than the white, is matured in cask. Wines not considered up to standard (for example the '77 and '80 vintages) are not bottled with the château name, but in general these are decent, fruity, early-maturing wines with a certain reputation.

Château Montalivet
Owners: **Pierre Coste, Pierre Dubourdieu, Robert Goffard. 14ha. Red: 4,000 cases; CS 70%, Mer 30%. White: 1,500 cases; Sém 80%, Sauv 20%.**
One of Pierre Coste's most successful châteaux, this property is situated in the commune of Pujols and produces stylish, fruity reds and Sémillon-based whites with plenty of varietal character.

Château Le Pavillon-de-Boyrein
Owner: **Société Pierre Bonnet et Fils. Red: 12ha; 11,000 cases; Mer 65%, CS 35%. White: 13ha; 12,000 cases; Sém 80%, Sauv 20%.** Second label: **Domaine des Lauriers.**
The best *cru* in its commune – Roaillan – this château produces wines similar in quality to many Crus Bourgeois of the northern Médoc. The red wines are the most pleasant, with a hint of *terroir* in the form of mineral and iron overtones.

Château Pessan-St-Hilaire
Owner: **Dominique Haverlan. Red: 10ha; 3,350 cases; Mer
60%, CS 35%, CF 5%. White: 4ha; 1,650 cases; Sém 80%,
Sauv 20%.**

The present owner bought Château Pessan-St-Hilaire in 1981 and
has since then expanded the vineyards and enlarged the *chai*. He is a
trained oenologist and makes attractive wines, both red and white
showing continual improvement.

Château Rahoul
Owner: **Alain Thiénot. Red: 11·5ha; 5,000 cases; Mer 60%,
CS 40%. White: 2·5ha; 1,000 cases; Sém 100%.**

This old property in Portets was bought by an Australian syndicate
in 1978. The Australians brought in a young Danish oenologist,
Peter Vinding-Diers, and invested in stainless steel and new oak. In
1982 they sold to another Dane, who in turn sold to the present
owner, a merchant from Champagne. He took over the management personally when Peter Vinding-Diers left in 1988 to run his
own property (*see* Château Landiras). Although the vineyard is not
in the best position, being low-lying with some drainage problems,
the care and expertise of the winemaking have been successful. One
of Vinding-Diers' most important contributions was the isolation
of 'R2', a pure strain of yeast found in the vineyard here. By
eliminating the other yeasts and using only this one, he found it was
possible to produce cleaner-tasting wines. 'R2' has since been used
as far afield as Australia. A proportion of new oak is used for the
maturation of both red and white wines after low-temperature
fermentations.

I find the white wines extremely elegant and long-flavoured,
only lacking perhaps the complexity and depth of the best Graves
further north. The reds are full of vivid spicy fruit and are at their
most delicious when young. This is an example of what investment
in expertise and the best equipment can achieve, and makes one
realize how much room for improvement there is at many better-
known and better-placed vineyards.

Château Respide-Médeville
Owner: **Christian Médeville. 7·5ha. Red: 1,000 cases; CS
and CF 65%, Mer 35%. White: 2,500 cases; Sém 50%, Sauv**

45%, Musc 5%.
This *cru* is situated on the ridge of gravelly clay in Toulenne. It has been built up by Christian Médeville of Château Gilette to earn its current high reputation. Of the white wines, the '78 and '85 are especially pleasing; the reds are also charming for young drinking.

Château de Roquetaillade-La-Grange
Owners: **Pierre & Jean Guignard. 36ha. Red: 12,000 cases; Mer 40%, CS 25%, CF 25%, Mal 5%, PV 5%. White: 2,200 cases; Sém 80%, Sauv 20%.** Second label: **Château Roquetaillade-Le-Bernet.**
The name of Roquetaillade is famous for the splendid mediaeval château built by a nephew of Pope Clement V at the beginning of the 14th century. It is regarded as the finest example of military architecture in the whole of southeastern France. But this property, lying on the hillsides to the east of the château, is actually unconnected with the château itself, which has no vineyards of importance. In recent years the owners (also owners of Château Rolland in Barsac) have raised the standard of the wines here to a high level, winning a number of medals in Paris and a deserved reputation as producers of one of the best red wines in southern Graves.

The red wines have real individuality and lovely mellow fruit on nose and palate – sometimes, in years like '79, with an unmistakeable hint of cherries, a fruit flavour most unusual for Bordeaux. The vintages of '78, '79, '81, '82, '83, '85 and '86 were especially successful. The white used to be pleasantly fruity without being special; but, with new controlled-temperature vinification, quality is likely to become more exciting.

Château St-Agrèves
Owners: **Claude & Marie-Christiane Landry. Red: 7·5ha; 3,750 cases; CS and CF 70%, Mer 30%. White: 2·5ha; 1,750 cases; Sauv 50%, Sém 50%.**
The red wines produced at Château St-Agrèves are unusual for this region in that they benefit from longer maturation than many of their neighbours. They are attractive wines though and show a good balance of fruit and tannin. The white wines are rather more coarse in style than those from nearby *crus*.

Château de St-Pierre
Owner: **Henri Dulac. 43ha. Red: 6,200 cases; CS 60%, Mer 40%. White: 13,800 cases; Sém 67%, Sauv 33%.** Second labels: **Clos d'Uza and Château Queyrats.**
This excellent property is run in conjunction with Château Les Queyrats by Henri Dulac. But here red as well as white wines are made. The vineyard is on ridges of clay and limestone in the southeast of the commune of St-Pierre-de-Mons, the most important wine-producing commune south of Sauternes. The wines are very carefully vinified. The whites, like those at Les Queyrats, were some of the first of the new-style Graves to emerge and have real finesse and character. The '82 won a gold medal in Paris. The reds are not as distinguished, but are vivid and quite generous, ageing well for this area. A *cru* with a long record for consistency.

Château Toumilon
Owner: **Jean Sévenet. 12ha. Red: 3,000 cases; CS 45%, Mer 35%, CF 20%. White: 2,500 cases; Sém 60%, Sauv 40%.**
Second label: **Château Cabanes.**
Another excellent *cru* in St-Pierre-de-Mons, the most important commune south of Sauternes. The property has been in the same family since 1783, and the vineyards are on gravelly ridges overlooking the Garonne. Since the 1983 vintage there has been a big improvement in the white wines due to new vinification facilities. Previously they were rather pedestrian with a soapy finish; now they have finesse and delicacy. The reds have finesse and personality and a real Graves character but without crudeness. The '80 vintage was delightful for the year and '81 was very fine.

Château Tourteau-Chollet
Owner: **SC du Château. 30ha. Red: 12,500 cases; CS 60%, Mer 40%. White: 4,170 cases; Sém 50%, Sauv 50%.**
This is another part ot the Mestrezat empire (*see* Grand-Puy-Ducasse and Rayne-Vigneau). The red wines carry a gold label, and the whites a white label. The commune of Arbanats is immediately to the southeast of Portets, and this is now the most important property there. Since taking over in 1977 the new owners have steadily improved the property, and pleasant fruity red wines and elegant dry whites are being made. A property to watch.

Sauternes and Barsac

Sauternes is produced in five communes: Sauternes, Barsac, Fargues-de-Langon, Bommes and Preignac. Barsac is also an *appellation* in its own right, and producers there can label their wines Barsac or Sauternes or (as many have begun to do) Sauternes-Barsac.

Traditional Sauternes is a luxury wine, and luxury wines have to be sold at luxury prices. If an article becomes unfashionable and can no longer command its former high price, something has to give, and that is likely to be quality. This, in a nutshell, has been the dilemma facing Sauternes since the late 1950s.

The top red growths can expect to make 40 hectolitres per hectare in a good vintage, sometimes more, and very seldom less than 30. At Yquem, the standard-bearer for Sauternes, over the past 20 years the average yield has been 7 hectolitres per hectare, in contrast with 25 allowed by the *appellation*. On this basis, Yquem's price would need to be around four times that of Lafite or Pétrus to produce the same income, in fact it is in the region of two and half times that amount. Costs are also much higher because of picking methods (*see* page 49), and there are years when frosts, hail or rain during the vintage mean that the wine is simply not good enough to go out under the famous label of Yquem.

The result of all this has been that only a few Sauternes properties have been able to continue to make wines in anything approaching the traditional way. Whatever short-cuts may be possible with the aid of modern technology, there can be no substitute for botrytis or *pourriture noble* (noble rot). This is what gives Sauternes its distinctive bouquet and flavour, its complex range of fruit, flavours and finesse. The short-cut of picking ripe but unaffected grapes and then chaptalizing, can only produce unsubtle sweet wines that may possibly be quite elegant and fresh, but will never develop into anything of interest.

Fortunately, there are signs that there are now enough lovers of the nectar that is true Sauternes who are willing to pay the price for a certain quantity of this style of wine, and enough dedicated proprietors with the financial strength to withstand the burdens of the bad years.

One way of helping to cover costs is to produce a certain

proportion of dry wine, or even red wine. Unfortunately, however good these may be, such efforts are hampered by the *appellation* system which will give only a simple Bordeaux AC to such wines (or Bordeaux Supérieur in the case of red wines). Ironically, in neighbouring Cérons, the producers of this sweet wine have been saved by having the right to the Graves AC for their dry whites and reds. This has so far been denied to the growers of Sauternes, apparently quite illogically.

The dividing-line between success and failure is a fine one. There are now 11 Premiers Crus. Ten years or so ago, only five of these were making wines that were up to standard. Since then the new owner of Guiraud has started to turn it around, and the Cordiers have reversed their previous policy at Lafaurie-Peyraguey. At the same time, changes at Coutet put a question mark against this property's future, though it has since returned to form. Most recently of all, Domaines Rothschild have secured the future of one of the best properties, Rieussec.

There are 14 Deuxièmes Crus, and of these there are probably eight owners who aim to produce quality wines to some extent, only half of these make more than 2,000 cases. On the other hand, the wines of one of the Deuxièmes Crus, Myrat, were pulled up in 1976, but happily replanted in 1988. Doisy-Daëne has been the Deuxième Cru most dedicated to quality over the past 20 years. And improvements also came in the 1970s, with Nairac being transformed by Tom Heeter; more recently Pierre Perromat has leased d'Arche and the Guignard brothers have begun promisingly at their part of Lamothe. There are three unclassified growths that now make wines of classified quality: Bastor-Lamontagne, Raymond-Lafon and Fargues.

Essentially Sauternes is a great dessert wine intended to be drunk at the end of a meal, and this clearly puts it into the special-occasions-only category. Of course it can be drunk as an aperitif; but it is not exactly designed to put an edge on your appetite, and the Bordelais habit of drinking it with a first course of *foie gras* hardly has a wide application. A more likely way forward is through the new devices for keeping open bottles under nitrogen, which make it possible for restaurant diners to order a single glass of Sauternes at the end of a meal. If this practice becomes widespread the future of Sauternes will look brighter. But unless more people are prepared to pay more and drink Sauternes more often, then the future for even a small number of quality *crus* will remain limited.

Château d'Arche
2e Cru Classé. Owner: **Bastit-St-Martin family.**
Administrator: **Pierre Perromat. 35·5ha. 4,500 cases. Sém 80%, Sauv 15%, Musc 5%.** Second label: **Château d'Arche-Lafaurie (not used since 1981).**
This is an old property, with a château dating from the 16th century and a reputation going back to the 18th. After a rather undistinguished period, Pierre Perromat, for 30 years president of the INAO, leased the property in 1981 and is determined to make classic Sauternes again. The traditional selections are now made in the vineyard again and, after fermentation in vat, the wine is matured for at least two years in casks – a small percentage are new.

The first wines of the new regime seem well-balanced, with nice fruit and sweetness and a certain fineness and breed. The vintages of '81 and '84 did well for these lesser years; '83 and '85 are also good wines, with the best vintages in '86 and '88.

Château Bastor-Lamontagne
Cru Bourgeois. Owner: **Crédit Foncier de France.**
Administrator: **Michel Garat. 48ha. 12,000 cases. Sém 78%, Sauv 17%, Musc 5%.**
This excellent *cru* is in Preignac, adjoining Suduiraut. It has for many years consistently produced excellent wines and is on the level of the Crus Classés, indeed better than some of them. The wines are very carefully and traditionally made, with three years' cask-ageing and a small proportion of new wood. The result is a rich, luscious wine with the aroma and flavour of apricots and all the stylishness of a top-rate Sauternes. Recently '75, '76, '79, '80, '81, '82, '83, '85, '86, '88 and '89 have all been highly successful vintages.

Château Broustet
2e Cru Classé. Owner: **Fournier family.** Administrator:
Eric Fournier. 16ha. 1,700 cases. Sém 63%, Sauv 25%, Musc 12%.
This very small property is not well known, mainly because its

production is small. But Eric Fournier (who also runs Château Canon in St-Emilion) is doing everything to produce quality wines here. It has belonged to the family since 1885, although they did not replant the vineyard until 1900. The wine is fermented in vat but matured in casks, of which a small percentage are new. The wines have a fine perfume and are generous and quite rich with a pleasing individuality and breed.

Château Caillou
2e Cru Classé. Owner: **Bravo GFA. 18ha. 3,300 cases. Sém 90%, Sauv 10%.**
A little-known property, because the wine is all sold by *vente directe* to private customers. So this is a place to visit if you have your car and room in the boot! The present owner has run the property since 1969 and keeps stocks of old vintages; I have memories of a wonderful bottle of 1920. The wines are carefully made, with fermentation in vat and maturation in casks, of which a small percentage are new, for up to three years. The wines have the reputation of being light, elegant and fruity.

Château Climens
1er Cru Classé. Owner: **SCEA du Château Climens.**
Administrator: **Lucien Lurton. 25ha. 4,500 cases. Sém 98%, Sauv 2%.**
For many, Climens is the best wine of the region after Yquem, not that the two can really be compared. The emphasis here is on elegance, breed and freshness, and Climens does not generally attempt to compete with Yquem's lusciousness. Since 1971 it has belonged to Lucien Lurton (*see* Brane-Cantenac, Durfort-Vivens etc), but the *régisseuse*, Mme Janin, has been here for 30 years, and her family for over 100 years. The soil is red sand and gravel over limestone. After pressing and settling for 24 hours in vat, the juice is fermented in casks, of which 25 percent are new, and matured for about two years before bottling.

The wines here are remarkably consistent in a region where it is not always easy to make good Sauternes. They are rather closed at first and usually need a minimum of ten years before they begin to give of their best. The great qualities here are balance, freshness, elegance and liquorousness in the great years. This makes it a very long-lived wine. Surprisingly acceptable light wines were made in '72 and '77, years not noted for Sauternes at all; '71, '75 and '76 are also outstanding wines for their vintages. '78 is without botrytis but elegant, '79 is light but very fine and can be drunk now; the '80 and '81 are also both very fine but the '82 is no more than average. Since 1983, the wines seem to have moved into another gear with a succession of outstanding wines: '83, '85, '86, '88 and '89, placing Climens second only to Yquem as the quality *cru* in Sauternes.

Château Coutet
1er Cru Classé. Owner: **Marcel Baly. 36ha. 7,000 cases. Sém 80%, Sauv 20%.**
The name of Coutet is always linked to that of Climens, the other great wine of Barsac. Generally Coutet is less powerful and often a little drier than Climens, which also tends to have more finesse in the great years. For 30 years the property was well run by the Rolland-Guy family, who sold in 1977 to Marcel Baly. The production methods here are traditional, with fermentation in casks, of which a third are new, and two years in cask before bottling.

Of the early vintages at Château Coutet, the '71 is very fine and the '73 one of the few fine wines in this mixed year. The last two vintages of the old regime were superb, the '75 a classic in a year when many wines were clumsy and unbalanced, while the '76 is perfumed and beautifully balanced but lighter. Since then '79 is elegant but rather dry, but '83 marked a return to form, and '88 and '89 were even better.

Château Doisy-Daëne
2e Cru Classé. Owner: **Pierre Dubourdieu. 14ha. 4,000 cases. Sém 100%.** Second labels: **Vin Sec de Doisy-Daëne, Château Cantegril.**
Once the three Doisys were one, and when they split up in the 19th century the first owner of this part was an Englishman called Deane, which has become corrupted to Daëne. Its present owner, Pierre Dubourdieu, is a great innovator, being one of the first to make a dry wine in Sauternes in 1962. The vinification methods here have been developed over a number of years and are special to Doisy-Daëne. The juice is fermented in vat at a controlled temperature of

not more than 18°C (64°F). Then, after 15 to 21 days when the balance between alcohol and sugar is judged correct, the temperature is lowered to 4°C (39°F) and the wine is sterile-filtered into new casks. Arresting the fermentation in this way much reduces the amount of sulphur needed. The process is repeated for the final *assemblage* the following March, and the wine is sterile-filtered again a year later.

All this gives Doisy-Daëne a freshness and elegance which I find delightful. The wines seem light to start but mature and keep very well, developing great finesse. Careful vinification certainly paid dividends with the difficult '75: for which this wine is much more elegant than most. Also fine are the '76, '78 (very late picked in November, still with no botrytis but very elegant), '79, '80, '81 and '82. '83 is elegant but '86 is finer, with '88 and '89 proving exceptional. This wine is finer than several Premiers Crus today.

Château Doisy-Dubroca
2e Cru Classé. Owner: **Lucien Lurton. 3·3ha. 750 cases. Sém 80%, Sauv 20%.**
This very small property has been run in conjunction with Climens for nearly 70 years. The vinification and maturation all take place at Climens with exactly the same care as the 1er *cru*. The distribution is exclusively handled by the aptly-named Louis Dubroca firm.

The wines here, as at Climens, are remarkably consistent. In style they are light and elegant and take time to evolve in bottle, but can be drunk young. '71, '75, '76, '79, '80 and '81 all produced good examples and '83, '85 and especially '86, were even better.

Château Doisy-Védrines
2e Cru Classé. Owner: **Pierre Castéja. 25ha. 2,500 cases. Sém 80%, Sauv 20%.** Second label: **Château La Tour-Védrines.**
This property contains the original Védrines château and *chai*. Pierre Castéja's family have inherited the property through several marriages since 1840, and he himself comes from an old family of proprietors. He also runs the *négociant* firm Roger Joanne. The wines are traditionally made with fermentation and maturation in casks, of which one-quarter are new.

There is a strong contrast between this and the other Doisys, which both concentrate on elegance and delicacy. Védrines is fuller and richer, but to my mind lacks the breed and stylishness of the others. Curiously enough I found the '75 here better balanced and finer than the '76, while at many properties the reverse is the case. Of some good wines in the 1980s, '89 was exceptional. There is also a red wine, La Tour-Védrines, but another wine, Chevalier Védrines, is a Joanne brand unconnected with this property.

Château de Fargues
Cru Bourgeois. Owner: **Comte Alexandre de Lur-Saluces. 13ha. 1,000 cases. Sém 80%, Sauv 20%.**
This tiny vineyard lies on the extremity of the commune of Fargues and of the Sauternes AC, and has belonged to the Lur-Saluces family for over 500 years. Under the present owner, Comte Alexandre de Lur-Saluces, the production of red wine has been abandoned, and they concentrate on producing the best possible Sauternes. Winemaking is identical to Yquem, with fermentation and maturation in new casks.

The wines, most of which are sold in the USA, combine lusciousness and elegance with great breed and finesse. The '67, '71, '75, '76, '80, '81, '83 and '85 are all great successes here, with the '76 finer than the '75 for me. This wine is of the standard of a top Premier Cru, and the price is correspondingly high – indeed higher than the Premiers Crus – at approximately half that of Yquem.

Château Filhot
2e Cru Classé. Owner: **Comte Henri de Vaucelles. 60ha. 12,500 cases. Sém 50%, Sauv 45%, Musc 5%.**
There are many beautiful properties in Sauternes, and this is one of the finest, an imposing late-18th-century mansion set among woods and fields. The wine is fermented in glass fibre vats and also matured in them: no wood is used. At its best this is a wine of individuality and great fruit but not necessarily great sweetness except in exceptional years. The higher than usual proportion of Sauvignon and the practice of keeping in vat help this tendency. Yet I cannot help feeling that the full potential here is not being realized. The '75 and '76 vintages are liquorous but lack style, while the '79 was still masked by sulphur when six years old. '83, '86, '88 and '89 produced raisin-like botrytized wines.

Château Gilette
Owner: **Christian Médeville. 3·5ha. 500–600 cases. Sém 90%, Sauv 8%, Musc 2%.**
This is a curiosity among the wines of Sauternes. Situated just outside the village of Preignac, it belongs to the Médeville family of Château Respide-Médeville in Graves. The soil here is sandy with a subsoil of rock and clay. Between three and seven pickings are made, with the earliest being of single berries affected by botrytis. Each picking is vinified separately with temperatures controlled at 24–25°C (75–77°F) during the first days of fermentation, and then brought down to 20°C (68°F) for the remainder of the time. The result is several different *cuvées* with differing characteristics, and normally two separate wines are made in each vintage. After the fermentation the wines are kept in small concrete vats for at least 20 years. The theory is that the large volume gives a mature flavour and bouquet while preserving fruit and freshness, so that the maturation process is slower than in a bottle.

In 1985 I was able to taste the '55 and '59 bottled in 1981, and the '49 and '50 bottled only six to seven years after the vintage. I thought the early bottlings were clearly superior to the later ones. In particular the '55 and '59 lack the bouquet and balance of the '49 and '50. In addition the '55 and '59 had great sweetness and concentration but rather lacked complexity. The '49 seemed the finest wine of all, and I preferred the '55 to the '59. So, while this system means you can find an old vintage more easily, it is far from clear that the result is actually as good as that achieved by earlier and more conventional bottlings.

Château Guiraud
1er Cru Classé. Owner: **SC Agricole.** Administrator: **Frank Narby. 118ha. Main wine: 7,000 cases; Sém 54%, Sauv 45%, Musc 1%. Dry white: 4,000 cases; Sauv 100%. Red: 8,000 cases; CS 50%, Mer 50%.** Secondary labels: **Le Dauphin de Lalague (Sauternes), 'G' Château Guiraud (Bordeaux Sec), Le Dauphin Château Guiraud (Bordeaux Supérieur, red).**
After some years in the doldrums, this famous old property received a shot in the arm when it was bought by the Narby family from Canada in 1981. Hamilton Narby, followed by his father in

1988, brought in an excellent *régisseur*, Xavier Planty, in 1983 and determined to impose the highest traditional standards for making classic Sauternes. Because of a shortage of money Guiraud had been reduced to maturing its wines in vat instead of cask, after a cask fermentation. Now 50 percent new wood is used for maturation. A dry white wine and a red wine are also made.

I remember this as a light, elegant wine which was less luscious than most Sauternes, but extremely fine in vintages such as '53, '55 and '62. Part of this distinctive character comes from the higher than usual proportion of Sauvignon. Now signs of this old distinction are returning. The successes of the new regime began with the '83, followed by '85, with the '86 even better than the '83; good wines were also made in '88, '89 and '90.

Château Guiteronde
Owner: **GFA du Hayot. 30ha. 7,500 cases. Sém 65%, Sauv 25%, Musc 10%.**
A well-known *cru* in Barsac, where André du Hayot makes some excellent wine. The '82 and '85 were fine vintages here, with all the finesse and breed typical of wines from this property. A wine to look out for, offering very good value for money.

Château Haut-Peyraguey
1er Cru Classé. Owner: **Jacques Pauly. 15ha. 3,000 cases. Sém 83%, Sauv 15%, Musc 2%.**
At the time of the 1855 classification this was a single *cru*, Château Peyraguey, and was divided in two in 1878. This is the smaller part with just a tower built in the manner of the older, grander one at Lafaurie recalling its origin. Jacques Pauly has been in charge since 1948. The fermentation is in vat, and after this the wine spends six months in vat and about 18 months in cask. The wines are light. They can be rather fine, but can also be inconsistent. '86 showed a marked improvement, but '88 is outstanding.

Château Les Justices
Owner: **Christian Médeville. 17ha. White: 8·5ha; 2,000 cases; Sém 88%, Sauv 8%, Musc 4%. Red: 6ha; 3,000 cases; CS 58%, Mer 42%.**
This property, run in harness with the same owners as Gilette, is

marketed in a more conventional manner. It has belonged to the family since 1710. The harvesting and vinification are basically the same as at Gilette, but the wines are bottled after only four years in small vats.

The '71 is superb, with a concentration of sweetness, a strong perfume and a lovely ripe fruitiness. It was perfection at nearly 14 years of age. The '80 and '81 are both promising, the '80 being very elegant with length and charming fruit and the '81 having more richness and concentration.

Château Lafaurie-Peyraguey
1er Cru Classé. Owner: **Cordier family. 20ha. 3,500 cases. Sém 90%, Sauv 5%, Musc 5%.**
After Yquem, the château here is the most spectacular in Sauternes, with its 13th-century fortifications and 17th-century buildings. It has belonged to the Cordiers since 1913 and is most carefully run. Recently the whole policy of winemaking here has changed significantly. The proportion of Sauvignon has been dropped from 30 percent to 5 percent, and the Sémillon increased from 70 to 90 percent. In 1967 a new system was introduced whereby the wines were kept in glass-lined vats under nitrogen after fermentation in cask. The result was that they became light and one-dimensional, quite lacking the distinction expected of a top Sauternes. Now they have returned to more traditional ways and are maturing in casks, of which a third are new. This, combined with the change in the vineyard, promises well for the future.

Much more interesting wines were been made here in '79, '80, '81 and especially '83. The '86 was finer still, with '88 and '89 following the same pattern of excellence. They have a honeyed bouquet, elegant fruit and breed, and will certainly be worth waiting for.

Château Lamothe
2e Cru Classé. Owner: **Jean Despujols. 8ha. 2,000 cases. Sém 70%, Sauv 20%, Musc 10%.**
This is another divided property. Lamothe used to belong to the same owners as Château d'Arche. Then in 1961 they sold half the property, including the château and half the cellars, to the Despujols family. They ferment in tank and then mature partly in tank and

partly in cask. The result is a rather light and dryish commercial Sauternes, which is decent but no more. A fine '86, however, may mark the beginning of better things, but in general there are more interesting wines among the Crus Bourgeois.

Château Lamothe-Guignard
2e Cru Classé. Owners: **Philippe & Jacques Guignard. 16ha. 3,000 cases. Sém 90%, Musc 5%, Sauv 5%.**
Lamothe as a single property belonged to the owners of d'Arche. In 1961 they sold a part of the property to the Despujols family, and continued to sell the wines from their portion as Lamothe-Bergey. Then in 1981 the Guignards bought Lamothe-Bergey and substituted their name for Bergey. The same family own Château Rolland. The first vintage of the new regime, '81, has elegance and ripeness, length and finesse, delectable fruit and moderate sweetness. '83, '86, '88 and '89 are also all very fine wines. Clearly a wine to watch with interest.

Château Liot
Owner: **J David. 21ha. 5,500 cases. Sém 80%, Sauv 15%, Musc 5%.**
Once bottled by Harveys of Bristol, these well-made wines are sold under the château label only in good vintages – the rest of the wine is sold in bulk. '88 was a particularly good vintage at this property.

Château de Malle
2e Cru Classé. Owner: **Comtesse de Bournazel. 26ha. 2,700 cases. Sém 75%, Sauv 22%, Musc 3%.** Second labels: **Château Ste-Hélène, Chevalier de Malle (white Graves, 3,000 cases), Château du Cardaillan (red Graves, 6,000 cases).**
This beautiful property is interesting to visit for the sake of the 17th-century château as well as the wine. The vineyard is partly in Sauternes and partly in Graves. Fermentation is in cask as well as vat, and the maturation follows a similar pattern. The wines have great elegance and charm, and are of a light style which is only moderately liquorous. It can be drunk young (three or four years old) but in good years gradually opens up in bottle and repays keeping. The '89 is exceptional.

Château du Mayne
Owner: **Jean Saunders. 8ha. 1,700 cases. Sém 80%, Sauv 20%.**
This small *cru* in Barsac produces wine that is full-bodied and perfumed but not luscious: classic in the drier style of Barsac. Some attractive wines have emerged from Château du Mayne. The '83 was especially good.

Château Menota
Owners: **M & Mme Noël Labat. 29ha. 6,600 cases. Sém 50%, Sauv 50%.**
A stunning château, dating from the 16th century, at which some very attractive wines are made. The property is well worth a visit, and the wines – with plenty of classic Sauvignon elegance – are stylish and seldom disappoint.

Château Myrat
2e Cru Classé. Owner: **Comte de Pontac.**
In 1975, the proprietor of this château pulled up all his vines as he was no longer able to afford to run the property. Fortunately his successor was able to begin replanting them just before the planting rights expired in 1988. It will be a while before new wines appear on the market.

Chateau Nairac
2e Cru Classé. Owner: **Nicole Heeter-Tari. 16ha. 2,000 cases. Sém 90%, Sauv 6%, Musc 4%.**
This is a heartening tale of restoration. Tom Heeter, a young American, came to work at Château Giscours to learn about wine, and in the process he carried off the daughter of the house; his father-in-law Nicolas Tari then spotted that Nairac, in the commune of Barsac, was for sale at a reasonable price. The couple finally took possession in 1972. With Professor Peynaud's guidance, Tom Heeter set out to make Barsac in a very traditional way, using only wood (65 percent new) to ferment and mature the wines. However, like Pierre Dubourdieu, he wanted to reduce the use of sulphur. He did not go to the extremes used at Doisy-Daëne, but by using vitamin B, an anti-oxidant, he had considerable success. Following their divorce (Tom Heeter finished with the '86 vintage)

Nicole has shown equal dedication and the '88 and '89 are as good as anything that went before.

The care of the winemaking has quickly won admirers for Nairac. The wines are not normally very liquorous, but are quite powerful and rich under the influence of new oak. The most successful years here before 1986 were '76, '79, '80 and '82. This is certainly a wine to watch out for.

Château Rabaud-Promis
1er Cru Classé. Owner: **GFA Rabaud-Promis.**
Administrator: **Philippe Dejean. 33ha. 5,000 cases. Sém 80%, Sauv 18%, Musc 2%.** Second label: **Château Jauga.**
Château Rabaud was a single property until 1903 when it was divided (*see also* Sigalas-Rabaud), and this part was bought by Adnen Promis. The château dates from the 18th century and is built in a fine hilltop position. This consists of two-thirds of the original property. The properties were reunited in 1929, but divided again in 1952. The Deuxième Cru Château Peixotto is now also incorporated into Rabaud-Promis. The grapes here, contrary to the tradition in Sauternes, are crushed before going into the presses, and the fermentation and maturation are carried out entirely in cement vats. Improvements came with a new generation of administration and now some casks are used. '83 was a fine stylish wine, '86 was powerfully botrytized, and the '88 set new standards of excellence, reviving memories of past glories.

Chateau Raymond-Lafon
Cru Bourgeois. Owner: **GFA Château Raymond-Lafon.**
Administrator: **Pierre Meslier. 20ha. 2,000 cases. Sém 80%, Sauv 20%.**
This property adjoins Yquem and since 1972 has belonged to Yquem's *régisseur*, Pierre Meslier. The vineyard is not only well-placed, with Yquem on one side and Sigalas-Rabaud on the other, but Pierre Meslier makes it with the same meticulous care he gives to Yquem. The wine is matured in cask with as much as a third in new oak. The resulting wines are already beginning to carve out a reputation for themselves as being well up to Cru Classé standards, fine, perfumed, and luscious. Fine wines were made in '75, '76, '79, '80, '81, '82, '83, '84, '85, '86 and '87. In the difficult '78 vintage,

with little or no botrytis, a particularly successful wine was made.

Château de Rayne-Vigneau
1er Cru Classé. Owner: **SC du Château.** Administrator: **Jean Pierre Angliviel de la Beaumelle. 78ha. 16,500 cases (including 4,000 cases dry). Sém 50%, Sauv 50%.** Dry wine: **Rayne Sec.**

The wines of Rayne-Vigneau enjoyed a great reputation in the 19th century and the first part of this century. Until 1961 it belonged to the Pontac family, who still own the actual château. In 1971 it was bought by the group that owns Château Grand-Puy-Ducasse and a number of other châteaux. Their properties are run and distributed by Mestrezat. The Sémillon and Sauvignon are pressed separately here, because some of the Sauvignon is also used for the dry wine (although most of this is made from less-ripe grapes picked earlier). The fermentation is in vat, then the wine goes into casks for maturation, of which 20 percent are new. Undoubtedly the property is now well-run again, but the yields were too high at first, and the wines tended to be correct but rather dull and uninspired. Certainly not up to the high standards of the past, these were frankly commercial wines. The '76 is the best of this period, but things began to improve with the '83 and '85. '86 and '88 have maintained this progress.

Château Rieussec
1er Cru Classé. Owner: **SA Château Rieussec. 66ha. 6,000 cases. Sém 80%, Sauv 18%, Musc 2%.** Second labels: **Clos Labère, Château Mayne des Carmes, 'R' (dry), Château Mayne des Carmes.**

This property is superbly placed on the highest hill in Sauternes after Yquem. The vineyard is in the commune of Sauternes, but the estate buildings are in Fargues. The soil here is particularly gravelly. Rieussec has always been regarded as one of the finest *crus* in Sauternes, producing wines of great individuality with an outstanding bouquet and great concentration of flavour, but also marked elegance and less lusciousness than some. In 1971 it was acquired by Albert Vuillier who determined to use the most traditional methods and produced wines that have been adored by some and disliked by others. In 1984 he sold to Domaines

Rothschild and sometime afterwards Charles Chevallier came from Lafite to run the property. The fermentation is in vat, then maturation is partly in large oak *foudres* (vats) and partly in casks, of which 50 percent are new.

After making a classic Rieussec in 1971, Albert Vuillier mostly made heavily botrytized wines, deep in colour, often with that dry nose and aftertaste associated with botrytis which in excess has the effect of cutting the sweetness at the finish owing to high volatile acidity. For this reason I dislike the '75 in spite of its obvious concentration. The '76 is very opulent and attractive but I think slightly unbalanced and therefore was at its best when young. '83 was Albert Vuillier's last and best vintage. Under the new regime there has been an acceleration of success. A lovely fresh, ripe '85 was followed by a concentrated '86 with real breed and finesse, then great wines in the three outstanding vintages of '88, '89 and '90.

Château de Rolland
Cru Bourgeois. Owners: **Jean & Pierre Guignard. 20ha. 4,000 cases. Sém 60%, Sauv 20%, Musc 20%.**
This *cru* in Barsac not only makes wine but is also a good restaurant and hotel, the only place to stay if you want to be in the middle of the Sauternes vineyards. The owners are also the proprietors of the excellent Château Roquetaillade-La-Grange in Graves. The wines enjoy a good reputation at the Cru Bourgeois level. Wines are vinified and matured in casks bought from Yquem.

Château Romer-du-Hayot
2e Cru Classé. Owner: **André du Hayot** (*see below*). **15ha. 4,000 cases. Sém 70%, Sauv 25%, Musc 5%.**
This *cru* deserves to be more widely known. The vineyard adjoins de Malle on the edge of the commune of Fargues. For some years the ownership has been divided between the du Hayot and Fargues families, but since 1977 the Fargues portion has been leased to the du Hayots, so that the property is now run as one, although there are two owners. The wine is both fermented and matured in vat, and bottling is done early. André du Hayot clearly knows how to make Sauternes because, both here and at Guiteronde in Barsac (where the wines are actually made), he is making excellent wines, of their sort, with limited resources. There is an emphasis on fruit and

freshness. Only in years like '76 is there a lot of sweetness, but the wines always seem well balanced and most attractive. Both '79 and '80 are successes, with the '79 fuller and richer; '88 and '89 are both fruity and stylish.

Château St-Amand
Owner: **Louis Ricard. 22ha. 4,500 cases. Sém 85%, Sauv 15%.** Second label: **Château La Chartreuse.**
Traditionally made and elegant, some fine Cru Bourgeois wines are produced at this property in Preignac. They are more commonly sold in England under the Château La Chartreuse label. '80, '81 and '83 are especially good vintages, though all are stylish and reliable.

Château Sigalas-Rabaud
1er Cru Classé. Owners: **Héritiers de la Marquise de Lambert des Granges. 14ha. 2,000 cases. Sém 88%, Sauv 12%.**
This *cru* formed part of the old property of Rabaud, which was divided in 1903. From 1929 to 1952 the properties were united again. The yields here are low and the traditional *trie* (selective picking of the ripest grapes) is made through the vineyard four or five times. The fermentation is in vat as is the maturation. I have found the wines usually very perfumed, elegant and quite delicate, yet liquorous and with real breed. For me the best and most typical vintages here have been the especially fine '67, and the '71,'75 and '81. The '83 and '86 follow in the same lines.

Château Suau
2e Cru Classé. Owner: **Roger Biarnès. 6·5ha. 1,500 cases. Sém 80%, Sauv 10%, Musc 10%.**
Probably the least known of the Crus Classés. The vineyard is in Barsac, but the present owners vinify the wine at their other property in Illats. Much of the wine is sold by *vente directe* in France. The wine is fermented in vats and then in used casks. The reputation is for rather ordinary, dull wines with an unbalanced sweetness and lacking breed but the '88 is delicate and fine.

Château Suduiraut
1er Cru Classé. Owner: **L Fonquernie. 70ha. 11,000 cases.**

Sém 80%, Sauv 20%.
This famous old *cru* adjoins Yquem and is partly in the commune of Sauternes and partly in that of Preignac. The Fonquernie family bought the property, with its lovely 17th-century château, in 1940 and have slowly nursed it back to quality and fame. It is normally the most liquorous and intensely rich wine after Yquem, and when at its best is also one of the very best Sauternes. The juice ferments in vats after a careful selection in the vineyard, and is then matured in casks, of which 35 percent are new. But one should note that Suduiraut went through a bad patch when there was little or no selection and virtually no cask-ageing. This affected the vintages from '71 to '75 inclusive.

The best Suduirauts are pale gold in colour, the bouquet is exquisitely perfumed and penetrating, and the flavour very rich and vigorous, distinctive, honeyed, with great finesse and breed. In good years the wines usually have 5 degrees Baumé or more. The '70 was one of the best examples of its vintage, and '76 produced a classic wine to stand beside the '59, '62 and '67. There have been good but not outstanding wines in '79 and '80. During the 1980s the wines have generally had less residual sugar than in the great vintages of the 1950s and 1960s, so one is left with an impression of alcohol at the finish. '83, '86, '88 and '89 were the best years.

Château La Tour-Blanche
1er Cru Classé. Owner: **Ministry of Agriculture.**
Administrator: **Jean Pierre Jausserand. 30ha. 5,600 cases. Sém 70%, Sauv 27·5%, Musc 2·5%.** Second label: **Cru St-Marc.**
The *cru* was placed at the head of the Premiers Crus in 1855 and since 1910 has belonged to the state, now being run as an agricultural school. Unfortunately its reputation is nowhere near what it should be, and there are Deuxièmes Crus and indeed unclassified wines that are better. The wine is fermented in vat and then matured in cask with 25 percent new wood. In 1988 a degree of cask fermentation was introduced. Considering the care taken in making the wine, it is hard to understand why it has been so uninspired. The present administration is keen to remedy matters however, and towards the end of the 1980s there have been clear signs of improvement. There was a rich, well-balanced '76 and a most attractive '81: rich, supple and attractive but rather forward.

Château d'Yquem
1er Grand Cru Classé 1855. Owner: **Comte Alexandre de Lur-Saluces. 102ha. 5,500 cases. Sém 80%, Sauv 20%.**
Second label: **'Y' (Bordeaux Blanc, 2,000 cases).**

In 1855, when the great sweet wines of Sauternes and Barsac were classified, Yquem was placed in a category of its own as the sole Premier Grand Cru, as distinct from the Premiers Crus. Its unique position has remained unassailed ever since. This is not only the greatest Sauternes, it is also the supreme dessert wine in the world. The Lur-Saluces family have owned it since 1785. None has been more dedicated than the present owner, Alexandre de Lur-Saluces, who succeeded his uncle in 1970. The château is a superb fortress commanding fine views over the region. The vineyard is carefully rotated, so that although there are 102 hectares under vine, only about 80 are actually producing the *grand vin*; the rest are young vines. The picking is carefully controlled, using only skilled workers, mostly from the 57 full-time estate workers, who go through the vineyard a number of times (anything from four to 11) selecting only overripe and botrytized berries. The aim is to pick at not less than 20 degrees and not more than 22 degrees Baumé. This produces the most balanced wines, which ferment to between 13·5 and 14 percent, leaving between four and seven degrees Beaumé unfermented sugar. The pressing is traditional and the musts are fermented in new oak, maturing in cask for three years prior to bottling. Yquem can never be sampled, even by its buyers. A dry wine, 'Y' or Ygrec, is made in some years. It has quite a honeyed nose, and is full-bodied and quite rich.

Yquem is the quintessence of Sauternes, with its colour turning gradually to pale gold, its intense honeyed bouquet, and the wonderful lusciousness and elegance of the flavour itself. It is always a privilege to drink this wine. One should not attempt to drink it before ten years of age, and it has a special charm of freshness for another decade after that. In the greatest years it can continue almost indefinitely. Wines at their peak now are '67 (a great year), '70 (very fine), '71 (a great wine), '73 (a good lesser vintage). Years to look forward to are '75 and '76 (exceptional), '80 and '81 (very good) and the '82 (exceptional for the year), '83 (a massive slow developer), '84 (exceptional for the year), '85 (small in quantity but excellent) and '86 (potentially the greatest Yquem for many years).

St-Emilion

What strikes one about St-Emilion as a district, compared to the other great regions, especially Médoc or Graves, is its smallness and compactness. One can walk straight out of the cramped mediaeval streets of St-Emilion and find all but one of the Premiers Crus Classés of the *côtes* are just a few minutes' walk away.

St-Emilion covers 5,000 hectares and is divided among 1,000 different *crus*, of which only a small proportion are actually classified. 1,150 hectares belong to the 330 members of the cooperative known as the Union des Producteurs. Another notable feature is the small size of the properties themselves. The average size of the 11 Premiers Grands Crus Classés is a bare 20 hectares, that of the Grands Crus Classés is less than ten hectares. Compare this with the vineyard sizes in Médoc. An analysis of the declarations made by growers for the '79 crop showed that out of 1,198, 843 were made by individuals, 330 by members of the cooperative, and 25 were for family consumption.

Another fundamental characteristic of St-Emilion is its complex variety of soils. For practical purposes these can be divided into three groups:

First, the limestone plateau (*plateau calcaire*) and the *côtes et pieds de côtes*, the hillsides and lower slopes. There is also an important element of clay in these soils. This covers the area around the town of St-Emilion, where all but two of the Premiers Grands Crus Classés are found.

Second, the *graves et sables anciens*, an area of gravel mixed with sand, but sand of an old windblown variety as distinct from the more recent alluvial kind. This is a small area near the border with Pomerol, where there are a succession of gravelly slopes covering about 60 hectares, in a sea of sandy soils. Cheval Blanc and Figeac dominate, and nearly all the other *crus* here are classified.

Third, the *sables anciens*, the area of sandy soils of the type already described. There are a number of good, attractive classified *crus* in this area, which lies between the first two.

In terms of *appellation* and geography, divisions are:

1 The **Grands Crus Classés**: allowed by a system of classification under the ultimate control of the INAO that is subject to revision

Appellations of the Libourne Region

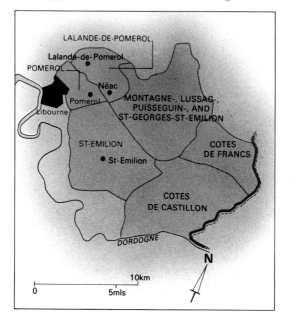

every ten years. In fact the original system of 1954 was revised in 1969, and the second revision came in 1985. This actually reduced the number of classified wines from 12 to 11 in the Premiers Grands Crus Classés, and from 72 to 63 in the Grands Crus Classés. All come from the commune of St-Emilion itself.

2 The **Grands Crus**: comprising some 200 *crus* that have to submit samples annually for tasting.

3 Wines bearing the simple St-Emilion *appellation*.

Geographically, although the best wines are to be found in the commune of St-Emilion itself, eight communes which come within the ancient jurisdiction of the Jurade de St-Emilion are also entitled to the *appellation*. In these communes the best wines come from St-Christophe-des-Bardes, St-Laurent-des-Combes, St-Hippolyte and St-Etienne-des-Lisses. The remaining four – St-Pey-d'Armens, Vignonet, St-Sulpice-de-Faleyrens and Libourne – are mostly on low-lying sandy soil or terraces of recent gravel and sand.

There was a time when St-Emilion was said to tend its vines better than anywhere else but not to be so good at making its wines. In the past years there has been a great improvement in this direction with many new *chais* and *cuviers* being built. Only the problems involved in commercializing so many small properties remain to be solved.

Château L'Angélus
Grand Cru Classé. Owner: **de Bouard de Laforest family. 24ha. 12,000 cases. CF 50%, Mer 45%, CS 5%.**
This is one of the most important estates on the St-Emilion *côtes*. Before buying L'Angelus in 1924, the de Bouard de Laforest family owned Château Mazerat, which they later incorporated, together with several other properties, into L'Angélus. The vineyard is on the lower slopes of the *côtes*, to the west of St-Emilion. There is a large modern *chai* and cask-maturing was introduced in 1980 – between 50 percent and two-thirds new oak is used. Before this the wines saw no wood at all.

The wines are characterized by a marked perfume and easy flattering fruit, but tend to lack depth. Prior to '83 many of these wines lacked concentration and needed to be drunk young. Since then they have had more solidity, while retaining their crunchy fruit and richness. '79 and '82 are the pick of the vintages so far, while '83, '85 and '86 promise interesting wines for the future.

Château L'Arrosée
Grand Cru Classé. Owner: **François Rodhain. 10ha. 5,000 cases. Mer 50%, CS 35%, CF 15%.**
A wine of growing reputation, the vineyard is well sited on the *côtes* above the cooperative and below Tertre-Daugay, just south-west of the town. The name means 'watered by springs'. The balance of the wine comes from its position: the *haute de côte* giving body and power, the *milieu de côte* providing the richness, and the *pied de côte* contributing finesse.

This is classic St-Emilion, rich and luscious, but with great depth, flavour and personality. Not easy to find, but well worth the effort.

Château Ausone

1er Grand Cru Classé. Owner: **Mme Dubois-Challon & Héritiers Vauthier. 7ha. 2,250 cases. Mer 50%, CF 50%.**

Named after the Roman poet Ausonius in the 18th century, this château has the remains of an important Roman villa nearby, that may well have belonged to the poet himself. It was only in the 1890s that Ausone was recognized as the first wine of the St-Emilion *côtes*, a position previously held by its larger neighbour, Belair. During the 1950s and 1960s the reputation of Ausone was not up to its rank as a Premier Cru, although in 1955 it was placed alongside Cheval Blanc at the head of the new classification by virtue of its undoubted intrinsic merits. In 1975 a new *régisseur*, Pascal Delbeck, arrived and took full control in 1976. Since then the reputation of Ausone has soared. Fermentation is now in stainless steel, and 100 percent new oak is used.

The essence of Ausone is the combination of delicacy and finesse with power, so that the concentration of complex perfumes on the nose is both lively and beautiful, while the sensation of multi-layered flavours on the palate is remarkable. The wines take longer to mature than other St-Emilions and have an ability to age which is unrivalled on this side of the river. Since the massive '75, there has been a fine '76, a great '78, a less monumental but glorious '79, a fine '80, an elegant and firm '81, a great '82 with opulence and concentration, a softer yet exotic '83, a top-quality '85 and a complex, densely rich '86. Everything seems set for Ausone to become the new Pétrus in terms of extraordinary wines produced in very small quantities. Let us hope that wine-lovers as well as collectors get a look-in.

Château Balestard-la-Tonnelle

Grand Cru Classé. Owner: **GFA Capdemourlin.**
Administrator: **Jacques Capdemourlin. 10·6ha. 5,000 cases. Mer 65%, CF 20%, CS 10%, Mal 5%.**

This estate lies at the limit of the *plateau calcaire*, to the east of St-Emilion and across the road from Soutard. A third of the maturation is in new wood, a third in one- or two-year-old wood and the remainder in *cuves*.

The wines here are consistent and most attractive, archetypal St-Emilion which is big, luscious and full-bodied, easy to drink, yet lasting longer than one might expect. The '78 is soft, ripe and full, ready to drink, the '79 had already developed complex overtones and was a luscious, attractive wine by '83; '80 is soft and full-flavoured and was also drinkable by '83, and '81 is rich and powerful but forward. The '82 shows real concentration with a rich meaty structure and will probably be ready to drink early. The '83 is high in extract and tannins, '85 is an opulent early-developer, and the '86 has real concentration with ripe, elegant tannins.

Château Les Baziliques
Owner: **SC du Château Le Couvent. 6ha. 3,500 cases. Mer 39%, CF 36%, CS 25%.**
The wines of this property have improved considerably since it was bought by the current owners. They have invested much in the *cru* and some delicious wines have resulted; '85 was a particularly good vintage here. A *cru* to look out for.

Château Beau Séjour Bécot
Grand Cru Classé. Owners: **Michel, Gérard and Dominique Bécot. 16·5ha. 6,600 cases. Mer 70%, CS 15%, CF 15%.**
This *cru* was classified in 1955 as a Premier Grand Cru, and in 1985 was demoted amidst a wealth of controversy. As this is written, Michel Bécot is appealing against the decision. In essence the demotion seems to be because Bécot added the vineyards of La Carte and Trois Moulins to the original ten hectares of Beau Séjour which he bought in 1970, although the merger was not effected until 1979. The vineyard is on the *plateau calcaire* and the fermentation is in stainless steel with fine underground cellars for maturation of the wines in bottle. 90 percent new wood is used.

The style of the wines here is very different from that of the other Beauséjour, more fleshy and rich, but with less tannin and style. They are very attractive, easy-to-drink wines but do lack distinction. It will be interesting to see what the outcome of it all is.

Château Beauséjour (Duffau-Lagarrosse)
1er Grand Cru Classé B. Owner: **Duffau-Lagarrosse.**
Administrator: **Jean-Michel Fernandez. 7ha. 3,000 cases. Mer 50%, CF 25%, CS 25%.** Second label: **Le Croix de Mazerat.**
Today the least-known of the Premiers Grands Crus. This is partly

because about half of its very small production is sold direct to private customers rather than through the trade. Beauséjour was a single property until 1869 when it was divided between two daughters. One married a doctor from St-Emilion, and this part now belongs to their heirs.

Long vatting here gives the wine breed and stylish fruit, but perhaps rather too much tannin for wines that are light in body. This is clearly a case of a wine essentially owing its classification to the vineyard site and a long tradition of respectable wines, because until recently the wines were good but not brilliant. After a very rich '82 with real 'race', '85 again had real concentration and the '86 was even more impressive, combining elegant fruit with rich concentrated fruit and tannins. '88 and '89 follow the same line of improvement. This is now a wine of real distinction.

Château Belair
1er Grand Cru Classé B. Owner: **Mme Dubois-Challon. 13ha. 4,000 cases. Mer 60%, CF 40%.**
Belair adjoins Ausone and its owner is also co-owner of Ausone. The two châteaux share the same outstanding *régisseur*, Pascal Delbeck. The major difference between Belair and Ausone is that, while Ausone is wholly on the *côtes*, the vineyard of Belair is divided between the *côtes* and the plateau above it. Having been made and kept in the Ausone cellars for many years, the wines of Belair returned to their own cellars in 1976, and the old wooden fermentation *cuves* were replaced by stainless steel vats after the 1980 vintage.

Today Belair is nearly always one of the best of the Premiers Grands Crus B group. The wines tend to be a little richer and more fleshy than Ausone, without quite the same intensity, but with real finesse and great vigour. Of recent vintages the '75 is firm and still backward, the '76 is charming and lightweight, for drinking now, while the '78 gets better all the time, '79 is outstanding and there is a good '80. '81 is fine and typical and the wines of '82, '83, '85 and '86 are exceptional.

Château Bellefont-Belcier
Grand Cru. Owner: **Héritiers J-L Faure.** Administrator: **Jean Labusquière. 13ha. 7,000 cases. Mer 70%, CS 20%, CF 10%.**

A good *cru* in St-Laurent-des-Combes, on the *côtes* and their lower slopes. The wines have a reputation for robustness and suppleness.

Château Bellevue
Grand Cru Classé. Owner: **SC du Château (M L Horeau).** Administrator: **René de Coninck. 6ha. 2,500 cases. Mer 70%, CF 15%, CS 15%.**
The vineyard lies on the limestone plateau and *côte* just to the west of Beauséjour. It must be one of the least-known of the Grands Crus today. It has the misfortune to have one of the commonest names in Bordeaux as there are 23 properties at present using it, several of which are in the St-Emilion region. This Château Bellevue is a very old property and has belonged to the same group of connected families since the 17th century.

For the '88 vintage a proportion of new oak was used for the first time, and from being a rather anonymous pleasant wine, one began to see the breed and style one would expect from a vineyard in this position. A *cru* of old repute, this was one of the 39 *crus* of St-Emilion that represented the region at the Paris Exhibition of 1867.

Château Bergat
Grand Cru Classé. Owner: **Mme Clause Bertin.** Administrator: **Emile Castéja. 4ha. 1,100 cases. Mer 50%, CF 25%, CS 25%.**
This is one of the smallest and least-known of the Grands Crus Classés. It lies to the east of St-Emilion at the edge of the plateau and *côtes*, overlooking the valley of Fougabaud. The property is farmed by Emile Castéja from nearby Trottevieille and distributed by his firm Borie-Manoux.

When I tasted the wine in 1984, the '79 was scented and full on the nose with a very distinctive spicy character on the palate, full-flavoured and still quite tough, promising a good bottle in 1986 or 1987. A bottle of Bergat should always be worth investigating.

Château Berliquet
Grand Cru Classé. Owners: **Vicomte & Vicomtesse Patrick de Lesque. 8·7ha. 4,500 cases. Mer 69%, CF and CS 31%.**
A very old *cru*, superbly placed on the *plateau calcaire* of St-Emilion

and the *côtes*, adjoining Magdelaine, Canon and Tertre Daugay. This *cru* was already regarded as one of the best in the 18th century, but had to wait until 1985 to become a Grand Cru Classé, and was the only one promoted that year. The reason for this neglect was that as a member of the cooperative its wines were vinified and matured there, until the '78 vintage. Then stainless steel fermentation vats were installed, the *chai* restored and the underground *cuves* made ready. Since 1978 all the wines have been vinified and matured here using a third new oak. All the supervision and work is still in the hands of the Union de Producteurs.

Judging by the wines now being produced, Berliquet well deserves its promotion. The '78 is mature and well-structured but still taut, with potential to develop further; '80 is stylish and pleasant, just ready in '85; '81 is very perfumed with verve and finesse, ready in '88; '82 is very dense, rich and powerful and needs time, and '83 had an intense bouquet of roses and tobacco plants and was rich, complex and powerful with a really lovely flavour. This is a *cru* with a growing reputation and considerable potential.

Château Cadet-Bon
Grand Cru. Owner: **Société Loriene. 6ha. 2,500 cases. Mer 75%, CS and CF 25%.**
This small property lies north of the town on the *plateau calcaire* and *côtes*. It lost its status as a Cru Classé in the 1985 revision. Tastings have shown that the wines can be rather rustic, with a coarse, stalky flavour suggesting poor vinification.

Château Cadet-Piola
Grand Cru Classé. Owners: **Jabiol family. 6·8ha. 3,500 cases. Mer 51%, CS 28%, CF 18%, Mal 3%.**
Cadet-Piola lies to the north of St-Emilion on the *plateau calcaire* and *côtes* at their culminating northern point. The present owners bought it in 1952 and run it in conjunction with another Grand Cru Classé, Faurie-de-Souchard. Vinification is in glass-lined vats and is carefully controlled. Maturation is in cellars quarried out under the vineyard, and 50 percent of the wood used is new.

The wines are certainly marked by their grape varieties. They need patience compared with many St-Emilions, being tightly knit and austere to start with, but with the structure and style of a wine of some distinction. The '76 is now exceptionally good for the year, and '78 was a big wine with structure and fruit and a promising future when five years old. '79 was still firm and austere and very undeveloped when four years old, and '80 was pleasantly open-textured and full-flavoured at three years. The '81 was still very tight and austere after a year in bottle, but with a fine depth of flavour. The '82 has great depth and concentration and '83 is scented, quite firm and tannic; '85 has more richness than usual, and '86 is tannic and rich but slightly austere. This wine needs waiting for, but should be worth it.

Château Canon
1er Grand Cru Classé B. Owner: **Eric Fournier. 18ha. 8,000 cases. Mer 55%, CF 40%, CS 5%.**
This is a beautifully placed property, with 13 hectares of its vineyard in a walled *clos* on the plateau just outside the walls of St-Emilion, and a very elegant little 18th-century château. The remainder of the vineyard is on the *côtes*. The wines are matured in as much as 40 percent new wood.

The wine is classic, beautifully perfumed, with great length of flavour, and can be almost silky in texture. There is an inner concentration of tannin and rich fruit that opens out only slowly. The wine always has immense breed, elegance and style. It is usually consistently one of the top St-Emilions, but is one you must wait for. The '75 is a long-term classic and the '76 charming to drink now; the '78 is rather austere and backward for the year and the '79 is outstanding. There is a classic '81 and the '82 and '83 are both superb – it is hard to say which will be the better. '85 is compact and fruity – a lovely wine – and '86 achieves the balance of power and finesse that is the hallmark of Eric Fournier's achievements here. Classic wines were produced in '88 and '89.

Château Canon-la-Gaffelière
Grand Cru Classé. Owner: **Comte de Neipperg. 19ha. 10,000 cases. Mer 55%, CF 40%, CS 5%.** Second label: **Château Le Mondotée.**
This property lies on the road which runs from the Libourne-Bergerac road to St-Emilion. It is at the southern foot of the *côtes* and on flat, sandy soil. The present owner has been here since 1971.

Maturation is in cask and *cuves*, with 50 percent new wood rotated with wine in vat.

This was an attractive, quick-maturing and easy to drink wine until transformed by changes in vinification and *élevage*, begun with the '85 vintage. Before this there was a good '82 with less concentration than the best wines but robust with plenty of character, and a supple, light '83. The wines are now showing clear signs of rather heavy oaking, which vintages such as '86 carry comfortably, but which in some others seems overdone. A wine to watch and wait for.

Château Cap-de-Mourlin
Grand Cru Classé. Owner: **Capdemourlin family.**
Administrator: **Jacques Capdemourlin. 14ha. 6,000 cases.**
Mer 60%, CF 25%, CS 12%, Mal 3%.
During the 1970s and until after the '82 vintage, this historic property was divided between two parts of the Capdemourlin family, and its wines were made and bottled separately, but used identical labels, the one difference being that one bore the name of Mme Jean Capdemourlin, the other that of her nephew Jacques, who also owns Balestard. Generally I have found the wines vinified by Jacques Capdemourlin to be superior during this period, and he is now responsible for the reunited whole. A third of the wood used for maturation is new. The vineyard is north of St-Emilion on the lower *côtes*. This is a classic St-Emilion, perfumed and fruity on the nose and with a generous, almost unctuous flavour, supported with a good structure. In recent years Jacques Capdemourlin made excellent wines in '78, '79, '81, '82, '83, '85 and '86. The future of the reunited property looks promising.

Château Cardinal-Villemaurine
Grand Cru. Owner: **J F & J M Carille. 18ha. 6,000 cases.**
Mer 75%, CF and CS 25%.
A domaine on the *plateau calcaire* just to the east of the town, with extensive underground cellars. The wines tend to be firm, tannic and a shade austere. They take time to mature. The '70, '75, '76, '79, '81 and '82 are fine examples.

Château Le Castelot
Grand Cru. Owner: **J Janoueix. 8·5ha. 3,000 cases. Mer 60%, CS 20%, CF 20%.**
The vineyards of Le Castelot are situated on the sandy plain of St-Sulpice-de-Faleyrens. The sand, gravel and iron traces give these wines noticeable *terroir* characteristics with an initially strong impact that usually softens as the wine ages. Careful vinification, using 20 percent new oak, is carried out by Paul Cazenave, *maître du chai* for all the Janoueix properties, as well as Château Canon. Once matured these wines are consistently delicious. Certainly a reliable property.

Château Chauvin
Grand Cru Classé. Owner: **Henri Ondet. 13ha. 4,200 cases. Mer 60%, CF 30%, CS 10%.**
This *cru* lies in what misleadingly used to be called the St-Emilion Graves. It is the most southeasterly of this group of *crus*, east of Ripeau and south of Corbin. The soil is sandy. A third of the casks for maturation are new. The wines are typical of this area near the Pomerol border, rich and dense in texture, quickly becoming mellow and unctuous in flavour, but with a touch of coarseness in their make-up. I have always found this to be a very attractive wine.

Château Cheval-Blanc
1er Grand Cru Classé A. Owner: **SC du Château Cheval Blanc.** Administrator: **M Lurton. 36ha. 12,000 cases. CF 66%, Mer 33%, Mal 1%.**
St-Emilion's two greatest wines, Ausone and Cheval-Blanc, are at opposite ends of the *appellation* and on quite different soils. Cheval-Blanc, the most famous of all St-Emilions, is a large property for the region, right on the border with Pomerol. Its reputation goes back to the 1921 vintage, and this was further strengthened by the legendary '47. The soil here is predominantly gravelly and sandy, but clay and sandstone with traces of iron are also present. The high proportion of Cabernet Franc at the expense of Merlot is an unusual feature. In 1956 the vineyard was seriously affected by the notorious February frost and took some time to recover. The vinification is in vat, with refrigeration available to control the temperature. 100 percent new oak is used for maturation. In 1989 Jacques Hébrard

retired, having successfully run the property on behalf of his wife's family since 1972. After a hiatus, the family turned to another family of château owners, the Lurtons of Clos Fourtet, to find a replacement.

The wines of Cheval-Blanc are famous for their powerful enveloping bouquet, which is rich and often spicy, and their very full, mellow, almost unctuous flavour. It is a particular quality of this *cru* that in very ripe years the wines can be drunk very young. This happened with the famous '47, which was delectable when a mere six or seven years old. At this stage the sheer animal vigour and stunning beauty of the wine is matched only by Pétrus, just across the border in Pomerol. Of course the wines keep and develop well according to the individuality of each year, but the early exuberance is not to be missed and Cheval-Blanc does not age as well as Ausone and some other wines of the *côtes*, becoming lacy and frail when over 40 years old. Great vintages worth looking out for from this property are '64, '66 and '70; other major years are '75, '78, '79 and '81, all of which are delicious to drink now. Of the more recent vintages the '82 is probably the best since '47, and the '83 is also very fine. The '85 is a bull's eye, with that opulence bordering on sweetness of the greatest years, and '86 is dense-textured with the style to suggest a great wine. '88 and '89 also promise great things.

Château Clos-des-Jacobins
Grand Cru Classé. Owner: **Domaine Cordier. 7·5ha. 4,500 cases. Mer 47%, CF 45%, CS 8%.**
The wines here have always been consistent and of attractive quality, but recent vintages have been more concentrated and impressive. There is a fine concentrated '78, a delightful '79, a lighter '85, and the '81, '82, '83, '86 and '88 are all excellent with great richness and opulence. Certainly this is one of the best *crus* in this section of St-Emilion.

Château La Clotte
Grand Cru Classé. Owner: **Héritiers Chailleau. 4·2ha. 1,550 cases. Mer 95%, CF 5%.**
This tiny vineyard is beautifully placed on the edge of the *plateau calcaire* and the *côtes*, just outside the walls of St-Emilion to the east. It is farmed by Ets J-P Moueix who take three-quarters of the crop

in return for running the vineyard and making the wine. They use ten percent new wood. The remainder of the crop is kept by the owners, who sell most of it in their popular restaurant, Logis de la Cadène, in St-Emilion.

The wines have real finesse and delicacy, and are fresh and supple with a lovely bouquet in the best style of the *côtes* wines. Occasionally in vintages such as '64 and '70 the wines have an extra dimension of richness and fleshiness. Owing to the very small quantities involved Ets J-P Moueix sell these wines on an exclusive basis in the USA and UK.

Château La Clusière
Grand Cru Classé. Owner: **Consorte Valette.** Administrator: **Jean-Paul Valette. 2·8ha. 1,000 cases. Mer 70%, CF 20%, CS 10%.**
This tiny vineyard forms a small enclave high up on the Côte de Pavie, among the wines of Pavie and under the same ownership and management. The vinification and *élevage* are carried out in the *chai* and cellars of Pavie, with 25 percent new wood being used.

The wines are solid, full-bodied and typically St-Emilion. They develop more quickly than those of Pavie-Decesse and are less tannic. The '78 and '79 are both good examples of these contrasting years, with the '78 being the more stylish. There is also an excellent '82 full of ripe, rich fruit and promising to be an early developer. '83 is concentrated and '85 is rich, if open-textured; the '86 is rather light. With its tiny production this is not an easy wine to find, but well worth it when you do.

Château Corbin
Grand Cru Classé. Owner: **Domaines Giraud. 15ha. 5,000 cases. Mer 50%, CF 25%, CS 25%.**
A good example of the curse of duplicated names in St-Emilion. In this area of St-Emilion near the Pomerol border there are five adjoining properties, all with Corbin in their names, all Grands Crus Classés, with two of them belonging to the Giraud family, to say nothing of others in Montagne-St-Emilion and Graves.

A small amount of new wood is used in the maturation, and the wines have a reputation for being rich and supple, characteristic of this area of sandy soils near Pomerol.

Château Corbin-Michotte
Grand Cru Classé. Owner: **Jean-Noël Boidron. 6·7ha. 3,000 cases. Mer 65%, CF 30%, CS 5%.**
There is a double confusion of names here. It is one of five adjoining properties – all Grands Crus Classés – with the name Corbin and one of two adjoining Michottes. This one lies immediately to the south of Croque-Michotte and east of La Dominique. The soil is basically sandy with some clay in the subsoil, containing iron traces, and with some surface gravel. Since acquiring this property in 1959, Jean-Noël Boidron has carried out many improvements, and the *chai* was entirely rebuilt in 1980. 20 percent of the wine is matured in new wood, rotated with wine held in stainless steel vats.

I have always been impressed with this wine. The rich, plummy texture, fat and very full and mellow in the mouth, is typical of the best wines from this corner of St-Emilion near Pomerol. Of recent vintages the '79 is especially good.

Château Cormeil-Figeac
Grand Cru. Owner: **Héritiers R & L Moreaud. 10ha. 3,500 cases. Mer 70%, CF 30%.**
A good vineyard on the sandy soils southeast of Château Figeac. Wood maturation is carried out and 15 percent new oak is used. The wines are very scented, supple and full-flavoured, delicious for early drinking with lots of vibrant fruit.

Château Côte-Baleau
Grand Cru. Owner: **Société des Grandes Murailles. 16ha. 8,500 cases. Mer 70%, CF 15%, CS 15%.**
This *cru* was classified in 1969, but then lost its position in 1985. It is on the lower slope of the *côtes* and on sandy soils, north of the town, adjoining Château Laniote. It is here that the wines of both Grands-Murailles and Clos St-Martin are actually made and kept. It is hard to say what was behind the thinking that demoted this *cru* and Grandes-Murailles, but retained Clos St-Martin. My own comparative tastings suggested that this was the best of the properties.

The wines have plenty of structure and richness of flavour, and require some ageing. '78, '79, '81 and '82 are all fine, powerful and stylish wines, and '80 is serious, full-flavoured and well-structured. The '85, however, was lighter.

Château Coudert
Grand Cru. Owner: **Jean-Claude Carles. 6ha. 3,000 cases. Mer 50%, CF and CS 50%.**
This *cru* in the commune of St-Christophe produces some stylish wines that are long on the palate, with some breed.

Château Coudert-Pelletan
Grand Cru. Owner: **Jean Lavau et Fils. 10ha. 4,000 cases. Mer 60%, CF 30%, CS 10%.**
A château producing classic St-Emilion wines with plenty of style and marvellous ageing potential. The '70, when over 15 years old, was still splendid.

Château La Couspaude
Grand Cru. Owners: **Vignobles Aubert. 7ha. 4,000 cases. Mer 60%, CF and CS 40%.**
A property on the *plateau calcaire* immediately to the east of the town, between Villemaurine and Trottevieille. It lost its place in the classification in 1985. The wines are bottled outside the district.

Château Coutet
Grand Cru. Owner: **J David Beaulieu. 11ha. 3,600 cases. Mer 45%, CF 45%, CS 5%, Mal 5%.**
This vineyard is on the *côte* to the west of the town. It lost its classified status in 1985. The wines seem light but lacking fruit, charm or depth of flavour.

Château Le Couvent
Grand Cru. Owner: **SC du Château Le Couvent. 0·4ha. 100 cases. Mer 55%, CF 25%, CS 20%.**
This tiny vineyard, actually within the town, changed hands shortly before the re-classification and did not apply to be considered for the revised classification. The soil is clay mixed with limestone. The maturation is in new casks, producing a wine which is supple but rich and well-structured.

Château Couvent-des-Jacobins
Grand Cru Classé. Owner: **Mme Joineau-Borde. 9ha. 3,500**

cases. Mer 65%, CF 25%, CS 9%, Mal 1%.
This is a very old property originally belonging to the Dominican friars. The house and *chai* are in the old town of St-Emilion, while the vineyard nestles beneath the eastern ramparts of the town on the edge of the *plateau calcaire* and on sandy soils. Secular owners took over in the 18th century and the present family have been here since 1902. It was added to the classification in 1969. This is a traditionally made wine, with 20 percent new wood used for the maturation.

In recent vintages I have found the wines to be consistent, well made, with a beautiful flavour and firm finish, quite taut and well structured. The '79 is less forward than the '81. There is a distinctive blue-black label. The wine is distributed by Dourthe Frères.

Château Croque-Michotte
Grand Cru Classé. Owner: **Mme Rigal. 14ha. 6,700 cases. Mer 90%, CS and CF 10%.**
This *cru* lies on the extreme northwest of St-Emilion where it borders on Pomerol. It has been in the same family since 1890. A third new wood is used for the maturation.

This seems to be a consistently well-made wine. The '78 is ripe and attractive, already drinking well, and the '79 is massive and dense with backbone and tannin, a wine with a future. The '81 is tannic and robust with a fine finish; the '83 is rich and complex and the '85 has a lovely opulent flavour of plums. This is a wine that is certainly above average in terms of quality and consistency.

Château Curé-Bon-La-Madeleine
Grand Cru Classé. Owner: **Maurice Landé. 5ha. 2,500 cases. Mer 95%, Mal 5%.**
This is a very well-placed vineyard on the *plateau calcaire*, a part of which forms the base of an old quarry. Its neighbours are Ausone, Belair and Canon. Maturation is in casks with a small percentage of new wood. The wines have a good reputation and tend to be quite firm in spite of the high proportion of Merlot, but they are also fleshy and generous with a distinctive bouquet, denoting breed.

Château Dassault
Grand Cru Classé. Owner: **SARL Château Dassault.** Administrator: **André Vergriette. 23ha. 9,000 cases.**

Mer 70%, CF 20%, CS 10%.
This was one of eight *crus* added to the classification in 1969.
Formerly known as Château Couperie, it was renamed in 1955.
Vinification is in stainless steel with maturation in wood, of which a
third is new oak.

The style of the wines is uncomplicated, full-flavoured and
supple, with charm and breed. They reflect very careful vinification
and *élevage* and are most consistent. There is a good '78 from this
property and the '79 is lighter and more forward than most wines of
this year in St-Emilion. '80 is a pleasing, ready-to-drink lightweight; '81 is full-flavoured and forward, and the '82 has beauty of
flavour combined with length and moderate concentration of fruit,
probably ready by '87; the '83 is rich, spicy and full of fruit and the
'85 is dense and powerful; the '86 is very firm, but with a delicious
vivid fruit flavour. These are pleasant middle-of-the-road wines.

Château La Dominique
Grand Cru Classé. Owner: **Clément Fayat. 18·5ha. 6,500
cases. Mer 76%, CF 8%, CS 8%, Mal 8%.**
This *cru* has always had the capacity to make exceptional wines, but
it was not consistent until the present owner took over in 1969.

The wines here are now an impressive blend of fruit, ripeness and
tannin which come together to produce remarkable opulence and
power-packed flavour, placing them at the very forefront of the
Grands Crus Classés. The '78 is open-textured and forward, and the
'79 is tannic and powerful, with dense fruit and length that
developed slowly. The '80 is very good for the year, very
perfumed, flowery and full of character; '81 is opulent with softer
fruit, promising earlier development; '82, '83, '85 and '86 are all
exceptional.

Château Faurie-de-Souchard
Grand Cru Classé. Owner: **Jabiol family. 11ha. 4,000 cases.
Mer 65%, CF 26%, CS 9%.**
The name is not to be confused with that of the neighbouring Petit-
Faurie-de-Soutard. Previously this property also had the prefix
'Petit', but this has been dropped. The vineyard is on the plateau
and *côtes* northeast of the town. Fermentation is in concrete vats,
and maturation is by rotating the wine between casks (of which a

third are new) and vats.

Although there is much more Merlot here than at Cadet-Piola, there are some similarities of style, especially a lack of flesh and a tightness of flavour. In recent tastings I found the '79 the most impressive recent vintage, with breed and style. Despite being rather undeveloped, it had a flavour that was very harmonious. The '81 was elegant but closed and lacking flesh after a year in bottle. There seems to be a lack of consistency and charm about these wines at present.

Château de Ferrand
Grand Cru. Owner: **Baron Marcel Bich.** Administrator: **Jean-Pierre Palatin. 30ha. 13,500 cases. Mer 65%, CF 20%, CS 15%.**

This is the most important property in St-Hippolyte, situated on the *plateau calcaire*. A lot of new wood is used for the maturation, not less than 50 percent and sometimes 100 percent. The aim is to produce rich, tannic wines that are suitable for ageing. The '85 is a serious wine of real character, but very harmonious in spite of the heavy dose of new oak.

Château Figeac
1er Grand Cru Classé B. Owner: **Thierry de Manoncourt. 40ha. 12,500 cases. CS 35%, CF 35%, Mer 30%.**

This fine old property is the remnant of a much larger estate, which in the 18th century included Cheval-Blanc and several others that now incorporate the name of Figeac. As with Cheval-Blanc, some two-thirds of the vineyard is on gravel and the remaining third on sandy soil. A fine new *chai* with a large underground section is the latest improvement here. Under Thierry de Manoncourt's direction the consistency and quality of winemaking has been of a high order. He has been in charge since 1947.

The similarities and differences between Figeac and Cheval-Blanc are always fascinating. The size of the vineyards and composition of the soils are strikingly similar, but the *encépagement* is notably different. Here an important role is given to Cabernet Sauvignon, while at Cheval-Blanc the Cabernet Franc reigns supreme. As a result, for all their similarities, Figeac seldom matches Cheval-Blanc for sheer weight and opulence of flavour, although it sometimes approaches it and occasionally (as in 1953 and 1955) can even surpass it. '75, '78, '79, '81, '82, '83, '85, '86 and '88 are superb wines. The '76 is rich, opulent and soft and at its best, and the '80 is charming and ready to drink.

Château La Fleur
Grand Cru. Owner: **Lily Lacoste. 6·5ha. 2,500 cases. Mer 75%, CF 25%.**
A good vineyard northeast of Soutard on sandy soils. The owner is better known as co-proprietor of Pétrus and owner of Latour à Pomerol. The wines are fleshy and quite rich – full of easy fruit and charm.

Château Fleur-Cardinale
Owner: **Claude Asséo. 9ha. 4,500 cases. Mer 70%, CF 15%, CS 15%.**
Situated on the clay-chalk soils of the *côte* at St-Etienne-de-Lisse, this *cru* produces wines that are traditionally vinified and matured in oak, but which need time to soften before drinking at their best.

Château La Fleur-Pourret
Grand Cru. Owner: **La Compagnie AXA.** Administrators: **Jean-Michel Cazes and Gilbert Xans. 6·5ha. 2,500 cases. Mer 50%, CS 50%.**
A property created by the grandfather of Bruno Prats in the 19th century, combining two *crus*: Clos Haut-Pourret and Château La Fleur. Now owned by AXA, the wines produced here have an unusually high proportion of Cabernet Sauvignon in their blend.

Château Fombrauge
Grand Cru. Owner: **Bordeaux Château Invest. 50ha. 25,000 cases. Mer 60%, CF 30%, CS 10%.**
An important *cru* in St-Christophe-des-Bardes, situated partly on the *plateau calcaire* and partly on the north-facing *côte* and its lower slopes. In 1987 the property was sold to its present owner, a Danish consortium. The wines are matured in cask with 25 percent new oak used. This wine has a long-established reputation in the UK for producing consistent, reliable wines.

Château Fonplégade
Grand Cru Classé. Owner: **Armand Moueix. 18ha. 7,500 cases. CF 35%, CS 5%, Mer 60%.**
These are firm, rather than tannic, wines that require time to show their style and finesse. The '78 was at its best after nine years but the '79 showed maturity and charm a little earlier. The '82 promises to be a long-term developer, with a powerful flavour and tannic undertones, and the '83 is a luscious early-drinker. '85 is surprisingly tannic for the year and the '86 is attractively scented and fruity, if characteristically firm. This is consistent and reliable wine, without the richness and charm of some, but rewarding to keep – solid and dependable, if lacking flair.

Château Fonroque
Grand Cru Classé. Owner: **GFA Château Fonroque.**
Administrators: **Ets J-P Moueix. 20ha. 8,000 cases. Mer 85%, CF 15%.**
The style here tends to be robust, and these are quite firm wines that need ageing to show at their best – not the flamboyant, early-drinking style at all. The '78 is finely perfumed, with personality and structure, nicely balanced fruit and tannin; ready in '86. The '79 is dense and powerful, but also has length and complexity – a wine worth waiting for. In contrast '81 has a fullness of flavour and fat but not the usual firmness; '82 is tannic and tough and is another wine to wait for. The '83 though looks outstanding, with a richness and concentration of flavour to match the tannin – perhaps better than '82? '85 is strong-flavoured and rich, yet austere for the year, and the '86 is predictably tannic but fruity.

Clos Fourtet
1er Grand Cru Classé B. Owner: **Lurton brothers (André, Dominique, Lucien, Simone). 17ha. 5,500 cases. Mer 60%, CS 20%, CF 20%.**
The reputation of this château was in decline until 1973 when extensive improvements were made and the proportion of Merlot increased.

There are distinct similarities of style between Clos Fourtet and its neighbour Canon. The wines tend to be tightly knit and slow to evolve, but recently richer and more open-textured than of old.

The '75 vintage here is good but not outstanding and the '76 too overblown to last. The '78 and '79 both have great promise, and the '81, '82 and '83 are all especially successful, the '81 having more weight than many of that year. The '85 is particularly good, having extra concentration and richness allied to a lovely flavour. This is certainly a château on its way up, and with the potential to improve its standing further.

Château Franc-Grâce-Dieu
Grand Cru. Owner: **Germain Siloret.** Administrator: **Eric Fournier. 8ha. 3,000 cases. Mer 52%, CF 41%, CS 7%.**
Until Eric Fournier from Premier Grand Cru Château Canon took over the farming and management here in 1981, the property was called Guadet-Franc-Grâce-Dieu. Then it was decided that this was rather a mouthful and the Guadet was dropped. Vinification is now in stainless steel with maturation in cask. I found Eric Fournier's first vintage, the '81, had finesse and style with intense, vibrant young fruit – better frankly than some Crus Classés.

Château Franc-Mayne
Grand Cru Classé. Owner: **AXA Millésimes.** Administrator: **J-M Cazes. 7ha. 3,000 cases. Mer 72%, CF 14%, CS 14%.**
This *cru* lies northwest of St-Emilion, just off the St-Emilion-Pomerol road, and is on the *côtes*. In recent years the proportion of Cabernet Franc has been increased, at the expense of the Cabernet Sauvignon, in order to produce less tannic and more elegant wine, and since AXA took over in 1987, some interesting wines have emerged. This *cru*'s reputation is modest and can only improve.

Château La Gaffelière
1er Grand Cru Classé B. Owner: **Vignobles Fomperier. 22ha. 10,000 cases. Mer 62%, CF 25%, CS 10%, Mal 3%.**
The reputation of La Gaffelière is mixed. It can produce marvellously perfumed, supple, rich and fleshy wines. But in the past there have been inconsistencies and the wines lacked the backbone and breed of some of the best *crus* on the *côtes* and plateau. The signs now are that there is more consistency and a high level of winemaking.

An excellent '71 was made at this property, and the '75 is also most attractive and successful. The '78 is rather lightweight but finer than the '79 which, though attractive, rather lacks concentration; the '81 is good and the '82 is reminiscent of the style of '47 with its dense, almost jammy concentration. The '83 is particularly successful here, wonderfully rich and complex with real 'race', and the '85 and '86 have benefited from increased selection, summer pruning of bunches, and longer maceration, their concentration and structure being much improved. A wine of enormous charm, which perhaps needs a degree of richness to give of its best, and one to watch.

Château La Grâce-Dieu-Les-Menuts
Grand Cru. Owner: **Max Pilotte. 13ha. 5,800 cases. Mer 65%, CF 30%, CS 5%.**
The name Grâce-Dieu comes from a Cisterian grange which was secularized in the 17th century and subsequently divided. Recently some new casks have been introduced for the maturation in wood, and the reputation of this *cru* is improving. It lies northwest of St-Emilion on the Libourne road, in the sector of sandy soils. The wines tend to be light-textured – suitable for young drinking.

Château Grand-Barrail-Lamarzelle-Figeac and Château La Marzelle
Grand Cru Classé. Owner: **Association E Carrère. 32ha. 10,900 cases. Mer 78%, CS 15%, CF 7%.**
There are two properties here, each a Grand Cru Classé in its own right, that are run together. They form a very important block of vineyards immediately south of Figeac, on mostly sandy soils, but with some gravel as well. No wood is used for the maturation. The Carrère family bought the properties in the disastrous year of 1956. The wines have a reputation for being supple, fruity and early-maturing. Given the position of the vineyard, one wonders if the full potential is as yet being realized. Château La Marzelle is distributed by Dourthe Frères.

Château Grand Corbin
Grand Cru Classé. Owner: **Alain Giraud. 13ha. 6,000 cases. Mer 50%, CF 25%, CS 25%.**
The history of this property is the same as that of Château Corbin, as is the ownership. It lies on sandy soils between Corbin and

Grand-Corbin-Despagne. Maturation is in casks of which 20 percent are new. The reputation is for wines that tend to be blander than those of Corbin and is certainly not of the same level as Grand-Corbin-Despagne.

Château Grand-Corbin-Despagne
Grand Cru Classé. Owner: **Despagne family. 31ha. 15,000 cases. Mer 75%, CF 20%, CS 5%.**
The wines here have a good reputation, and recent tastings confirm that this is deserved. The '79 is an opulent wine with iron undertones, powerful and assertive, a shade rustic in contrast with the '81 which I found to be particularly good, with rich fruit on the nose, a delicious flavour that was ripe and opulent, and more body than many '81s – altogether a very attractive wine with nice firm undertones.

Château Grandes Murailles
Grand Cru. Owner: **SC du Château. 2ha. Mer 80%, CF 20%.**
This tiny vineyard adjoins Clos Fourtet where the *plateau calcaire* begins to fall away to the *côte*. There is a curious situation here. The wine is made and kept at the cellars of Baleau, the largest of the three properties owned by this company, but Grandes Murailles and Baleau lost their classified status as a result of the 1985 revision.

I have found the wines rich and opulent in style, and quick to mature. Delicious wines were made in '78, '79, '81 and '82.

Château Grand-Mayne
Grand Cru Classé. Owner: **Jean-Pierre Nony. 17ha. 11,000 cases. Mer 50%, CF 40%, CS 10%.** Second labels: **Châteaux Beau Mazerat and Cassevert.**
This old domaine lies on the western *côte* and its lower slopes. Stainless steel vats replaced the traditional wooden ones in 1975. Maturation is in casks of which 20 percent are new.

At a recent tasting the '79 had a very dry finish and seemed to lack middle fruit and ripeness – odd in a vintage such as this. '81 had a complex bouquet, a long flavour and elegant, crisp fruit – a very stylish and attractive wine. If future vintages follow the '81 this should be a good middle-of-the-road wine to watch.

Château Grand-Pontet
Grand Cru Classé. Owner: **Bécot and Pourquet families.**
14ha. 6,500 cases. Mer 70%, CF 15%, CS 15%.
This château, at the foot of the *côtes*, lies just outside St-Emilion on
the Libourne road. From 1965 to 1980 it belonged to Barton &
Guestier, who completely modernized the property. One of the
two present partners also owns nearby Beau Séjour Bécot.

Under the Barton & Guestier regime, sound but unexciting
wines were made. It is now said that quality has improved under the
new management, so the wines should be worth watching.

Château Guadet-St-Julien
Grand Cru Classé. Owner: **Robert Lignac. 5·5ha. 2,000**
cases. Mer 75%, CS and CF 25%.
Generally this is an attractive, supple wine, showing unmistakable
class and maturing quickly. The '78 is now most attractive with a
firm flavour and fruit, balanced by structure. It can be enjoyed now
or kept. The '79 was still tough and somewhat astringent after two
years in bottle and the '80 and '81, ready by 1986, also fall into this
category.

Château Haut-Badette
Owner: **J-F Janoueix. 4·5ha. 2,500 cases. Mer 90%, CS 10%.**
The wines of Haut-Badette are of better quality than many of
Grand Cru status. They are charmingly perfumed with an
abundance of fruit and body, combining the fruit and qualities of a
young-drinking wine with the ability to mature well. '78 and '83
were especially good vintages.

Château Haut-Corbin
Grand Cru Classé. Owner: **A M du Batiment et Travaux**
Publics. Administrator: **Domaines Cordier. 4·5ha. 2,500**
cases. Mer 67%, CS 33%.
This small property, near the border with Montagne-St-Emilion,
lies north and east of the other Corbins on sandy soil. It was the only
cru in this part of the *appellation* to be upgraded to Grand Cru Classé
in 1969. The wines are matured in cask, but no new wood is used.

I found the '79 hard and edgy – disappointing for the vintage and
for a Grand Cru Classé. The '81 was crisp, clear, simple,

straightforward and well-balanced. Since the new management took over in 1986 there has been a dramatic improvement, with rich, meaty wines in '86, '88 and '89.

Château Haut-Gueyrot
Owner: **Jean-Marcel Gombeau. 7ha. 3,500 cases. Mer 85%, CF 15%.**
This small vineyard on the lower slopes and the plain of St-Laurent-des-Combes produces consistently attractive, rich, fruity, quite luscious and typical wines, usually delicious after three years.

Château Haut-Pontet
Grand Cru. Owner: **Limouzin Frères. 5·2ha. 2,500 cases. Mer 75%, CF and CS 25%.**
This small *cru* is on the lower slopes of the *côte* north of St-Emilion. This is well-made wine, distinctive, rich and full-flavoured with a good backbone. Very consistent.

Château Haut-Sarpe
Grand Cru Classé. Owner: **J-F Janoueix. 12·5ha. 6,000 cases. Mer 70%, CF 30%.**
Tastings of a number of recent vintages over a period of years have confirmed that this is a wine of character and breed. The '78 is a rather austere and dry wine, but the '79 is luscious and chewy, very St-Emilion; the stylish '81 developed slowly and the '82 promises something special; '83 is a rich tannic wine, and '85 is concentrated and relatively firm for the year; the '86 is oustanding and has a lovely flavour and richness.

Château Jean-Faure
Grand Cru. Owner: **Michel Amart. 17ha. 5,600 cases. CF 60%, Mer 30%, Mal 10%.**
For many years this *cru*, lying on sandy soils between Cheval-Blanc and Ripeau, belonged to Ripeau and the properties were run together until the present owner bought it in 1976. The wine is distributed by Dourthe Frères. The *cru* lost its classified status in the revision of 1985. The aim is to produce full-bodied wines which are also elegant. My limited experience of them is that they are either tough and ferrous or soft and lacking personality and style.

Château Lagrange-de-Lescure
Grand Cru. Owner: **SC du Château Le Couvent. 17ha.**
8,500 cases. CS 37·5%, CF 37·5%, Mer 25%.
Situated on some of the best land in the commune of St-Sulpice-de-
Faleyrens – gravel and sand terraces of recent deposition – this
property yields some very attractive wines. They are supple and
fruity with good depth of flavour, likely to show improvement
over the next few vintages.

Château Laniote
Grand Cru Classé. Owner: **Freymond-Rouja family. 5ha.**
3,000 cases. Mer 70%, CS 20%, CF 10%.
This is not a big beefy St-Emilion but it has great finesse. It is very
perfumed and intense, with a long, refined and beautiful flavour,
and with real 'race'. It has a most enchanting texture, lush and silky,
which makes the wines very exciting. The '79, '81, '82 and '83 are
all superb.

Château Larcis-Ducasse
Grand Cru Classé. Owner: **Mme Hélène Gratiot**
Alphandéry. 11ha. 4,160 cases. Mer 65%, CF 25%, CS 10%.
The wines here have been noted for their breed and charm, but have
sometimes been rather light. Recent vintages have shown a marked
improvement in consistency and quality. The '78 has concentration, personality and charm; the '79 is rather backward, with
tannin but still some elegance and finesse; '80 is an attractive wine
and '81 is finely balanced, with depth and length of flavour. '82 is
exceptional with layers of flavour and real complexity, richness and
length, and the '83 has concentration and tannin with the breed
shining through. '85 and '86 both have good concentration with
lovely ripe tannins and fruit.

Château Larmande
Grand Cru Classé. Owner: **SCE des Vignobles Méneret-**
Capdemourlin. 22ha. 10,000 cases. Mer 60%, CF 35%, CS
5%. Second label: **Château des Templiers.**
This fine property lies north of St-Emilion looking towards St-
Georges. It marks the end of the *côtes* and the beginning of the sandy
soils. The last decade has been one of progress here. The vineyard

has been enlarged and the proportion of Merlot increased at the expense of Cabernet Franc and, to an even greater extent, Cabernet Sauvignon. A new *cuvier* equipped with stainless steel fermentation vats was built in 1975.

This wine has won many accolades of late, and consistently does well in blind tastings. The bouquet tends to be perfumed, full and vibrant, the wine rich, full-flavoured, quite spicy and with depth, harmony and style. '79 and '81 are both excellent, with power and charm, and there is a good '80. The '82 is fine and typical of its vintage, while '83 is especially good for the year. '85 is rich and well structured and '86 is a genuine *vin de garde*.

Chateau Laroque
Grand Cru. Owners: **SCA Château Laroque.** Distribution: **Alexis Lichine & Cie. 53ha. 20,000 cases. Mer 77%, CF 13%, CS 10%.**
This large property is in the commune of St-Christophe-des-Bardes where it occupies an exceptional site on the *plateau calcaire* and *côte*. New fermentation *cuves* were installed in 1969. The maturing wine is rotated between vats and casks. The wines have a good reputation.

Château Laroze
Grand Cru Classé. Owner: **Georges Meslin. 30ha. 11,000 cases. Mer 50%, CF 40%, CS 10%.**
The wines here are characterized by their very fresh, clean, up-front fruit. They are perfumed, supple and very easy to drink, maturing quite quickly (over three to five years) and usually at their best at around five to eight years. These are delicious, flattering, fruity wines sold at very reasonable prices. The '78, '79, '80, '81, '82, '83, '85 and '86 are all good examples of these vintages, and all but the '86 can now be drunk.

Clos La Madeleine
Grand Cru Classé. Owner: **Hubert Pistouley. 2ha. 1,000 cases. Mer 50%, CF 50%.**
This tiny property is well placed on the southern edge of the plateau of La Madeleine and on the *côte* below it. Most of the production is sold in Belgium. The wines are carefully made and have all the

refinement and breed one would expect from such a site. They are
finely perfumed, have charming fruit and are light and easy to
drink. The '79 and '81 were both ready to drink in '84 and are good
examples of these vintages.

Château Magdelaine
1er Grand Cru Classé B. Owner: **Ets J-P Moueix. 11ha.
4,000 cases. Mer 90%, CF 10%.**
The hallmark of Magdelaine is its great delicacy and breed and
refinement of flavour. There was an exceptionally attractive '75 and
very fine wines were made in '78, '79, '81, '82, '83, '85, '86 and '88.
The personality of the *cru* is very interesting, because it is more
charming than the straight plateau wines such as Canon but less
fleshy and more elegant than a lower *côtes* such as La Gaffelière. For
me this is one of the most rewarding wines of the St-Emilion *côtes*.

Château Matras
Grand Cru Classé. Owner: **Jean Bernard-Lefèbvre. 18ha.
6,000 cases. Mer 33%, CF 33%, CS 33%, Mal 1%.**
If you stand on the promontory at Tertre Daugay and look across
the *côte* northwards, you will see a battery of tanks standing beside
some modest buildings. This is Matras. It is southwest of the town
and occupies a hollow on the *côtes* and the lower slope. The
proprietor is an oenologist. Ageing is in casks – 25 percent new.

Unfortunately the wines are not as interesting as the history of
the property. I found both the '79 and '81 had an unpleasantly
marked iron taste and were tough and charmless. The impression is
that all is not well with the winemaking, especially as the site is so
good. Something of a cautionary tale for oenologists!

Château Mauvezin
**Grand Cru Classé. Owner: Pierre Cassat. 4ha. 4,500 cases.
CF 50%, Mer 40%, CS 10%.**
This small vineyard lies east of St-Emilion at the limits of the *plateau
calcaire*, between Haut-Sarpe and Balestard-La-Tonnelle. Since the
present owner took over in 1968 there has been much replanting of
the old vineyard, and the yields have increased accordingly. A high
percentage of new wood is used in the maturation. The many gold
medals won by this *cru* attest to the quality of its wines.

Château Monbousquet
Grand Cru. Owner: **Querre family. 30ha. 12,000 cases. Mer 50%, CF 40%, CS 10%.**
These are attractive, rich, supple wines with a distinctive character, sometimes a hint of tobacco on the nose – and a strong, rather earthy flavour. They just lack the ultimate breed of the best St-Emilions, but are nevertheless highly enjoyable wines.

Château Montlabert
Grand Cru. Owner: **SC du Château.** Administrator: **Jacques Barrière. 11ha. 6,000 cases. Mer 50%, CF 40%, CS 10%.**
This property lies on sandy soils northwest of St-Emilion near Figeac. Since 1967 it has belonged to a company of which Jacques Barrière is a partner and acts as administrator. The distribution is in the hands of the *négociants* A & R Barrière. The wines have a good reputation and are widely exported.

Château Moulin du Cadet
Grand Cru Classé. Owner: **Ets J-P Moueix. 5ha. 1,800 cases. Mer 90%, CF 10%.**
A very small property on the *plateau calcaire*, north of St-Emilion and adjoining the Moueix property of Fonroque. The wines bear all the hallmarks of the impeccable care which Ets J-P Moueix take of all the properties they own or farm. Recently a small percentage of new wood has been introduced to the cask maturation. The wines are little known because of the very small production, but I have been impressed by their perfume, breed and elegance. They can be rather finer than those at neighbouring Fonroque, but less powerful and robust.

Château Moulin-St-Georges
Grand Cru. Owner: **Alain Vauthier. 6·5ha. 2,500 cases. Mer 60%, CF 40%.**
Some stylish wines are produced at this property; past vintages have shown the ability to age well, also being very pleasant to drink when young. Alain Vauthier's family are co-owners of Ausone.

Clos L'Oratoire
Grand Cru Classé. Owner: **SC Peyreau.** Administrator:

Michel Boutet. 10ha. 5,000 cases. Mer 75%, CF 25%.
This property lies northeast of the town where the lower slope of
the *côte* gives way to the sandy soils, close to the border with St-
Christophe-des-Bardes. It is run with the larger Château Peyreau
which is an unclassified Grand Cru. 25 percent new casks are used
for the maturation.

These are rich, concentrated wines, very Merlot in style with a
good depth of flavour; what one thinks of as a typical St-Emilion.
They develop quite quickly. '78 and '79 are both rich and very
drinkable. '80 is forward and attractive. '81 is excellent and '82 was
an early developer.

Château Palais-Cardinal-La-Fuie
Grand Cru. Owner: **Gérard Frétier. 16ha. 7,500 cases. Mer
50%, CF 35%, CS 15%.**
This *cru* is situated in the commune of St-Sulpice-de-Faleyrens. It
produces wines that are very pleasant to drink young but which age
rather rapidly in years of high production.

Château Patris
Grand Cru. Owner: **Michel Querre. 13ha. 7,000 cases. Mer
92%, CS 8%.**
This *cru* lies on sandy soils of the little valley of Mazerat, just at the
southwest base of the *côte* of St-Emilion. The property is run with
the same care as the owners' *cru* in Pomerol, Château Mazeyres.
Two-thirds of the wine is matured in casks, of which a third are
new, the rest in vats. Perfumed, supple wines of good repute are
made.

Château Pavie
1er Grand Cru Classé B. Owner: **Consorts Valette.**
Administrator: **Jean-Paul Valette. 37·5ha. 12,000 cases. Mer
55%, CF 25%, CS 20%.**
This is the largest vineyard on the *côtes*, and is splendidly placed on a
long, south-facing slope southeast of the town of St-Emilion. In
recent years Jean-Paul Valette, the member of the family in charge,
has done much to improve the quality of the vines here. It is
probable that the land at the foot of the *côtes* on sandy soil reduces
the overall quality of the wines, which while full of charm have a

tendency to lack concentration.

Of the recent vintages the '75 is less concentrated and more attractive than most, '76 is rather lightweight and the '78 is understated but fine. The '79 is soft and easy and the '81 is quite lovely. A marvellously opulent '82 was followed by the outstandingly successful '83 and a classic '85, charming with real richness and style; the '86 was one of the greats of its vintage, with opulent fruit allied to lots of tannin and structure. This is the most improved *cru* among the Premiers.

Château Pavie-Decesse
Grand Cru Classé. Owner: **Valette family.** Administrator: **Jean-Paul Valette. 9ha. 4,500 cases. Mer 65%, CF 20%, CS 15%.**
This is fine classic *côtes* wine, with power and breed. Sometimes one is more conscious of the tannin than with Pavie because the wine has less opulence and fat. Yet sometimes – as in '82 – it can actually have more alcohol. At this property the '78 vintage is unusual in that it is better than the '79, and there is a stylish and delicious '80. As in Pavie, the '81, '82, '83, '85 and '86 are all successful.

Château Pavie-Macquin
Grand Cru Classé. Owner: **Corre family.** Administrator: **Maryse Barre. 14ha. 4,000 cases. Mer 70%, CF 25%, CS 5%.**
Named after Albert Macquin who was a pioneer of the processes used to graft European vines onto American root-stocks to combat the phylloxera. This *cru* is on the plateau above the Côte de Pavie, and between Pavie, Troplong-Mondot and the town. The wines are elegant and pleasant, of good average quality and sold at very reasonable prices.

Château Pavillon-Cadet
Grand Cru Classé. Owner: **Anne Llammas. 3·5ha. 1,500 cases. Mer 70%, CF 30%.**
This very small property is on the hill of Cadet, just north of the town. It is one of the least-known of the Grands Crus Classés. The wine is matured in cask, but I have never tasted it and information is scant.

Château Petit-Faurie-de-Soutard
Grand Cru Classé. Owner: **Mme Françoise Capdemourlin.**
Administrator: **Jacques Capdemourlin. 8ha. 3,500 cases. Mer 60%, CF 30%, CS 10%.**
Until 1850 this formed part of Soutard. It lies in a fine position on the *plateau calcaire* and the *côtes*.

This is a stylish wine with real breed and finesse. Because of the soil here, with its high limestone content, the wines are less luscious but have more structure and are perhaps finer than at Balestard. The '78 is surprisingly forward and lightweight, not a keeper; '79 is rich and full, attractive, with real class; '80 is delicious, stylish and ready to drink, and '81 is more structured and closed with finesse and breed. The '82 has a marked character and a fine middle flavour and richness – there is noticeable breed but this is not a heavyweight wine.

Château Pipeau
Grand Cru. Owner: **Pierre Mestreguilhem. 30ha. 13,000 cases. Mer 75%, CF 20%, CS 5%.**
Pierre Mestreguilhem's aim is to produce wines with body and suppleness and which mature well. The resulting wines are often superior to some senior *crus*.

Château Pontet-Clauzure
Grand Cru. Owner: **SC du Château Le Couvent. 9ha. 5,000 cases. CF 48%, Mer 46%, CS 6%.**
Since the owners purchased this château in 1981, they have made considerable improvements to it. The differences are very noticeable in the wines too, the '83 being considerably better than the '81. A *cru* with a fine future ahead of it.

Château de Pressac
Grand Cru. Owner: **Jacques Pouey. 35ha. 14,000 cases. Mer 50%, CF 30%, CS 20%.**
A fine feudal château overlooks this *cru*, which is situated on the chalky soils of the plateau in St-Etienne-de-Lisse. It was here, in the late 1730s, that the Auxerrois or 'Noir de Pressac' grape was introduced to Bordeaux. Now better known as the Malbec, it was an important contributor to the wines of this region. At this

château, wines with a fine reputation are produced, using traditional methods of vinification.

Château Le Prieuré
Grand Cru Classé. Owner: **SCE Baronne Guichard. 5ha. 1,500 cases. Mer 70%, CF 30%.**
This property on the *plateau calcaire* is on high ground, on a site set apart, between Trottevieille and Troplong-Mondot. The owners also have an important property in Lalande de Pomerol, and also Château Siaurac and Château Vrai-Croix-de-Gay in Pomerol. Château Le Prieuré once belonged to the Franciscan house in St-Emilion, the Cordeliers. A proportion of 25 percent new wood is used in the maturation. I have found the wines attractive, elegant, on the light side, good breed but not above average. The '79 is very good, the '81 is pretty but lacks depth of flavour.

Château Ripeau
Grand Cru Classé. Owner: **Michel Janoueix de Wilde. 16ha. 6,000 cases. Mer 60%, CF and CF 40%.**
An important *cru* on the sandy soils near the border with Pomerol, it lies southeast of Cheval-Blanc and La Dominique. Since the present owners took over in 1976 they have considerably expanded the *cuvier* and *chai*.

It is a sure sign of the progress being made here in restoring the reputation of this fine *cru* that the '81 is better than the '79. I particularly liked its perfumed spicy bouquet: better-balanced and finer than the '79, with complexity and firm undertones.

Château Rozier
Grand Cru. Owner: **Jean Saby. 17ha. 10,000 cases. Mer 65%, CF and CS 35%.**
A *cru* in the commune of St-Laurent-des-Combes, that produces appealingly fruity wines. They respond well to ageing and have plenty of character.

Château St-Georges-Côte-Pavie
Grand Cru Classé. Owner: **Jacques Masson. 5·5ha. 2,500 cases. Mer 60%, CF 40%.**
A small, very well-placed *cru* on the western end of the Côte de

Pavie and its lower slope. La Gaffelière is on the other side, and there are views across to Ausone. The fermentation is in stainless steel, and maturation is in cask. The wines are notable for their delicious easy fruit and marked character and breed. They are high-toned and flavoured and are delightful to drink when four to seven years old. The '79 is scented and opulent, the '81 more spicy, luscious and stylish. The sort of joyous St-Emilion that is irresistible.

Clos St-Martin
Grand Cru Classé. Owner: **SC des Grands Murailles. 3·5ha. 1,600 cases. Mer 66%, CF 17%, CS 17%.**
Three *crus* – this one, Grandes Murailles and Côte Baleau – were, until recently, all managed together, with the wine made and kept at Côte Baleau. In 1985 however, the other two *crus* lost their Grand Cru Classé status in a revision of the classification system, and since then the proprietors have made a determined effort to improve matters. Clos St-Martin now has separate facilities, and the '86 has consequently shown a big step forward in quality, with a bouquet full of vivid, scented fruit, breed, elegance and balanced tannins. This improvement was maintained in the '88 and '89. Before this, the wines were rather uneven. The best vintages were the '79 and '82. For each vintage 25 percent of the casks are new.

Château Sansonnet
Grand Cru Classé. Owner: **Francis Robin. 8ha. 3,300 cases. Mer 60%, CF 20%, CS 20%.**
This *cru* is on the *plateau calcaire* east of St-Emilion on its eastern culminating point, and just north of Trottevieille. There is clay mixed with limestone here, on rocky subsoil. The wine is matured in cask. These are firm wines which are not particularly rich or luscious and need time to unfold and develop. The '79 was still firm with an iron flavour but some balancing fat when five years old, and still needed time. The '81 was lighter and less concentrated with nice fruit that developed and filled out in the glass, indicating that it was still evolving.

Château La Serre
Grand Cru Classé. Owner: **Bernard d'Arfeuille.**
Administrator: **Luc d'Arfeuille. 6ha. 3,000 cases.**

Mer 80%, CF 20%.
This is a wine with structure, depth of flavour and a finely perfumed bouquet, a wine of individuality, typical of the plateau around St-Emilion. It is a solid, reliable Grand Cru Classé of good average quality – not a high-flyer but thoroughly worthy. Very good wines were made in '83 and '85, while '82 and '86 are outstanding.

Château Soutard
Grand Cru Classé. Owners: **Comte François & Comtesse Isabelle des Ligneris. 28ha. 8,000 cases. Mer 60%, CF 35%, CS 5%.**
The aim at Soutard is to make traditional, long-keeping wines and the result is uncompromising and requires patience. My own feeling is that sometimes the fruit and natural charm of St-Emilion are unnecessarily sacrificed and that often the wines would benefit from earlier bottling and a lighter touch – but these are matters of taste. The stylishness comes through, but the wines often seem lean and ungrateful. This was certainly true of the '79 when six years old. But the '81 was better-balanced, rather light but with attractive fruit not crushed by wood.

Château Tertre-Daugay
Grand Cru Classé. Owner: **Comte Leo de Malet Roquefort. 16ha. 6,000 cases. Mer 60%, CF 30%, CS 10%.**
The property was in an appalling state of neglect when Comte Leo de Malet-Roquefort bought it in 1978. From then until the reconstruction of the *cuvier* and *chai* in 1984 the wines had to be made and kept at La Gaffelière. This property now receives the same care and attention as the Premier Grand Cru, but with a third new wood used for the maturation.

There can be no doubting the potential of this *cru* to be one of the very best of the Grands Crus Classés. The wines are gloriously perfumed and spicy on the nose, with tannic and rich, ripe fruitiness well matched to give a fine, powerful, complex flavour with stylish breed shining through. The '78, '80 and '81 are all excellent examples of these years, with good keeping qualities. The '78, the first year of the new regime, is delicious but forward and lighter. The future here looks to be full of promise.

Château Tertre-Rôteboeuf
Owner: **François Mitjavile. 4·5ha. 2,000 cases. Mer 80%, CF 20%.**
The name of this château derives from the oxen which were once used to plough the steep slopes of this property. Exposed to the hot sun while they worked, the oxen roasted in the heat – hence 'roast beef'. François Mitjavile has been the proprietor of this château since 1978, and by late harvesting and long vatting he aims to produce serious wines that age well. His wines have great individuality, the '85 and '86 responding well to new oak and also retaining plenty of fruitiness and structure.

Château Toinet-Fombrauge
Owner: **Bernard Sierra. 8ha. 2,900 cases. Mer 85%, CF and CS 15%.**
This *cru* is in St-Christophe-des-Bardes and lies below the north *côte* on mostly sandy soils. It produces rich, full-flavoured, rather soft wines of marked character, usually very drinkable after three or at most four years.

Château La Tonnelle
Owner: **Guy Arnaud et Fils. 15ha. Mer 65%, CS 30%, CF 5%.**
This *cru* is in the commune of Vignonet on the terraces of gravel and sand in the plain of the Dordogne. The wine is vinified and bottled at the cooperative and is compact and firm, developing style.

Château La Tour-Figeac
Grand Cru Classé. Owner: **SC du Château.** Administrator: **Michel Boutet. 13·5ha. 6,000 cases. Mer 60%, CF 40%.**
This property lies on the border with Pomerol and was part of Figeac until 1879. Three years later the two La Tour-du-Pin-Figeacs were also hived off.

 This is a powerful yet stylish wine, rich and scented on the nose, with real length of flavour, marked by elegant breed. Its recent vintages have consistently done well in blind tastings, being placed with La Tour-du-Pin-Figeac (Moueix) and La Dominique as one of the leaders among the Grands Crus Classés. '78, '79, '80, '81 and '82 are excellent wines.

Château La Tour-du-Pin-Figeac
Grand Cru Classé. Owner: **Héritiers Marcel Moueix.** Administrator: **A Mouiex. 9ha. 4,000 cases. Mer 60%, CF 30%, Mal and CS 10%.**
These are powerful, robust, full-flavoured wines of style, which have consistently come out well in blind tastings in recent years. Together with its neighbours, La Tour-Figeac and La Dominique, it is one of the outstanding *crus* in this area adjoining Pomerol, and indeed stands with them among the top Grands Crus Classés. The '78, '79, '80, and '81 are all distinguished wines, and the '82 is especially fine. '83 is aromatic but rather tannic and the '85 is impressively rich with a lovely taste of prunes. The '86 is solid and powerful.

Château La Tour-du-Pin-Figeac (Giraud-Bélivier)
Grand Cru Classé. Owner: **GFA Giraud-Bélivier. 10·5ha. 4,000 cases. Mer 75%, CF 25%.**
This property is not nearly as well-known or as well-reputed as its neighbour of the same name, owned by the A Moueix firm of Château Taillefer, though they shared a common history until 1882. The Giraud family bought the property from the Béliviers in 1972, but there is no sign that this has resulted in wines worthy of its excellent site.

Château Trimoulet
Grand Cru Classé. Owner: **Michel Jean. 17ha. 8,000. Mer 60%, CF 30%, CS 10%.**
This property lies north-northeast of St-Emilion, near the boundary with St-Georges. The soils here are sandy mixed with clay and traces of iron. It has belonged to the same family for several generations and 100 percent new wood is used for the maturation.

Whenever I have drunk mature bottles in France I have found this to be an attractive St-Emilion. When young the wines can look rather rustic. I found the '79 disappointing – short and rather coarse and stalky – though the '81 had a good fruity flavour and was well structured.

Château Troplong-Mondot
Grand Cru Classé. Owner: **Claude Valette.** Administrator:

Christine Fabre. 30ha. 13,500 cases. Mer 65%, CF 15%, CS 15%, Mal 5%.

This is one of the most important properties in St-Emilion on the *côte* and plateau. It should be one of the best *crus* in St-Emilion and if sites play a part should be challenging for a position as a Premier Grand Cru. But until recently the full potential was not realized in terms of consistency and quality. Then for the marvellous '86, 50 percent new oak was used and all the wines were kept in cask instead of rotating between cask and vat. This vintage has proved a watershed. The '88, '89 and '90 have produced wines that are increasingly on a level with the Premiers Crus Classés. This has all been the devoted work of the owner's daughter, Christine Fabre. Before this the best vintages were '70, '78, '79, '82 and '83.

Château Trottevieille
1er Grand Cru Classé B. Owner: **Castéja family.**
Administrator: **Philippe Castéja. 10ha. 4,500 cases. Mer 60%, CF 25%, CS 15%.**

This is the only Premier Grand Cru to be owned by a Bordeaux *négociant*. The vineyard is apart from the other Premiers on the plateau to the east of St-Emilion, somewhat below Troplong-Mondot. The soil is a mixture of limestone and clay. The reputation of Trottevieille has been disappointing in recent years, and does not correspond to some of the rich, concentrated wines I recall before the 1956 frost. Too often the wines were either coarse and dull, or disappointingly diluted. The '75 and '79 are the best of the vintages of this time.

Then Philippe Castéja introduced 100 percent new oak for the '85 vintage, and began producing much more concentrated wines. The difference between '82 and '83 on the one hand, and the '85, '86 and '88 on the other, is very marked. Now the wines have more breed and concentration, and are again mostly Premiers Crus, recalling the great vintages of the past.

Union des Producteurs de St-Emilion
Members: **330.** Director: **Jacques Baugier. 1,150ha. 550,000 cases.**

There is no other cooperative in Bordeaux that produces as much high-quality wine as this one, lying just at the southern foot of the

The St-Emilion plateau

côtes, between the town and the Libourne–Bergerac road. In 1985 it saw one of its 330 members, Château Berliquet, become a Grand Cru Classé (*see* Château Berliquet).

There are four important wines, all entitled to the Grand Cru status, which are sold under trademarks:

Royal St-Emilion This is made from properties on the plain. The wine is full, robust and open-textured with a certain coarseness typical of its origins, but attractive.

Côtes Rocheuses As the name implies, this comes from properties in the *côtes* area. This is a wine which takes longer to develop its richness, and has more power. Some 120,000 cases are produced annually.

Haut Quercus Quercus is the Latin for oak. This brand was launched in 1978, and the wine is aged in new oak. At present 2,500 cases, all in numbered bottles, are produced annually. The wines have real intensity and are quite tannic with a very classic flavour. They take time to mature.

Cuvée Galius This is a special selection of cask-aged wines. The first vintage was 1982, and it was selected at a blind tasting as one of the 12 best wines for the Trophée des Honneurs in 1984.

The quality of these branded wines is frequently superior to that of many small *crus* made at the property, and certainly more saleable. It is an invaluable source of good, typical, sound St-Emilion.

In addition, a large number of château wines are individually made and bottled under their respective labels. These are labelled as *mis à propriété*.

Vieux Château Mazerat
Owners: **Francis and Christian Gouteyron. 11ha. 6,000 cases. Mer 60%, CF 30%, CS 10%.**
This is the only unclassified *cru* in its sector of vineyards, west of St-Emilion, but it certainly has the potential for this to change. The wines are most attractive and good vintages in '79, '82, '83, '85 and '86 are proof of their consistently high quality.

Château Vieux Sarpe
Grand Cru. Owner: **J-F Janoueix. 6·5ha. 4,000 cases. Mer 70%, CF 20%, CS 10%.**
A property run in conjunction with Château Haut-Sarpe – also owned by the Janoueix family – producing wines with their own distinctive character. Excellent fruit structure and balance enable them to age particularly well. '82, '85 and '86 are all very good vintages.

Château Villemaurine
Grand Cru Classé. Owner: **Robert Giraud. 7ha. 3,800 cases.**

Mer 70%, CS 30%.
The name is derived from Ville Maure, meaning Moorish city, the name given to the place where the Saracens camped in the eighth century. Great efforts are being made to improve the quality here, and there is certainly potential, though whether they are right to have so much Cabernet Sauvignon must be open to question. The '79 was still firm and very young, but had already developed a lovely flavour after five years. The '82 is perfumed and rich with an attractive flavour, and long, with a taste of cinnamon: spicy and complex. The '83 is extremely tannic but rich and fat, it could do well. If more wines like this can be produced, Villemaurine will soon re-establish its reputation.

Château Yon-Figeac
Grand Cru Classé. Owners: **Vins René Germain. 24ha. 7,500 cases. Mer 34%, CF 33%, CS 33%.**
This large vineyard lies northwest of St-Emilion on the road to Pomerol, between Laroze and Grand-Barrail-Larmarzelle-Figeac on sandy soil. The Lussiez family were owners here for four generations before selling to their distributors.

The wines spend only about six months in cask, the rest of the time in vat. They have been noted for their consistency and typical attractive characteristics for many years. They tend to be very scented, soft, rich and full-flavoured, with a nice underlying firmness. The '79 is a big wine, typical of the property, and the '81 is a good straightforward example.

The St-Emilion Satellites

Outside the St-Emilion *appellation* to the north and northeast lie the so-called St-Emilion satellites. While they have been excluded from the straightforward St-Emilion AC, they have the right to add the name St-Emilion to their own communal names. Some of these wines are in fact superior to St-Emilions produced from the plain of the Dordogne, and there is a much higher proportion of large domaines than in St-Emilion and Pomerol. Many of the small owners are members of the cooperatives of Montagne and Lussac-

Puisseguin. The satellite communes are as follows:

Montagne-St-Emilion The small communes of St-Georges and Parsac were joined to Montagne in 1972, but some growers in St-Georges continue to exercise their option of using the St-Georges-St-Emilion *appellation*. The AC now covers around 1,500 hectares of vineyard. The soils are *plateau calcaires* but with more clay than in St-Emilion.

Lussac-St-Emilion Here there are around 1,100 hectares of vines, on the *plateau calcaires* of the type found in St-Emilion and St-Christophe. But below these are the *côtes* of 'sables du Périgord' which are less favourable for viticulture. This is the most northerly of these *appellations*.

Puisseguin-St-Emilion. This lies northeast of St-Emilion with around 650 hectares of vines. There is a large *plateau calcaire* and its *côtes*, which provide good viticultural land.

Châteaux Belair-Montaiguillon and Belair St-Georges
Owners: **Nadine Pocci & Yannick Le Menn. 10ha. 4,700 cases. Mer 75%, CF and CS 20%, Mal 5%.**
This excellent *cru* is situated on one of the highest points in the commune of St-Georges, facing south towards St-Emilion on limestone and clay soils. Really delicious wines are now being made here. They are full of rich, supple fruit and have marked character – comparable to the best St-Emilion Grands Crus. Since the '88 vintage, two separate wines have been made. The Belair St-Georges is a selection from the oldest vines, aged in cask with some new oak. This wine is slower-developing, so needs longer ageing than the Belair-Montaiguillon, which sees no wood but has lots of fruit.

Château Bel-Air
Owner: **Robert Adove. 12ha. 6,000 cases. Mer 70%, CF 30%.**
A *cru* at the most northerly part of the region, in the commune of Puisseguin. Some attractive wines of good fruit and substance are produced here.

Château Calon
Owner: **Jean-Noël Boidron. Montagne vineyard: 35ha;**

15,000 cases; Mer 70%, CF 15%, CS 13%, Mal 2%. St-Georges vineyard: 5ha; 2,600 cases; Mer 80%, CF 10%, CS 10%.
Some cause for confusion here! This is basically one property with land in two communes, Montagne and St-Georges. The label is the same but both *appellations* are used, although the whole production could now be sold as Montagne. The owner also owns Château Corbin-Michotte, which produces well-made wine that has a good reputation.

Château Guibeau
Owner: **Bourbin family.** Administrator: **Henri-François Bourbin. 41ha. 25,000 cases. Mer 66%, CF 17%, CS 17%.**
Second labels: **Château Guibeau-la-Fourvieille, Le Vieux Château Guibeau, Château La Fourvieille, Château Les Barrails.**
Situated on the limestone plateau near Puisseguin, the wines of this large *cru* are of good quality – on a par with the St-Emilion Grands Crus even – and reflect the attention to detail shown by the Bourbin family, who have invested much in restoring and modernizing this property.

Château Laroze-Bayard
Owner: **Laporte family. 30ha. 15,000 cases. Mer 70%, CF 15%, CS 15%.** Second label: **Château Le Tuileries-de-Bayard.**
An old property in the hamlet of Bayard, which has been owned by the Laporte family since 1700. *Cuve*-matured wines, rich in colour and fruit, are produced here. They are well-structured with good body.

Château des Laurets
Owner: **GFA du Domaine des Laurets et de Malengin. 60ha. 30,000 cases. Mer 70%, CF 15%, CS 13%, Mal 2%.**
Second labels: **Châteaux La Rochette and Maison-Rose.**
This is the most important property in Puisseguin and one of the largest in the St-Emilion satellites. The vineyards are on the *plateau calcaire* and the *côtes* south of Puisseguin. These are well-reputed, robust and attractive wines.

Château du Lyonnat
Owner: **GFA des Vignobles Jean Milhade. 50ha. 25,000 cases. Mer 50%, CF 50%.** Second label: **Château La Rose-Peruchon.**
This is one of the largest and best-known domaines of the St-Emilion satellites. It lies to the east of Lussac on the *plateau calcaire*. This is very reliable, fairly light-textured, stylish wine which nevertheless keeps quite well. The standard is comparable to a good Grand Cru of St-Emilion.

Château Macquin St-Georges
Owner: **François Corre.** Administrator: **Denis Corre. 30ha. 15,000 cases. Mer 70%, CF and CS 30%.** Second label: **Château Bellonne St-Georges.**
This well-known *cru* is on hillside sites near St-Georges. The wines are bottled and distributed by Ets J-P Moueix. (*See* Château Pavie-Macquin for information on Macquin.) Fine, attractive, luscious wines are consistently made here. They are up to good St-Emilion Grand Cru standards.

Château Maison-Blanche
Owners: **Gérard & Françoise Despagne. 30ha. 15,000 cases. Mer 40%, CF 30%, CS 30%.**
This important domaine is on the *côte* to the west of Montagne. The wines are richly perfumed and very attractive for early drinking.

Les Productions Réunies de Puisseguin et Lussac-St-Emilion
Members: **150. 600ha. 300,000 cases. Mer 70%, CF and CS 30%.**
Wines from this cooperative are mostly sold under two separate labels, one for each of the two communes. Lussac accounts for about 75 percent of this production and Puisseguin for the other 25 percent. There are also 21 *crus* that are vinified here separately and marketed under their own château labels.

Château de Roques
Owner: **Michel Sublett. 25ha. 12,000 cases. Mer 60%, CF and CS 40%.** Second labels: **Châteaux Vieux-Moulin, des**

Aubarèdes and Roc du Creuzelat.

The name derives from a former proprietor – Jean de Roques – who was a close acquaintance of Henri IV. There is an attractive château on this site and some delicious wines are made here. The '75 was especially good, although almost all the vintages are comparable to Grand Cru St-Emilions.

Château Roudier

Owner: **Jacques Capdemourlin. 30ha. 15,000 cases. Mer 60%, CF 25%, CS 15%.**

This fine and important property is on the *côte* (limestone and clay) facing south towards St-Emilion. The proprietor also owns Balestard-la-Tonnelle and manages Capdemourlin. The wines are of a high standard; there is a marvellously rich, gamey flavour. The '79 was ideal drinking when six years old. Easily up to the best St-Emilion Grand Cru standard.

Château St-André-Corbin

Owner: **Robert Carré. 25ha. 12,000 cases. Mer 75%, CF 20%, CS 5%.**

A *cru* of comparable quality to the St-Emilion Grands Crus, producing charming wines which have spiciness, fruit and a good balanced structure. These wines have been marketed by J-P Moueix for some years now.

Château St-Georges

Owner: **M Desbois-Pétrus. 45ha. 25,000 cases. Mer 60%, CS 20%, CF 20%.** Second label: **Puy-St-Georges.**

Certainly one of the most spectacular properties in the whole region, with a truly palatial château built in 1774 by Victor Louis, architect of the Grand Theatre, in the purest classical style. Its vineyards are on south-facing *côtes* looking towards St-Emilion. These are elegant but well-constructed wines that have a considerable life span. 50 percent of the maturation casks used each year are of new oak. If this was in St-Emilion it is hard to think it would not be a Grand Cru Classé. As it is the wines have a great reputation, especially in France, where much is sold by mail-order.

Château Tour-du-Pas-St-Georges

Owner: **Mme Dubois-Challon. 15ha. 8,000 cases. Mer 54%, CF 33%, CS 13%.**

This property lies on south-facing slopes of limestone and clay in St-Georges. It is now farmed by Mme Dubois-Challon, which means that the gifted Pascal Delbeck, *régisseur* of Ausone and Belair, is making the wine. The results look promising. I found the '81, bottled in April '84, deliciously fruity, very easy and evolved after a year in bottle.

La Tour Mont d'Or

Members: **60. 160ha. 90,000 cases. Mer 80%, CF 10%, CS 10%.**

A cooperative in Montagne-St-Emilion, producing well-reputed wines in the classic style of the St-Emilion satellites. Two individual labels, Châteaux La Picherie and Baudron, are also vinified here.

Château Tour-Musset

Owner: **Henri Guiter.** Administrator: **Maurice Guiter. 25ha. 12,000 cases. Mer 50%, CS 50%.**

Some unusual wines are produced at this *cru* near Parsac. They are tannic with a strong, fruity flavour, probably derived from the high proportion of Cabernet Sauvignon. Wines that age well.

Château des Tours

Owner: **Marne et Champagne. 72ha. 45,000 cases. Mer 34%, CF and CS 33%, Mal 33%.** Second label: **Château La Croix-Blanche.**

This is the largest domaine in Montagne and also has the most imposing 14th-century château. The vineyards are on the *côte* east of Montagne, facing St-Emilion. The *chai* is modern and well equipped to handle the large production. There is storage capacity for over 80,000 cases. The present owners bought the property, which forms the flagship of their Bordeaux group (*see* Pontet-Clauzure, Le Couvent, Lagrange-de-Lescure, Les Baziliques), in 1983. Their offices are also here. There has been considerable investment and the wines are now aged in cask and quite transformed. They are well structured and rich, with vivid fruit character. Certainly a wine to watch from '85 onwards.

Pomerol

This is easily the smallest of the great red wine districts of Bordeaux. It measures only four by three kilometres and covers an area of only about 730 hectares, producing on average a little less than 30,000 hectolitres per year, which is roughly comparable with St-Julien in the Médoc. But a complexity of soils gives these wines an individuality and originality that sets them apart, enabling them to produce some of Bordeaux's most remarkable wines.

The best Pomerols are more intense, richer, denser and more tannic than most St-Emilions. Although the Merlot is even more predominant here than in St-Emilion, because of the clay and generally cold soils, many wines go through a stage in early maturity when they can look remarkably like Médocs, which shows how soil can change the character of grape varieties. The majority of wines become enjoyable to drink when four to seven years old, but a few top growths will take longer. The best vintages

Château Pétrus – Pomerol's most distinguished *cru*

keep very well. The '55s, '64s and '70s are still excellent.

There is no classification in Pomerol, nor will there be, since there is no desire for one locally. After Pétrus, universally acknowledged as *hors classe*, the following wines are generally recognized as the leading ones, in alphabetical order: Certan-de-May, La Conseillante, L'Evangile, La Fleur-Pétrus, Gazin, Lafleur, Latour à Pomerol, Petit-Village, Trotanoy, Vieux Château Certan.

Château Beauregard
Owner: **Héritiers Clauzel. 13ha. 4,500 cases. Mer 48%, CF 44%, CS 6%, Mal 2%.** Second label: **Domaine des Douves.**
This counts as a large property by Pomerol standards and has a fine château dating from the 17th and 18th centuries. A replica was erected on Long Island, New York, for the Guggenheims in the 1920s, an unusual compliment for a Bordeaux château, and is called Mille-Fleurs.

The vineyard is on the high plateau of Pomerol, with some sand mixed with the gravel. This is a well-run and well-reputed *cru*; 25 percent new wood is used for its maturation. While not among the leading dozen *crus* of Pomerol, it is a good wine in the second flight, rich and full-flavoured. It develops quite quickly and has real breed and charm.

Château Le Bon-Pasteur
Owners: **Dupuy-Rolland.** Administrator: **Michel Rolland. 7ha. 3,500 cases. Mer 75%, CF 25%.**
This *cru* is right on the Pomerol St-Emilion border in the north-west of the *appellation*, between Gazin and Croque-Michotte. Since the present owners took over this property it has established quite a reputation for itself in the USA. But the wines were rich and enticing before that – I recall a splendid '70. Now 35 percent new wood is being used for the cask maturation. The wines are very attractive, supple and rich. The best-reputed of recent vintages are the '78, '81, '82, '83, '85, '86 and '88.

Château Bonalgue
Owner: **Pierre Bourotte. 6·5ha. 2,500 cases. Mer 75%, CF and Mal 20%, CS 5%.** Second label: **Château Burgrave.**
This château was built in 1815 by Antoine Rabioun and is situated

on the sand and gravel soils of the plateau, in the south of the *appellation*. The Bourotte family have owned this property since 1926 and produce some very attractive wines. Fermentation takes place in modern stainless steel vats and a high proportion of new oak is used for maturation. The wines have ample fruit and weight to balance the oak flavours but need five to seven years before they drink at their best.

Château Bourgneuf-Vayron
Owners: **Charles & Xavier Vayron. 9ha. 5,000 cases. Mer 89%, CF 11%.**
A property on the western side of the high plateau of Pomerol as it slopes away in that direction. Here the gravelly soils are mixed with sand. This is a good *cru* placed by Alexis Lichine in the third category of Pomerols. The wines tend to become supple and enjoyable quite quickly and lack the concentration of the leading wines, while showing definite breed.

Château La Cabanne
Owner: **Jean-Pierre Estager. 10ha. 5,000 cases. Mer 90%, CF 10%.** Second label: **Domaine de Compostelle.**
La Cabanne is situated on the high terrace of Pomerol, on soils of gravel and clay, which overlie an iron-pan or *crasse de fer*. Jean-Pierre Estager bought this property in 1966 and has since modernized the *cuvier* and *chai*, installing vats of lined concrete and of stainless steel. Care is taken that the grapes are fully matured and that as much tannin as possible is extracted from them to balance the high proportion of new oak used here. The results are reliable wines with concentrated fruit character. They are not yet widely known but their reputation is growing.

Château Certan-de-May
Owner: **Mme Odette Barreau-Badar. 5ha. 1,750 cases. Mer 70%, CF 25%, CS and Mal 5%.**
This minute vineyard is typical of a number of properties at the heart of Pomerol's high plateau, its very size combined with the devotion of its owners creates something individual and personal. Originally part of Vieux Château Certan, the soil here has clay mixed with the predominant gravel. It lies in the area, close to

Cheval-Blanc, where nearly all the best Pomerols are to be found. In recent vintages this *cru* has re-emerged from the shadows and has rapidly taken its place again among the leading wines of the district. A proportion of 25 percent new oak is used for the maturation. The wines have an opulence, richness and power that are reminiscent of Trotanoy rather than its more compact neighbour, Vieux Château Certan. '76, '78, '79, '81, '82, '83, '85, '86 and '88 are splendid wines, with the first of these – the '76 – still the most drinkable. Certainly this is a wine to snatch up when you can.

Château Certan-Giraud
Owner: **Domaines Giraud. 6ha. 2,000 cases. Mer 70%, CF 30%. Part of crop sold as Certan-Marzelle.**
With neighbours like Pétrus and Vieux Château Certan, this small *cru* situated on the very best gravel mixed with clay in the heart of the Pomerol high plateau should be among the very top wines of the region. But, while the wines are good, they have yet to rise to the same heights as their illustrious neighbours. Only ten percent new wood is used for the maturation. Domaines Giraud also own Château Corbin in St-Emilion. '82 and '83 both have depth of fruit and a fine flavour with real breed. A wine to watch.

Château Clinet
Owner: **Georges Audy. 7ha. 3,000 cases. Mer 75%, CS 15%, CF 10%.**
This *cru*, belonging to Libourne *négociants* Audy, is near the church of Pomerol on the high plateau with its gravelly soil mixed with sand. For years there was too much Cabernet Sauvignon in the vineyards here and the wines were tough and charmless. Then Jean-Michel Arcaute took over the management of all Audy's vineyards in the mid-1970s. First he tackled the vineyard problem by increasing the Merlot and reducing the Cabernet, then, in consultation with oenologist Michel Rolland, in '85 he changed his pattern of working, going for late picking – maximum maturation – selection of grapes prior to vinification, long vatting and the use of plenty of new oak. The difference has been dramatic, with '86 easily the best claret I have ever tasted, followed by the fine example of '87, and the classic wines of '88 and '89.

This is now one of the rising stars of Pomerol.

Clos du Clocher

Owner: **Ets J-B Audy. 6ha. 3,000 cases. Mer 80%, CF 20%.**
This property was established in 1931 by Jean-Baptiste Audy. It is now a well-known and reliable *cru*, its wines being vinified with much care and attention to detail. Blending or *assemblage* is carried out by Michel Rolland of Château Le Bon Pasteur. '61, '80 and '87 are some of this property's better vintages.

Château La Conseillante

Owners: **Héritiers Louis Nicolas.** Administrator: **Bernard Nicolas. 13ha. 5,000 cases. Mer 45%, CF 45%, Mal 10%.**
This is always one of the best two or three wines in Pomerol after Pétrus, year after year. Added to the consistency is the strong personality of the wine. It combines concentration and breed on the nose with a superb flavour of real originality, unctuous yet firm-centred, and great persistence of flavour. Its neighbour L'Evangile is clearly from the same stable, but at present is less consistent and tends to be more massive but less fine. On the other side there are similarities with Petit-Village as the wine improves. The outstanding vintages here are '70, '75, '76, '79, '81, '82, '83, '85, '86, '88 and '89. Lesser years like '73, '77 and '80 have still provided some delicious bottles.

Château La Croix

Owner: **SC J Janoueix. 14ha. 6,100 cases. Mer 60%, CF 20%, CS 20%.**
These are very well-balanced attractive wines that are enjoyable after four or five years, yet also keep well, acquiring delicacy and a spicy complexity. The '71 was keeping well and had fined down, developing a lovely flavour, mellow but with a good backbone when 14 years old. I found the '79 had lots of fruit and flavour but was already open-textured and forward at six years. Since then excellent examples have been the '81, '82, '83, '85 and '86. If you can sort this château out from all the others in Pomerol with 'Croix' in their names, it is a wine worth looking out for.

Château La Croix-de-Gay

Owner: **Noel Raynaud. 12ha. 6,500 cases. Mer 90%, CS and CF 10%.** Second label: **Château La Fleur de Gay.**

This property is on the northern borders of the plateau of Pomerol where the predominantly gravelly soils mingle with sand. For the maturation 30 percent new wood is used. This is stylish, attractive wine that lacks the richness and concentration of it neighbour, Le Gay, and is made for young drinking. Nevertheless it is the sort of fruity, supple wine that has a wide appeal.

Château La Croix-du-Casse
Owner: **Ets G A M Audy. 9ha. 4,500 cases. Mer 60%, CF 40%.**
La Croix-du-Casse is under the same management as Château Clinet but produces wines of a totally different style. Benefiting from the gravel soils and underlying iron-pan, they are attractively perfumed, full-flavoured and have a delicious fruit quality.

Château La Croix-St-Georges
Owner: **SC J Janoueix. 4ha. 2,500 cases. Mer 60%, CF 20%, CS 20%.**
This property is run in conjunction with Château La Croix, the main differences in their wines being derived from the variations in the *terroirs* of their respective vineyards. La Croix-St-Georges is situated on the plateau and therefore is based mainly on gravel. The vintages of '79, '81, and '85 are the most attractive produced here recently, they have both suppleness and finesse.

Château La Croix-Toulifaut
Owner: **SC J Janoueix. 1·5ha. 1,000 cases. Mer 100%.**
This property is situated in the commune of Beauregard, on the *sables anciens*, similar to that found in St-Emilion. The wines produced here are well-oaked, deep in colour and have an attractive, dense fruitiness, usually needing five or six years before optimum drinking.

Domaine de l'Eglise
Owners: **Philippe Castéja & Mme Peter Preben Hansen. 7ha. 3,500 cases. Mer 85%, CF 10%, CS 5%.**
Not surprisingly this vineyard is near the church on the high plateau, and the soil is deep gravel with traces of iron deposit which gives the wines a certain brilliance and depth of colour. The Castéjas

bought the property, whose wine they had distributed for many years, in 1972. The wines tend to be light in style yet fine, perfumed and elegant. But with the '86 vintage, Philippe Castéja began making much more concentrated wines using new oak for the maturation casks – a third being new each year. This is good second-tier Pomerol.

Clos L'Eglise
Owners: **Moreau family.** Administrators: **Michel & Francis Moreau. 6ha. 2,800 cases. Mer 50%, CS 36%, CF 14%.**
This small vineyard lies near the church on the high plateau where the predominantly gravelly soil is mixed with sand. This is a well-run property where stainless steel fermentation vats were introduced in 1983. The wines are matured in wood with a small percentage of new oak. The wines here are fine and rather more delicate than some Pomerols, with a particularly lovely bouquet. Their fine-textured quality with length and beauty of flavour provides an attractive contrast with some of the heavyweights. It keeps well in spite of its lighter weight. Among recent vintages the '79 is particularly outstanding. A wine to watch.

Château L'Eglise-Clinet
Owner: **Mme Durantou. 4·5ha. 1,850 cases. Mer 60%, CF 30%, Mal 10%.**
This small vineyard has for many years been farmed by the Lasseire family of Clos René. It is near the church on the high plateau. There the soil is mainly gravelly mixed with sand. An important point here is that the vines are older than in most Pomerol domaines because they were not pulled up after the '56 frost but left to recover, which most of them did. The wines are very carefully made and a small amount of new wood is used for the cask maturation. The reputation of the wine has long been high amongst its devotees. This is classic Pomerol and is rich, supple and very fruity. The '78 is ready to drink and the '81, '82 and '83 are all reported to be delightful. Unfortunately this is a wine that takes some finding.

Château L'Enclos
Owner: **SC Château L'Enclos.** Administrator: **Hugues**

Weydert. 10·5ha. 4,600 cases. Mer 90%, CF 9·5%, Mal 0·5%.
This good *cru* lies on the far side of the N89 Libourne–Périgueux road from the main vineyards of the high plateau of Pomerol. Here the soil is predominantly sandy, but there is an important gravelly outcrop which occurs here, at the neighbouring Clos René, and further away, at Moulinet.

The wines here have been well made and are of high quality in the second tier of Pomerol wines. I have memories of a wonderful '29. Today the style of the wines is rather similar to Close René, dense-textured, succulent and fruity, drinkable quite young but also possessing the capacity to age. This is fine classic Pomerol which is thoroughly reliable and enjoyable.

Château L'Evangile
Owner: **Domaines Rothschild.** Administrator: **Mme Louis Ducasse. 14ha. 5,000 cases. Mer 66%, CF 34%.**
This is one of the leading *crus* of Pomerol, situated near the edge of the high plateau adjoining La Conseillante and Vieux Château Certan. The predominantly gravelly soil is here mixed with some clay and sand, the feature responsible for the unique quality of Pétrus (where the vineyard is almost entirely clay and gravel). The style of the wines most resembles La Conseillante, but has a different emphasis owing to the high proportion of Merlot, the presence of clay in the soil and the fact that only 20 percent new oak is used here for the maturation. The submerged cap system of vinification is used and results in high colour extraction. The wines tend to be more massive and chewy in texture, yet sometimes lack the firmness of La Conseillante. In 1990 all the shareholders except Madame Ducasse sold to Domaines Rothschild; Rothschilds now distribute the wine, but Madame Ducasse continues to run the property using Michel Rolland as consultant oenologist. There have in the past been some inconsistencies but the recent record is impressive. '81 is a fine example of the year, '82 is luscious and ripe and '83 big and firm. The '85 is generous and fine, but the '86 shows some dilution. '87 is good for the year and the '88 is also very fine; '89 and '90 are exceptional wines. The future of this property looks bright indeed.

Château Feytit-Clinet
Owners: **Succésseurs Tane-Domergue.** Administrator: **Ets J-P Moueix. 7ha. 3,000 cases. Mer 85%, CF 15%.**
A property on the northwestern edge of the plateau where the predominantly gravelly soil is mixed with sand. It is entirely run by the highly efficient Moueix organization presided over by Christian Moueix and his oenologist Jean-Claude Berrouet. While the wine is all plummy fruit on the nose, the flavour is more elegant than one expects, with good length and a firm finish, an excellent second-tier Pomerol, and naturally, from such a stable, most consistent.

Château La Fleur-de-Gay
Owners: **Raynaud family. 1·75ha. 1,000 cases. Mer 100%.**
The Raynaud family have set this vineyard aside specifically for the Merlot grape. Benefiting from deep gravelly soils, the Merlot wines are full of flavour and concentrated fruit. Their vinification is monitored by Michel Rolland and Pascal Ribéreau-Gayon and is unusual in that it is carried out at fairly high temperatures. These are very special wines and have a fine future ahead of them.

Château La Fleur-Pétrus
Owner: **SC du Château.** Administrator: **Jean-Pierre Moueix. 7ha. 3,200 cases. Mer 85%, CF 15%.**
One of the leading *crus* of Pomerol, situated just across the road from Pétrus, but on quite different soil. Here the soil is very stony with large gravel but no clay or sand. In recent years the reputation of this wine has steadily grown, and this is now one of the flagships of the Moueix empire and almost certainly the finest Pomerol on purely gravelly soil, all the others having some clay in their make-up, except for Latour à Pomerol. A third of the wood used here for maturation is new. The wines are gorgeous, perfumed, powerful and elegant on the nose, with great complexity, richness and power of flavour which is so obviously of the highest quality. The wines of this property are consistently good: '70 is an impressive wine, and '71 was lovely too, though now not quite what it was, some of the sheen having gone. Lovely examples were the '78, '79, '81, '82, '83, '85 (quite exceptional) and '86. Not as massive as most of the other leading *crus*, but there is no doubting the breed and beauty of this wine.

Château Le Gay
Owner: **Marie Robin. 8ha. 2,000 cases. Mer 50%, CF and CS 50%.**
This *cru* lies on the northern side of the high plateau on gravelly soils, near to the owner's other *cru*, Lafleur. For many years its wines have been exclusively distributed by Ets J-P Moueix, but the Robin sisters ran the properties themselves. However, since the death of Thérèse Robin the Moueix team have taken over the management of both properties. Le Gay has always produced big, dense, firm-textured wines that age very well, as bottles of '64 and '66 still demonstrate. Now things can only get better and no doubt the wines will be polished up a little and show some consistency. Recent successes have been the '79, '82, '83, '85 and '86.

Château Gazin
Owner: **Etienne de Bailliencourt. 20ha. 8,300 cases. Mer 80%, CF 15%, CS 5%.**
This is the largest of the leading Pomerols, situated on the north-eastern corner of the high plateau on gravelly soils. In the late 1960s a portion of the vineyard adjoining Pétrus, with the same clay in the soil, was sold to Pétrus. Only a very small percentage of new oak is used for the maturation in cask. I find Gazin a difficult wine to assess. It is undeniably rich and opulent with an extraordinarily vivid and forceful character when young. There is a touch of coarseness but this perhaps is merely a part of a highly extrovert personality that demands attention. There has been a shortage of money here, due to inheritance problems, but from '85 onwards greater concentration and more style have been achieved. Before this the pick of the bunch were the '78, '81, '82 and '83. The '85 is very concentrated, rich and firm, the '86 is rather austerely tannic while the '88 has a lovely rich aftertaste and is very stylish, the '89 is very impressive indeed. It is good to see this distinguished *cru* returning to form.

Château La Grave Trigant de Boisset
Owner: **Christian Moueix. 8ha. 3,300 cases. Mer 90%, CF 10%.**
This small vineyard has been the personal property of Christian Moueix of Ets J-P Moueix since 1971. The firm owns many properties, and farms or manages many others, with Christian

Moueix heading their team. The property is on gravelly soil on the middle plateau in the northwest of Pomerol, just before the Libourne-Périgueux road. The name is something of a handicap, the words 'Château La Grave' appearing in large characters on the label, with 'Trigant de Boisset' in smaller ones underneath. For maturation in cask 25 percent new oak is used. The wine is quite rich, tannic and fine but less spectacular than that of the leading *crus*, making this a good second-tier Pomerol. The '78, '79, '81, '82, '83, '85 and '86 are all very successful here – beautifully made and consistent wines.

Château Lafleur
Owner: **Marie Robin**. Administrator: **Sylvie & Jacques Guinaudeau. 4ha. 1,500 cases. Mer 50%, CF 50%.**
This minute but superb property is on the gravelly high plateau, with some of the precious clay soils found at the best *crus* making up its vineyards. It is next to La Fleur-Pétrus but their subsoils differ considerably due to the patchwork of other Pomerol soils in this area, La Fleur-Pétrus having none of the clay deposits. In 1985 the Guinaudeaus assumed responsibility, running the property for Mlle Robin, and have further enhanced the already great reputation of this *cru*. Unfortunately, with so little wine produced, it is rare as well as expensive. The style is all opulent charm and great finesse with a lovely bouquet. The '79, '82, '83, '85, '86 and '88 all have great reputations.

Château Lafleur Gazin
Owner: **Maurice Borderie**. Administrator: **Ets J-P Moueix. 7·8ha. 3,500 cases. Mer 70%, CF 30%.**
A property on the northeastern limits of the plateau next to Gazin. Here the predominantly gravelly soil is mixed with sand. This *cru* has come into great prominence since Ets J-P Moueix became '*fermiers*' here in 1976. It is run with all the usual meticulous care associated with the Moueix team under Christian Moueix and his oenologist Jean-Claude Berrouet. The wine is rich and quite powerful with an underlying firmness. In the '79 I detected a certain coarseness which differentiated it from the best *crus*, but in the very supple and ripe '83 I saw no sign of this. An indication of the vintage or of the château's progress. A serious wine worth following.

Château Lagrange
Owner: **Ets Jean-Pierre Moueix. 8ha. 2,600 cases. Mer 90%, CF 10%.**
Another Moueix property on the gravelly high plateau. There is some new wood used for the cask maturation. The wines seem to have a certain originality of flavour, a breeding allied to charm and structure, which marks them out as very fine wines. The '82, '83, '85 and '86 are all most impressive. A good second-tier Pomerol.

Château Latour à Pomerol
Owner: **Mme Lily Lacoste.** Administrator: **Ets J-P Moueix. 8ha. 2,400 cases. Mer 80%, CF 20%.**
This fine property lies on the gravelly high plateau, northwest of the church. Its owner is also co-proprietor of Pétrus, and it is managed and distributed by Ets J-P Moueix. 25 percent new oak is used for the cask maturation. This property has noticeably improved throughout the 1970s. In the past there were inconsistencies and fine bottles were interspersed with disappointments. More recently the wines have been marked by a wonderful perfume, and a delectable beauty of flavour, power and finesse. There is now a clear similarity of style with La Fleur-Pétrus, and with the '83 I even thought Latour the better wine. The '78, '79, '81 and '82 were all wonderful wines and the '85, '86 and '88 are all concentrated and impressive. This is now indisputably among the leading *crus* of Pomerol.

Clos des Litanies
Owner: **J Janoueix. 0·8ha. 400 cases. Mer 100%.**
The name of this *cru* derives from a very conscientious 16th-century monk, Brother Mathieu Bossuet, who used frequently to recite his breviary at this *clos*. Some lovely wines are produced here, from vineyards entirely planted with Merlot.

Château Mazeyres
Owner: **SC (Querre family). 9ha. 5,000 cases. Mer 70%, CF 30%.**
This property lies on the recent gravel and sand of the lower plateau north of Libourne and at the western extremity of the *appellation*. Two-thirds of the wine produced is matured in casks (of which 25

percent are renewed annually), and a third in vats. The wines are consistent and well made, with a good colour, quite light-textured but full-flavoured with lovely easy, attractive fruit. A delicious '80 was made here. A very good lesser *cru*.

Château Moulinet
Owner: **SC du Château.** Administrator: **Armand Moueix. 17·5ha. 8,000 cases. Mer 60%, CS 30%, CF 10%.**
This relatively large property lies beyond the Libourne-Périgueux road on the gravelly sandy soils of the middle plateau. This is one of Armand Moueix's well-run properties. A third of the wood used for maturation is new. The wines are very scented and charming. The '82, for example, is delicious for drinking now. A pleasant, widely distributed wine.

Château Nenin
François Despujol. 27ha. 10,000 cases. Mer 50%, CF 30%, CS 20%.
This is one of the largest and best-known Pomerol properties. It lies on lower ground northwest of the high plateau, on sandy gravelly soils. Unfortunately tastings and a visit to this property have indicated that all is not well here. I suspect the major problem is one of old casks in poor condition, as a result of which the wines often seem coarse and can leave one with a dirty woody aftertaste. This is a pity as in cask the raw materials are rich and powerful. The '79 is most disappointing and the '81 tasted very dry and ungrateful before bottling. The '82 is certainly suspect but some improvement was apparent with the '85 and '86 vintages. A mechanical harvester was used at this property for the first time in 1982.

Château Petit-Village
Owner: **AXA Millésimes.** Administrator: **J-M Cazes. 11ha. 3,900 cases. Mer 82%, CF 9%, CS 9%.**
A finely placed vineyard on the high plateau, with gravelly clay soils, close to La Conseillante and St-Emilion. Previous owners, the Prats family (*see* Cos d'Estournel), sold to AXA (*see* Pichon-Baron) in 1989. One problem here has been that after the '56 frost the vineyard was largely replanted and the mistake of planting too much Cabernet Sauvignon was then made. This has now been

corrected and the wines are getting better and better. A minimum of 50 percent new wood is used, sometimes more, according to the year. The style is closest to that of La Conseillante, especially since '78. The wines have a lovely aroma and are very rich and deep, firm-centred, with a lovely flavour and great breed. '79, '81, '82, '83 and '87 are the great recent successes here. On this form Petit Village is back in its rightful place among the leading *crus*.

Château Pétrus
Owners: **Mme L P Lacoste & J-P Moueix.** Administrator: **Christian Moueix. 11·4ha. 3,700 cases. Mer 95%, CF 5%.**
40 years ago Pétrus was unknown outside a small circle of wine-lovers in Bordeaux but has lately become one of the region's great names; unfortunately it is more talked about than drunk, due to its price and rarity.

This is the world's greatest Merlot wine and shows what can be done with this grape variety when conditions are just right. There is an unctuous and almost chewy quality of richness and power which has some similarity with that of Cheval-Blanc, but Pétrus tends to be more concentrated, firmer and slower to develop. The complexity and nuances of flavour that develop with age are astonishing. Some vintages like '67 and '71 could already be enjoyed when only seven to ten years old, but then go on to surprise one with their further development; while some great years like '64 are still flexing their muscles. Of the vintages still drinking today the '71 is remarkable if controversial and the '73 and '76 are also good. '75, '78, '79 and '81 are all great wines and the '82 is already acquiring legendary status and prices to match. The '83 is not far behind the '82, and the '85 has a lovely ripe supple character, but without the concentration of its two fine predecessors. The '86 is enormously concentrated and tannic, a great *vin de garde*. Pétrus is a wine which every wine-lover should find a way of experiencing.

Le Pin
Owner: **Thienpont family. 1·2ha. 1,500 cases. Mer 88%, CF 12%.**
The wines of this tiny property have developed great prestige since the Thienpont family took over in 1979. They are attractive wines, almost Californian in style, and are sold at particularly high prices.

Château Plince
Owner: **Moreau family. 8·3ha. 4,600 cases. Mer 68%, CF 24%, CS 8%.**
A good lesser *cru* situated on the sandy soils in the southwest of Pomerol behind Nenin. The Moreau family also own the excellent Clos L'Eglise. A small amount of new oak is used for the cask maturation. This property has long had the reputation for producing deliciously fruity supple wines. The marvellous '47 remained fresh and opulent for over 30 years. After some ups and downs, good wines are now being made here, and they are excellent value for a *cru* on the sand, making the most of its high potential.

Château La Pointe
Owner: **Bernard d'Arfeuille. 25ha. 9,000 cases. Mer 80%, CF 15%, Mal 5%.**
This large property is on the sandy, gravelly soils of the middle plateau opposite Nenin though on slightly lower ground. The property is well known and the wines widely distributed by the *négociants* d'Arfeuille in Libourne. For the maturation 35 percent new wood is used. A retrospective tasting in 1983 confirmed my suspicions that this wine is not as good as it used to be. The splendid '70 cast a shadow over the rest of the decade, making '75 look tannic and lacking in fruit, and '78 and '79 seem only moderate, if charming, lightweights.

A certain lightness, allied to finesse and stylishness, has long been the mark of La Pointe but they always had a certain balance and flair which somehow seems missing now, even with the '82. '86 however, showed a marked improvement in the quality of these wines.

Château Prieurs de la Commanderie
Owner: **Clément Fayat. 3·5ha. 1,200 cases. Mer 80%, CF and CS 20%.**
Situated on Pomerol's middle terrace, this *cru* is an amalgamation of several small plots, formed in 1984 by Clément Fayat. A new *cuvier* and *chai* have been built, incorporating the most modern winemaking equipment – including automatically temperature-cooled *cuves*. It is early yet to judge these wines, which are rich-textured

and marked by oak, but they appear to be improving with every vintage.

Clos René
Owner: **Pierre Lasserre. 11ha. 5,500 cases. Mer 60%, CF 30%, Mal 10%.** Alternative label: **Château Moulinet-Lasserre.**
This is a wonderfully perfumed, dense, rich, plummy Pomerol which seldom disappoints. The '75 is a rich, powerful, tannic wine which is now very harmonious and can be drunk with enjoyment. The '76 is delicious for drinking now and the '78 is good too, better than the '79 which lacks concentration. The '81 is also extremely fine, very rich with a slightly roasted flavour. '82 has a smell of prunes and an incredibly dense, rich but supple flavour, the superb '83 is more tannic and alcoholic than this and the '85 has the richness and charm of its year. '86 is exceptional, with intense fruit and a lovely smell of damsons, yet is very tannic. This is a very good second-tier Pomerol. For fiscal and family reasons, a part of the crop is sold as Moulinet-Lasserre. The wines are the same – this is not a second label, but an alternative one.

Château Rouget
Owner: **François-Jean Brochet. 16ha. 6,250 cases. Mer 88%, CF 12%.**
This is an interesting property on sandy and gravelly soils, with some clay, at the northern limit of the high plateau. The wine is very traditionally made and a third of the wood used for the cask maturation is new. An unusual feature here is that the proprietor and his uncle before him have kept large stocks of old wines, so you can sometimes see these on restaurant lists in Bordeaux.

This is really a wine that takes time to develop. Even in a ripe flattering vintage like '79 the Rouget has a dense, austere nose and is quite powerful with lots of fat. '85 is in a more opulent flattering style, and is developing more quickly. This is real *vin de garde* wine in all good years.

Château de Sales
Owner: **GFA du Château de Sales – Les Héritiers de Laage.** Administrators: **Henri & Bruno de Lambert. 47·5ha. 22,500**

cases. **Mer 66%, CF 17%, CS 17%.** Second label: **Château Chantalouette.**

This is the largest property in Pomerol by a comfortable margin and lies on sandy soils with some recent gravel, in the northwest corner of the *appellation* near the Libourne-Pouis road. There is an impressive château (17th and 18th century) in a park. It has belonged to the same family for almost 400 years; Henri de Lambert's wife is a de Laage. Their son Bruno is a qualified oenologist.

The wines are alternated between vats and used casks for the maturation. There was a very noticeable improvement in quality here from 1970 onwards. The wines are now scented, rich, plummy and powerful with a pleasant stylishness. They develop quite quickly. Good reliable Pomerol at a reasonable price.

Château du Tailhas
Owner: **GFA du Tailhas.** Administrator: **Daniel Nébout. 10·5ha. 4,000 cases. Mer 76%, CF 12%, CS 12%.**

This property is on sandy soils in the extreme southwest corner of the *appellation* and near to Figeac, just the other side of the stream which is also called Tailhas. 50 percent new wood is used for the cask maturation. This is well-made and well-reputed second-tier Pomerol. The wines have a very full colour, a highlighted bouquet which is most attractive, and lots of young fruit with that slightly earthy taste which occurs in some growths in Pomerol where there are iron deposits in the subsoil. There is now a pleasing degree of consistency – a very good '80 was made and '82 is a compact solid wine that has matured slowly.

Château Taillefer
Owners: **Héritiers Marcel Moueix.** Administrators: **Bernard & Jean-Michel Moueix. 18ha. 7,500 cases. Mer 50%, CF 30%, CS 15%, Mal 5%.**

An attractive 19th-century château and park dominate this *cru*, which is one of the largest in Pomerol. A Moueix et Fils have their headquarters here and produce some light-bodied, fruity wines from their very modern winery. The vintages '82, '86 and '87 are particularly elegant wines.

Château Trotanoy

Owner: **Ets J-P Moueix. 7·5ha. 3,000 cases. Mer 90%, CF 10%.**

This leading *cru* is on gravel and clay soils at the western edge of the high plateau. Apart from being one of the most illustrious jewels in the Moueix crown, it is also the home of Jean-Jacques Moueix, nephew of the legendary Jean-Pierre Moueix. Of course the care of this *cru* stands very high among the priorities for Christian Moueix and his oenologist Jean-Claude Berrouet. A proportion of 50 percent new wood is used for the cask maturation.

The reputation of Trotanoy is now higher than ever before, as can be seen from the prices collectors are prepared to pay for its mature vintages at auction. The style of the wine is for me more reminiscent of Pétrus than any other Pomerol, with its dense colour, rich spicy enveloping bouquet, and opulent fleshy body which develops an enchanting flavour of exceptional length. The '70 and '71 are both wonderful wines of contrasting style, and the '79 is rather soft-centred and therefore the only recent vintage that is currently drinkable. Great and often exceptional vintages were the '75, '78, '79, '81, '82, '83, '85, '86 and '88.

Vieux Château Certan

Owner: **Héritiers Georges Thienpont. 13·6ha. 5,500 cases. Mer 50%, CF 25%, CS 20%, Mal 5%.**

Until the rise of Pétrus, this fine *cru* was long regarded as the leading one in Pomerol. It is splendidly placed on the high plateau with sandy clay mixed with its gravel, and Pétrus, La Conseillante and L'Evangile are neighbours, with Cheval Blanc not far away. The small but aristocratic 17th-century château is the only one of note among these leading Pomerol *crus*; until the end of the 18th century the estate was actually much larger. It has belonged to the Belgian Thienponts since 1924 and Leon Thienpont ran the property from 1943 until his death in 1985 and has been succeeded by his son Alexandre, who had the useful experience of working at La Gaffelière from 1982 until this time. The *chai* and *cuvier* were enlarged and modernized in the early 1970s, though wooden vats were kept. A third of the wood used for the maturation is new.

This is a wine of marked individuality. It is very perfumed, less dense in colour than other leading Pomerols, very compact and firm on the palate, with a complexity, finesse and flavour that set it apart. It lacks the opulence of Trotanoy, and while it has something of the structure of La Conseillante, it lacks its unctuousness. Harmony, 'race' and finesse are the great hallmarks here. The '78, '79 and '81 are classic wines from this *cru*; the '82 with its great richness and '83 with its unusual power are two exceptional vintages and the '85 has all the seductive charm one would hope for from this *cru* in this year. The '86 has great power and concentration and is also an exceptional wine. Evolution tends to be slow; the '71 is still at its peak and the '80 needs longer keeping than most from this year. For individuality this is still one of the best Pomerols.

Château Vraye-Croix-de-Gay
Owner: **Baronne Guichard. 3·7ha. 1,200 cases. Mer 55%, CF 40%, CS 5%.**
This small *cru* is on gravelly soils on the edge of the high plateau near Le Gay and Domaine L'Eglise. Its owner also has the excellent Château Siaurac in Lalande-de-Pomerol. In style the wines are closest to those of Le Gay, very powerful and densely textured, needing time to show worth. The wines have been inconsistent, but with recent improvements. The '86 shows great promise.

Lalande-de-Pomerol

This is an *appellation* of growing importance, covering about 950 hectares of vines, of which roughly 60 percent are in the commune of Lalande and 40 percent in that of Néac. In Lalande the vineyards are on recent gravel and sand terraces, which are relatively low-lying. However in Néac there is a high plateau with those *crus* facing south towards Pomerol being on very good gravel. The best wines are close in quality to lesser Pomerols, with less power and tannin, developing quickly, but attractive, with finesse and style.

Château des Annereaux
Owner: **M Hessel-Milhade. 22ha. 11,000 cases.**
A good *cru* on the gravel and sandy soils of the lower plateau. Very elegant, attractive wines are made. There was a delicious '79, but the '82 seems forward and lacks stuffing.

Château de Bel-Air
Owner: **L & Jean-Pierre Musset. 12ha. 5,000 cases. Mer 60%, CF 15%, Mal 15%, CS 10%.**
This well-reputed *cru* is on the gravel and sand of the middle plateau, opposite Moulinet (Pomerol). It has long been considered one of the *appellation*'s leading *crus*.

Château Haut-Chaigneau
Owner: **André Chatonnet. 20ha. 10,000 cases. Mer 60%, CF 20%, CS 20%.**
A good *cru* in the commune of Néac. Rich, plummy and attractive wines are made here. '81, '82, '83 and '85 are all of a high standard.

Chateau Les Hauts-Conseillants and Les Hauts-Tuileries
Owner: **Leopold Figeac. 8ha. 3,000 cases. Mer 60%, CS 25%, CF 15%.**
This very good *cru* is in Néac. The Les Hauts-Conseillants name is used *vente-direct* in France, the Hauts-Tuileries for export sales. A third of the wood used for the cask-maturation is new. The wines are well made and have a marvellous opulent, perfumed bouquet and a seductively silky texture with good concentration worthy of a Pomerol. Very good vintages were the '79, '81, '82, '83 and '86.

Château Moncets
Owner: **Baronne de Jerphanion. 16ha. 7,000 cases.** Second label: **Gardour.**
An excellent *cru* on the gravel and sand at the edge of the plateau in the best southern part of Néac. The wines are bottled in Libourne by Ets J-P Moueix. They are rich and velvety in texture with style and breed placing them in the category of good lesser Pomerols.

Château Siaurac
Owner: **Baronne Guichard. 25ha. 10,000 cases. Mer 50%, CF 40%, CS 10%.**
This important *cru* is in Néac, in the south of the commune on gravel and sand at the edge of the plateau. It is one of the best known *crus* in this *appellation*, consistently producing firm, fruity wines which are most attractive.

Minor Appellations

The following section covers some of the *appellations* that do not belong to the major league of Bordeaux regions but which contain many wines that are worth investigating. These wines tend to mature earlier than the Grands Crus of the well-known *appellations*, which makes them extremely useful commercially. Among them are wines of great charm and personality that it would be a pity to overlook.

Côtes de Bourg

The attractive, hilly and often wooded countryside of the Côtes de Bourg has seen something of a revival in the past decade. There are now over 3,000 hectares of vines, this area showing an increase of 14 percent between 1981 and 1988. The soils are mostly of limestone and clay, and gravel and clay on a limestone subsoil. The traditional *encépagement* was a third each of Cabernet Sauvignon, Merlot and Malbec (still to be found at Château Guerry), but in most properties the role of the Malbec has been reduced and that of the Merlot increased. This factor, together with the inability today of many owners to afford casks for maturation, has meant that something of the distinctively rich fruitiness of the Bourg has inevitably been lost. But good and attractive wines are being made here, in increasing quantities, and as the demand for good, reasonably priced red Bordeaux grows, Bourg should prosper.

Château de Barbé
Owner: **Savary de Beauregard family.** Administrator: **Louis Savary de Beauregard. 56ha. 32,000 cases. Mer 70%, CF and CS 25%, Mal 5%.**
One of the largest, finest and best-reputed properties in the region. There is no wood-ageing, and the wines are light-textured, fruity and charming with some 'race'. Essentially for young-drinking (after two to four years).

Château Guerry
Owner: **SC du Château Guerry.** Administrator: **Bertrand de**

Rivoyre. 22ha. 12,000 cases. CS 36%, Mer 36%, Mal 28%.
A *cru* which shows what Bourg is capable of. There are two
distinctive features: the position of the Malbec as a major variety is
retained, and this is one of the last *crus* in Bourg where all the wines
are matured in cask. The result is a wine which combines richness
and suppleness, power and finesse. Distribution is exclusively
through Ets de Rivoyre-Diprovin and Louis Dubroca.

Château Guionne
Owner: **Richard Porcher. 12ha. 6,250 cases. CF and CS
50%, Mer 45%, Mal 5%.**
This *cru* is all château-bottled and produces fruity, attractive and
quite elegant wines.

Château Mendoce
Owner: **Philippe Darricarrère. 14ha. 6,600 cases. CS 57%,
Mer 43%.**
This is one of the best-known and best-reputed wines in the region.
There is a fine château, parts of which date from the 15th century.
The owners are also proprietors of Château Moulin-à-Vent in
Moulis. The wines are supple with some richness, and mature
rapidly.

Château Peychaud
Owner: **Jacques & Bernard Germain. 34ha. 16,600 cases.
Mer 40%, CF and CS 50%, Mal 10%.**
This large and well-known property was acquired by the owners in
1971. It has a good reputation for supple, pleasing wines.

Château Rousset
Owner: **M & Mme Teisseire.** Administrator: **Gérard
Teisseire. 23ha. 12,000 cases. Mer 46%, CS 37%, Mal 13%,
CF 4%.**
Situated in the commune of Samonac, this is certainly one of the
best *crus* of Bourg. The wines have richness and length of flavour
which place them above the general run of wines from this area.

Château Tour-de-Tourteau
Owner: **GAEC Chagnaud Père & Fils. 16ha. 8,000 cases.**

Mer 60%, CF and CS 35%, Mal 5%.
This excellent *cru* was once part of Rousset. All the wines are château-bottled and distributed by Calvet and Ets de Rivoyre & Diprovin-Louis Dubroca. The wines are unusually rich and powerful, even pungent, making delicious drinking when three to four years old.

Premières Côtes de Blaye

This region forms the northward extension of the Côtes de Bourg. Although the region is larger than the Bourg, the parts suited to the vine are smaller. The area of vineyards has, however, more than doubled over the last 20 years, now covering over 3,000 hectares. The output consists predominantly of red wine with only a small and unimportant production of white. The soil here is of limestone and clay, and the Merlot is more predominant than in Bourg.

The prices achieved are often no more than for Bordeaux Supérieur, and some growers take advantage of the higher permitted yields for the lesser *appellation* and declare their wines as Bordeaux Supérieur instead of Premières Côtes de Blaye. This is a good source of fruity, easy-to-drink red Bordeaux.

Château Bourdieu
Owner: **Jean Kléber Michaud. 33ha. Red: 15,000 cases; Mer 50%, CS 40%, CF 10%. White: 5,000 cases; Sém 80%, Sauv and Col 20%.**
A well-known and well-reputed *cru*, unusual in its high proportion of Cabernet Sauvignon and in using wood maturation. The result is a wine above average in character and quality.

Château Charron
Owner: **Marc Doudet-Beaudry. 25ha. Red: 11,250 cases; Mer 80%, CF and CS 20%. White: 1,250 cases; Sém 65%, Sauv 35%.**
A well-reputed *cru* that uses wood maturation and even some new oak. The result is a wine with more colour and richness than average.

Château L'Escadre
Owners: **GFA L'Escadre**. Administrator: **Jean-Marie Carreau. 32ha. 5,800 cases; Mer 70%, CS 20%, Mal 10%. White: 400 cases; Mer Blanc 40%, Sém 30%, Col 20%, Ugni Blanc 10%.**
This very good *cru* in the commune of Cars has acquired an excellent reputation for consistency over the last 20 years. Some wood maturation is used, and the wines are charmingly fruity and stylish.

Château Segonzac
Owner: **Mme Pierre Dupuy**. Administrator: **Nicolas Leclair. 32ha. 12,250 cases (red and white). Mer 60%, CS 25%, CF 10%, Mal 5%.**
This *cru* in the commune of St-Genès-de-Blaye produces very fruity, light, supple wines for early drinking.

Fronsac

In the early 18th and 19th centuries, Fronsac was the most reputed of the Libournais wines, fetching higher prices than those of St-Emilion. Now, after a long period of obscurity, it is slowly re-emerging as a quality region. In total there are about 1,100 hectares of vines divided between the *appellations* of Canon-Fronsac (27 percent of the area) and Fronsac (73 percent). These vineyards, like those of the St-Emilion *côtes*, are wines of the plateau and *côtes*, only more spectacularly so. The vineyards of the Canon-Fronsac are on a *plateau calcaire* and on outcrops and *côtes* of sandstone, while those of the Fronsac AC are mostly on a *plateau calcaire* covered with red soils similar to those of St-Christophe.

The vineyards here tend to be small, but there are some lovely buildings, such as the châteaux at La Rivière and La Dauphine. The Merlot now dominates, but the Cabernet Sauvignon also has an important place in some of the best vineyards. There has been a tendency to use too much old wood and keep the wines in cask too long, and many château-bottled wines have looked rustic, but now things seem to be improving. With Ets J-P Moueix now taking an increasing interest in the region, better quality should lead to better prices and a wider interest. So there could be a brighter future ahead for Fronsac.

Château Cardeneau
Owner: **Jean-Noël Hervé. 14ha. 6,000 cases. Mer 65%, CF 20%, CS 10%, Mal 5%.**
A *cru* showing much promise. The vineyard was replanted in the early 1980s and yields wines which are notably tannic, yet fruity in character, both on the nose and the palate. From such young vines these are qualities that bode well for an excellent future.

Château de Carles
Owner: **Antoine Chastenet de Castaing. 18ha. 8,000 cases. Mer 65%, CF and CS 35%.**
Charlemagne is said to have camped here *en route* to Spain, and it is to this visit that Château de Carles owes its name. Its 15th-century château is especially attractive. The wines have not been particularly impressive but, as the J-P Moueix empire is now taking an interest in the property, they could be worth watching.

Château Dalem
Owner: **Michel Rullier. 13ha. 6,500 cases. Mer 70%, CF 20%, CS 10%.**
An important property on the *côte*, just out of Saillans to the southeast. It produces perfumed wines with real charm. They develop soft, ripe, fruity flavours when young, but they last well; I was interested to note that, while the '78 was already very pleasing when four years old, '64, '67 and '70 were also still full of fruit and not drying up at all. The '82, '83, '85 and '86 are also very impressive wines. All the wine is château-bottled.

Château de la Dauphine
Owner: **Ets J-P Moueix. 10ha. 4,500 cases. Mer 60%, CF 40%.**
One of the best-known *crus* of Fronsac, situated on the lower *côte* west of the town of Fronsac. The wines are very well made. A proportion of 20 percent new wood is used, and the wines are bottled at the right time. This all leads to delicious, fruity wines with character, which can be drunk young.

Château Fontenil
Owner: **Michel Rolland. 7ha. 3,500 cases. Mer 86%, CS 14%.**
Fontenil is in the commune of Saillans; it comprises plots from several different growers which were amalgamated by Michel Rolland to create this *cru* in 1986. A winemaker with an excellent reputation, Rolland's first few vintages have shown progressive improvements and make this a property to watch for the future.

Château Gagnard
Owner: **Mme Bouyge-Barthe. 18ha. 8,000 cases. Mer 50%, CS 25%, CF 25%.**
This *cru* is situated on the sandstone terrace north of Fronsac. Its wines are classics in the Fronsac style and have attractive perfumed fruit, sound structure and good breed. Also sold under the La Croix-Bertrand label.

Château Jeandeman
Owner: **M Roy-Trocard. 30ha. 15,000 cases. Mer 80%, CS and CF 20%.**
This is the largest vineyard in Fronsac, and is on the *plateau calcaire* with red soil, in the commune of St-Aignan. The wines are distinctly perfumed and have a delicious fruitiness on the palate that makes them very drinkable after three to four years.

Château Mayne-Vieil
Owner: **Sèze family. 24ha. 12,000 cases. Mer 79%, CF 21%.**
An important and well-distributed *cru*. The vineyard is on sand and clay producing very attractive wines with a rich middle flavour, good structure and character, very drinkable in three to four years.

Château Moulin Haut-Laroque
Owner: **Jean-Noël Hervé. 14ha. 6,000 cases. Mer 65%, CF 20%, CS 10%, Mal 5%.**
This important Fronsac *cru* is on the *plateau calcaire* and *côte* south-west of Saillans. The wines are very perfumed with more power and structure than many straight Fronsacs. Tannin and fruit are well matched and the wines are slower to develop than some (four to five years).

Château Moulin-Haut-Villars
Owner: **Madame Brigitte Gaudrie. 4ha. 2,000 cases. Mer 70%, CF 30%.**
The recent adoption of new oak for maturing these wines has changed their character considerably. Once light-bodied and pleasantly young-drinking, they are at present somewhat over-powered by tannins. The '86 and '87 exemplified this particularly, but it may be that they will develop when older.

Château Plain-Point
Owner: **Denis Ardon. 32ha. 8,000 cases. Mer 75%, CF and CS 25%.**
Once an important mediaeval fortress, this ancient château overlooks the property and much of the surrounding Fronsac countryside. Its vineyards are on the chalky soils of the *plateau calcaire* and have recently been considerably expanded. '82 and '83 were good vintages at this *cru* but others have been disappointing. There is certainly the potential for these wines to do well.

Château Puyguilhem
Owner: **Janine Mothes. 10ha. 4,000 cases. Mer 60%, CF 20%, Mal 20%.**
A *cru* in Saillans with vineyards on the *côte* and on the limestone plateau. The wines produced here have a tendency to be tannic, but the high proportion of Merlot in the blend can soften this harshness in good vintages. '85 was a good year here.

Château La Rivière
Owner: **Jacques Borie. 47ha. 20,000 cases. Mer 60%, CS 30%, CF 5%, Mal 5%.**
A very grand château, superbly sited and complete with huge underground cellars. The vineyard is on the *plateau calcaire* and *côte*. A proportion of 30 to 40 percent new wood is used, and the wines are powerful and tannic and age very well. '87, '83 and '85 are the best recent vintages.

Château Rouet
Owner: **Patrick Danglade. 10ha. 5,000 cases. Mer 65%, CF 35%.**
Situated on the edge of the plateau in St-Germain-la-Rivière, this *cru* has a superb view over the surrounding countryside. Patrick Danglade works hard to promote both his own wines and those of the region. Unfortunately, the samples I have seen do not seem to live up to their generally good reputation, though the '85 was said to be quite fine.

Château La Valade
Owner: **Bernard Roux. 15ha. 7,500 cases. Mer 70%, CF and CS 30%.**
This *cru* is on the *plateau calcaire* and *côte* of the commune of Fronsac. The wines are perfumed and vigorous, well balanced with lots of character and quite fine.

Château La Vieille Cure
Owner: **The Old Parsonage (C Ferenbach, P Sachs, B Soulan). 16ha. 7,000 cases. Mer 75%, CF 20%, CS 5%.**
Second label: **Château Coutreau.**
A *cru* with a bright future ahead of it. La Vieille Cure is well situated: its vineyards on the *plateau calcaire* and *côte* produce some luscious Merlot-based wines, full of varietal character. An American syndicate took over in 1986, and since then the winery has been thoroughly modernized. Winemaking is now controlled by Michel Rolland of Château Le Bon Pasteur, and new oak casks are used for maturation. '83 and '85 were good vintages at this property.

Château Villars
Owner: **Jean-Claude Gaudrie. 25ha. 11,500 cases. Mer 60%, CF 30%, CS 10%.**
This *cru* is in the commune of Saillans, on the *plateau calcaire* and *côte*. For the maturation a third of the wood used is new. The wines have a lot of fruit but tend to be rather soft and develop quickly (over about three years).

Canon-Fronsac

The *appellation* Canon-Fronsac, or Côtes de Canon-Fronsac, is a small island of about 300 hectares in the middle of the Fronsac *appellation* consisting of parts of the communes of Fronsac and St-Michel-de-Fronsac. Although the outstanding *crus* are in Canon-Fronsac rather than Fronsac the two areas can in practice be treated as one *appellation*.

Château Barrabaque
Owner: **Achille Noël-Vincent. 9ha. 4,500 cases. Mer 60%, CF 30%, CS 10%.**
This property is on Fronsac's mid-*côte* and produces wines which have shown much improvement over recent vintages. The '83 had a certain earthiness, which was balanced by attractive fruit and tannins; '86 and '87 had fuller, plummier fruit qualities. These are improving wines, of some originality.

Château Canon
Owner: **Christian Moueix.** Administrator: **J-P Moueix. 1·1ha. 500 cases. Mer 80%, CF 20%.**
'82 and '85 were both stunning vintages from this property, full of the breed and style expected from a *cru* such as this, on one of Fronsac's best sites. It was the Moueix family's first château in this *appellation*, and their wines are well made and beginning to realize their full potential.

Château Canon
Owner: **Mlle Henriette Horeau. 10ha. 44,000 cases. Mer 95%, CF 5%.**
Château Canon is one of the leading properties in this *appellation*, it has an extensive history, dating back to the early 1700s, and once belonged to the Fontémoing family. All the wines are marketed by the Libourne firm of *négociants* Horeau-Beylot.

Château Canon-de-Brem
Owner: **Ets J-P Moueix. 20ha. 8,000 cases. Mer 67%, CF 33%.**
One of the best known and best reputed of all Fronsacs. The wines

have remarkable concentration of fruit and flavour, and are rich and supple with great style and character. This really shows what the *appellation* is capable of. The wines need four to five years to show at their best, and will keep well. Bought by Ets J-P Moueix in 1985.

Château Canon-Moueix (formerly Pichelèbre)
Owner: **J-P Moueix. 12ha. 5,500 cases.**
This property belonged to the de Brem family of Canon-de-Brem fame, until sold by them to J-P Moueix in 1985. The wines under the de Brems were full of character, powerful, and long-keeping. The first Moueix vintage, '85, was rich and deep-flavoured, softer and more generous early than Canon-de-Brem. The vineyard is on the *côte* and must now be reckoned among the leading *crus* of the *appellation*.

Château Cassagne-Haut-Canon
Owner: **Jean-Jacques Dubris. 10·5ha. 4,250 cases. Mer 70%, CF 25%, CS 5%.** Second label: **La Truffière.**
This château also produces wines under the label La Truffière, a name derived from the truffle oaks growing on the property. Some rather poor wines were produced here in the early 1980s; they were rank-flavoured and rather coarse. The '86 and '87 however, are a lot more appealing with spiciness and voluptuous fruit character.

Château Copet-Bégaud
Owner: **Alain Roux. 4ha. Mer 80%, CS and CF 20%.**
The '82 vintage from this château was particularly outstanding, with rich, ripe fruit flavours, balanced by a good tannic background. The '85 was similar in style but slightly mellower.

Château Coustolle
Owner: **Alain Roux. 16ha. 6,600 cases. Mer 60%, CF 30%, CS and Mal 10%.**
A fine *cru* on the *côte* north of Fronsac. For the maturation 20 percent new wood is used, and the result is a wine of concentration and richness which holds very well and develops character and some distinction. The '71 was still excellent when 11 years old.

Château La Fleur–Cailleau
Owner: **Paul Barre. 3ha. 1,500 cases. Mer 90%, CF 10%.**
Some highly individual and quite delightful wines are produced at
this small property. A distinctive bouquet of wild cherries, rich
tannins and elegant fruit flavours are noticeable in good vintages.
'83, '86, and '87 are especially attractive. Certainly a wine to look
out for.

Château La Fleur–Canon
Owner: **A de Coninck. 7ha. 3,500 cases. Mer 90%, CF and
CS 10%.**
A small *cru* in the commune of St-Michel, making some pleasantly
fruity wines, which are unusual in that they mature quickly,
drinking earlier than those of their neighbours.

Château du Gaby
Owner: **Yves & Henri de Kermoal. 9ha. 5,000 cases.**
A good *cru* on the *côte* and *plateau calcaire* northwest of Fronsac. The
wines are rich and powerful with lots of extract, needing time to
develop, and can keep very well. The '62 was still delicious when 20
years old.

Château du Gazin
Owner: **Henri Robert. 30ha. 15,000 cases. Mer 50%,
CF 50%.**
This is the *appellation*'s largest property and is situated on the
limestone plateau of St-Michel. Its wines look to have a very
promising future, they are beautifully scented, firm but with plenty
of breed and elegance. '85 was an especially good vintage.

Château Grand–Renouil
Owners: **J-F and M Ponty. 5ha. 2,500 cases. Mer 70%,
CF 30%.**
Another *cru* in the commune of St-Michel. This property is situated
on the *côte* and produces some attractive wines, that are certainly
worth looking out for. The '82 was particularly rich and the '86
powerful and tannic.

Château Haut-Mazeris
Owner: **Mme Bleynie. 20ha. 4,000 cases. Mer 70%,
CF and CS 30%.**
Haut-Mazeris is situated on the *plateau calcaire* in the commune of
St-Michel. Its wines are assertive with consistent balance and
quality.

Château Junayme
Owner: **Héritiers de Coninck.** Administrator: **René de
Coninck. 18ha. 8,500 cases. Mer 80%, CF 14% and CS 6%.**
This well-known *cru* is on the *côte* of Canon. Its wines are less
powerful than the best *crus* today in Canon-Fronsac, but have a
wide following.

Château Mausse
Owner: **Guy Janoueix. 10ha. 4,500 cases. Mer 50%, CS and
CF 50%.**
A good *cru* on the *plateau calcaire* northeast of St-Michel. This
property produces very perfumed wines with richness and some
concentration, which develop pleasing suppleness after four to five
years.

Château Mazeris
Owner: **Christian de Cournuaud. 14ha. 5,000 cases. Mer
80%, CF 10%, CS 10%.**
This *cru* is one of the best in its *appellation*. Its wines have marked
individuality, as was recognized by *négociants* J-P Moueix, who
bought the property's entire crop in 1985. The proprietors are
planning to expand the vineyard to 20 hectares; they are producing
wines with a great richness and concentration of flavour. This is one
of the rising stars of the area.

Château Mazeris-Bellevue
Owner: **Jacques Bussier. 11·5ha. 5,000 cases. Mer 45%, CS
40%, CF 15%.**
A fine *cru* on the *plateau calcaire* and *côte*. Unusually, the Cabernet
Sauvignon is in the ascendancy here, and the result is a distinguished
and fine flavour with lots of character and style.

Château Toumalin
Owner: **Bernard d'Arfeuille. 8ha. 4,000 cases. Mer 75%, CF 25%.**
This *cru* is on the *côte* above the valley of the river Isle north of Fronsac, and belongs to the well-known Libourne *négociants* who also own La Poir (Pomerol) and La Serre (St-Emilion). Lovely vivid, fruity wines with the necessary balance to be enjoyed young.

Château Vray-Canon-Boyer
Owners: **Coninck family. 10ha. 3,500 cases. Mer 90%, CS 5%, CF 5%.**
Owned by Horeau-Beylot, the oldest firm of Libourne *négociants*, this excellently situated *cru* produces wines with elegance and finesse, and which also mature very successfully. The '82 and '83 vintages are particularly good.

Entre-Deux-Mers

This huge area is the largest source of good dry white wines in Bordeaux. There are now 2,590 hectares benefiting from the AC (including the small Haut-Benauge AC), considerably more than there were 15 years ago. This is a region of large estates with mechanical harvesting now widely used and cool fermentation the rule. Much good red wine is also made, but this is only entitled to the *appellation* Bordeaux or Bordeaux Supérieur.

Château Bonnet
Owner: **André Lurton. Red: 80ha; 45,000 cases; CF and CS 60%, Mer 40%. White: 40ha; 40,000 cases; Sém 60%, Sauv 20%, Musc 20%. Rosé: 1,000 cases.** Second labels: **Châteaux Tour-de-Bonnet, Gournlin, and Peyraud.**
One of the most impressive properties in Entre-Deux-Mers, with an elegant 18th-century château and enormous vineyard. It is in Grézillac, due south of St-Emilion. The *chai* and *cuvier* are as well equipped as André Lurton's prestigious Graves properties. The white wine is cold-fermented at 16–18°C (61–64°F), and some of the red wine is matured in cask and sold in special numbered bottles. With its interesting mixture of *cépages*, the white wine is very

perfumed and full of elegant, fruity flavours. The red grapes are mechanically harvested, and the red wines are thoroughly attractive with quite a pronounced character.

Château Fondarzac
Owner: **J-C Barthe. 56ha. White 50% (Sauv, Sém and Musc). Red 50%.**
This *cru* has been owned by the Barthe family since the 17th century; their winemaking skills have manifested themselves in more recent generations and Jean-Claude Barthe has shown himself to be a particularly talented oenologist. The wines have a delicious bouquet and plenty of fruit.

Château Fongrave
Owner: **Pierre Perromat.** Second label: **Château de La Sablière-Fongrave (for red wines).**
This *cru* at Gornac is run by Pierre Perromat, who also owns Château d'Arche and was president of the INAO for many years. The property has been in his family since the 1600s and produces some attractively-scented wines – both red and white.

Château Launay
Owner: **Rémy Greffier. 105ha. Red: 17,000 cases; CS 50%, Mer 50%. White: 40,500 cases; Sém 34%, Sauv 33%, Musc 33%.** Second labels: **White: Châteaux Dubory, Braidoire and La Vaillante. Red: Châteaux Haut Castenet and Haut-Courgeaux.**
This very large property is at Soussac, on the road between Pellegrue and Sauveterre in the eastern Entre-Deux-Mers. All the wine is château-bottled. The wines are well reputed.

Château Moulin-de-Launay
Owners: **Claude & Bernard Greffier. 75ha. 45,000 cases. Sém 40%, Sauv 30%, Musc 20%, Ugni Blanc 10%.** Second labels: **Châteaux Tertre-de-Launay, Plessis, La Vigerie and de Tuilerie.**
This large property at Soussac in eastern Entre-Deux-Mers between Pellegrue and Sauveterre is entirely consecrated to the production of white wines – fruity, with elegance and length.

Château de la Rose
Owner: **Jean Faure.**
Situated in the north of the region, this property is small compared with most in Entre-Deux-Mers. Its wines are most attractive with a charming bouquet and with floweriness and fruit on the palate.

Château Thieuley
Owner: **Francis Courselle. Red: 8,300 cases; Mer 68%, CF 18%, CS 14%. White: 12,500 cases; Sauv 64%, Sém 36%.**
The proprietor here is a professor of viticulture. The property is at La Sauve near Créon in western Entre-Deux-Mers. The white wines, made from 100 percent Sauvignon, have a most attractive fruit, without exaggerated acidity, and are light and fresh.

Château de Toutigeac
Owner: **René Mazeau. Red: 100ha: 45,000 cases; CF 70%, CS 25%, Mer 5%. White: 50ha; 25,000 cases; Sém 100%.**
One of the best-known properties to use the sub-*appellation* Entre-Deux-Mers-Haut-Benauge. The *appellation* can be used only for white wines. Both red and white wines here are well reputed and all are château-bottled.

Premières Côtes de Bordeaux

This attractive area runs from the suburbs of Bordeaux southwards down the right bank of the Garonne to the sweet wine regions of Loupiac and Ste-Croix-du-Mont. It produces moderately sweet white wines and fruity, vivacious reds for early drinking. 15 years ago there was a slightly greater vineyard area devoted to white than to red wine production, but today the situation has reversed and the red vineyards have increased by 44 percent over the past eight years to 2,130 hectares, while those covered by white vines have decreased to 725 hectares, a reduction of nine percent. The best whites in the south of the area carry the superior AC Cadillac, but the idea has not really caught on. The real future of the region seems to rest more with its very pleasant red wines.

Château Birot
Owner: **Jacques Boireau. 34·5ha. Red: 5,000 cases. White: 15,000 cases.**
This *cru* in the commune of Béguey is best known for its fresh, fruity whites, with well-balanced acidity, sweetness and elegance.

Château Brethous
Owner: **Denise Verdier. 13ha. Mer 45%, CF 25%, CS 20%, Mal 10%.**
This good *cru* at Camblanes produces wines which are deliciously fruity and scented. They drink well when two to three years old, but can still be fresh and delicious after eight years.

Château Cayla
Owner: **Patrick Doche. 24ha. Red: 24ha; CS 34%, CF 33%, Mer 33%. White: 12ha; Sém 75%, Sauv 25%.**
Since 1985, this property at Rions has been transformed by the present owner. The red wines have varied fruit, delicious when three years old; whites are rotated through ten percent new oak after a cool fermentation and pre-fermentation skin contact.

Château de Chastelet
Owner: **Jean Estausau. 7ha. Mer 50%, CS 45%, CF 5%.**
A *cru* at Quinsac producing wine that needs three to five years to achieve harmony, it has solid fruit with plenty of charm.

Château Fayau
Owner: **Jean Médeville & Fils. 36ha. Red: 27ha; 13,500 cases; CS 60%, Mer 30%, CF 10%. White: 9ha; 4,500 cases; Sém 48%, Sauv 32%, Musc 20%.**
This excellent *cru* in Cadillac is carefully run by the Médeville family who make a particularly good sweet white Cadillac, with fruit and style, which ages well.

Château Le Gardera, Château Laurétan, Château Tanesse
Owner: **Domaines Cordier.**
For many years Domaines Cordier have run these adjoining properties in the Premières Côtes as a single production centre, producing several different *appellations*. Since 1983 the production

of Château Laurétan has ceased, and this has been changed into a brand, Laurétan Rouge and Laurétan Blanc, with the simple Bordeaux *appellation*. The other two châteaux are as follows:

Château Le Gardera: 25ha. Red (AC Bordeaux Supérieur); 11,500 cases; Mer 60%, CS 40%.
Château Tanesse: Red (AC Premières Côtes de Bordeaux); 35ha; 12,000 cases; CS 55%, Mer 35%, CF 10%. White (AC Bordeaux Blanc): 20ha; 12,000 cases; Sauv 85%, Sem 15%.
Le Gardera now produces an attractive, light-bodied Merlot-dominated red wine. Tanesse makes a more Cabernet-dominated red wine together with a flowery, fresh, Sauvignon-style white.

Château de Haux
Owners: **Jorgensen brothers. Red: 20ha; Mer 30%, CS 30%, CF 30%, Mal 10%. White: 5ha; Sém and Sauv.**
In 1985 two brothers, wine merchants from Denmark, bought this property at Haux and have rapidly transformed it. Their red wine is rich and solid with attractive fruit and definite character, the white is exceptionally attractive, with long-flavoured, crisp fruit.

Château Lagarosse
Owner: **M Ottari.** Administrator: **G Laurenciu. 32ha. Red: Mer 80%, CS and CF 20%. White: Sém 80%, Sauv 20%.**
This property at Tabanac was bought in 1987 by a Japanese importer of agricultural machinery. The red wines have intense fruit, a rich, solid flavour and a suggestion of liquorice. The whites have a big broad flavour with lots of fruit and character.

Château Laroche-Bel-Air
Owner: **Martine Palau. 25ha. Red: Mer 55%, CS and CF 40%, Mal 5%. White: Sém and Sauv.**
This *cru* at Baurech produces stylish, fruity but quite tannic wines that need four to five years' maturation before being ready.

Château de la Meulière
Owner: **Jacques Fourès. 34·5ha. Mer 38%, CS 33%, CF 27%, Mal 2%.**
Jacques Fourès, inventor of the famous Cruover now much used for conserving wines in bars and restaurants, has developed this, the

family property, as a fine *cru* since taking over in 1987. The vineyard is in three different locations: in Canac (15 hectares), Bouliac (seven hectares) and Camblanes (12·5 hectares). He produces concentrated, powerful wines, marked by dense, ripe tannins. The '85 was delicious, with ripe, supple fruit and marked character when four years old.

Château Nenin
Owner: **Francis Fouquet. 8ha. CF 45%, Mer 35%, CS 20%.**
This vineyard at Baurech is the retirement home and hobby of a man who spent his career as a *négociant* at Borie-Manoux and Gilbey de Loudenne. He believes the Cabernet Franc suits the particular *terroir* of his vineyard, and makes charmingly fruity, scented wines, ideal for early drinking.

Château Plaisance
Owner: **Patrick Bayle. 25ha. Mer 50%, CS 30%, CF 20%.**
Patrick Bayle left a business career to run this property at Capian in 1985. His wines have a rich, berryish fruit that needs three or four years to mature. There is also a cask-fermented white wine.

Château de Plassan
Owner: **Jean Brianceau. 35ha. Red: CS and CF 50%, Mer 45%, Mal 5%. White: Sém 50%, Sauv 40%, Musc 10%.**
This fine property at Tabanac has one of the region's rare Palladium buildings, with château and *chais* forming a harmonious whole. The reds are concentrated and solid but with good fruit, serious wines needing time, except for a delicious '87. The white wines are now cask-fermented.

Château Reynon
Owner: **Denis & Florence Dubourdieu-David. 40ha. Red: 9,000 cases; Mer 50%, CS 40%, CF 10%. White: 12,500 cases; Sauv 100%.**
This well-known and well-distributed *cru* is the most important property in the commune of Béguey, very near to Cadillac. Here an excellent red wine is made, possessing the almost startling fruitiness which characterizes the area. The whites are well regarded and fruity but are designed for drinking very young.

Ste-Croix-du-Mont

The two *appellations* of Ste-Croix-du-Mont and Loupiac are situated on some spectacular hillsides and the plateau, just across the Garonne from Sauternes and Barsac, affording a splendid panorama of the whole Graves-Sauternes region. They also provide the best sweet wines outside Sauternes. In fact the best properties are able to make wines which can be better than the lesser Sauternes, given grapes properly affected by rot. They tend to be lighter and less rich than Sauternes, but are very fruity and long-lived. The cooperative at Ste-Croix-du-Mont produces wines of a good standard. The area under vine is 417 hectares.

Château Loubens
Owner: **Arnaud de Sèze. 4,500 cases. Red: 6ha; CS 50%, Mer 42%, CF 8%. White: 15·5ha; Sém 97%, Sauv 3%.**
Second labels: **Château Terfort and Fleuron Blanc de Château Loubens.**
This has long been one of the best *crus* of the *appellation*. The sweet wines have an elegant fruit and freshness about them and are well made with well-balanced sweetness. The vineyard is finely placed at the top of the *côte*. There is an attractive dry wine, sold under the name of Fleuron Blanc, and another sweet wine, Château Terfort, which also maintains an excellent standard.

Château de Tastes
Owner: **Domaines Prats. White: 1ha; 400 cases; Sauv 100%.**
This historic domaine with its superbly positioned château and vineyard on the summit of the *côte* commands splendid views across the Garonne and over the Sauternes and Graves. Sadly, little of this very fine wine is made today.

Loupiac

Apart from the fact that they lie in different communes, there is in fact no useful distinction to be made between the Loupiac *appellation* and that of its neighbour, Ste-Croix-du-Mont. Loupiac has 336 hectares under vine.

Chateau Loupiac-Gaudiet
Owner: **Marc Ducau. 45ha. Red: 15ha; 900 cases. White: 30ha; 10,000 cases; Sém 85%, Sauv 15%.**
This has been one of the best and most consistent wines of Loupiac for many years. The wines are mostly aged in vat. They have delicacy and finesse with a fruity sweetness, and age very well.

Château de Ricaud
Owner: **SC Garreau-Ricard.** Administrator: **Alain Thienot. 45ha. Red: 5,750 cases. White: 10,000 cases.**
This is the most famous *cru* in Loupiac, and many of the historic vintages (such as '29 and '47) are still superb. Unfortunately in the last years of the previous ownership the property was neglected and run down, but since the new owners from Champagne took over in 1980 there has been steady progress. The Loupiac is finely perfumed with finesse, real elegance and richness. Some new wood is now used for the maturation. Fine examples were made in '81, '82 and '83 but the real breakthrough came with a gloriously botrytized '86 which could well pass for a good Barsac. There is a rather traditional Sémillon-dominated dry white with the Bordeaux AC, and a very fruity, attractive red wine which has the Premières Côtes AC in the best years ('81 and '82) and otherwise the Bordeaux Supérieur AC. Again these wines are matured in cask. The property has rapidly regained its former reputation.

Bordeaux Côtes de Castillon

This region lies between the St-Emilionnais and the boundary of the Gironde and Dordogne departments, and used to be included in the St-Emilionnais before the *appellations* came into force. It produces some of the very best Bordeaux Supérieur, with body and some character, much of it from a very good *cave coopérative*. With 2,637 hectares of vines, the area has more than doubled since 1974.

The following châteaux, among others, are worth looking out for: de Belcier, Castegens (also sold as Fontenay), Chante-Grive, de Clotte, L'Estang, Haut-Tuquet, Lardit, Moulin-Rouge, Pitray, Puycarpin, Rocher-Bellevue, Roquevieille, Ste-Colombe, Thibaud-Bellevue, La Treille-des-Girondiers.

Index

This does not include names of châteaux, which are listed in the A–Z, pages 68–86.

Index